Typing: Two-in-One Course
Second Edition

Typing
Two-in-One Course
Second Edition

Archie Drummond

Anne Coles-Mogford
Oxford and County Secretarial College

McGRAW-HILL BOOK COMPANY

London · New York · St Louis · San Francisco · Auckland · Bogotá · Caracas
Hamburg · Lisbon · Madrid · Mexico · Milan · Montreal · New Delhi · Panama
Paris · San Juan · São Paulo · Singapore · Sydney · Tokyo · Toronto

Published by
McGRAW-HILL Book Company Europe
Shoppenhangers Road, Maidenhead, Berkshire, SL6 2QL England
Telephone 0628 23432   Fax 0628 770224

British Library Cataloguing in Publication Data
Drummond, A. M. (Archibald Manson),
  Typing: Two-in-One Course. – 2nd ed.
  1. Typing
  I. Title II. Coles-Mogford, Anne
  652.3

  ISBN 0-07-707254-5

Library of Congress Cataloging-in-Publication Data
Drummond, Archie.
  Typing: Two-in-one course/Archie Drummond, Anne Coles-Mogford. – 2nd ed.
  p. cm.
  ISBN 0-07-707254-5
  1. Typewriting. I. Coles-Mogford, Anne. II. Title.
Z49.D8 1990   652.3-dc20   89-13314 CIP

3 4 5 IP 9 3 2

Typeset by Eta Services (Typesetters) Ltd, Beccles, Suffolk
Printed and bound in Malta by Interprint Limited

INDEX

PREFACE

Typing: Two-in-One Course, Second Edition, is a completely revised and up-to-date programme for the learning and application of typing skills and techniques. It is similar to the first edition in that it includes the successful and popular keyboard approach used in the first edition—apart from minor alterations and additions—and covers the elementary and intermediate levels of any typewriting syllabus.

In addition, all production exercises are new and many cover topics dealing with word and data processing which will enable students to prepare more fully for the electronic office and for today's examinations in typewriting at elementary and intermediate levels, as well as for examinations in word processing.

New features of the second edition

SKILL MEASUREMENT As only the student and/or tutor will know whether, at any given time, the student should be practising for speed or accuracy, we have called the speed/accuracy material **skill measurement**, and a choice must be made as to whether the practice should aim at increasing speed or working for greater accuracy. After **skill measurement** exercise 11 (SM11), the remaining exercises are on pages 158–163. There is a **skill measurement chart** in the *Workguide and Resource Material* and this may be duplicated and completed by the student, or tutor, to show the standard reached at any given stage.

RECORD YOUR PROGRESS In this edition, each **record your progress** exercise contains every letter of the alphabet. The usual **record your progress chart**, which may be duplicated, will be found in the *Workguide and Resource Material.* After **record your progress** exercise 6 (R6), the remaining exercises are on pages 164–169.

KEYBOARDING SKILLS Directions for typing **keyboarding skills** (which include **skill measurement** and **record your progress** exercises, **techniques** and **reviews** and **language arts** drills) are given at the top of the first page of each unit.

PERSONAL LETTERS As some learners may not wish to have a great deal of formal tuition beyond the keyboard stage, we have presented display and personal letters immediately after the figures and symbol keys.

DATA FILES In order to develop a student's initiative in the finding and utilizing of information, twenty-two exercises have details that need to be verified. The student is instructed to refer to the **data files**, each of which is given a filename and presented in alphabetical order on pages 173 and 174. Other exercises may refer to details given on previous pages in the textbook, eg names and addresses, dates, etc.

WORD PROCESSING PROCEDURES Although students may not have access to word processors, electronic typewriters and computers with word processing capabilities, they should take every opportunity to familiarize themselves with the terminology. We have included word processing and data processing terminology throughout the text, and wherever we considered it appropriate, we have mentioned word processing concepts and applications that would apply to the operations being practised. We hope these points will enable students to prepare more fully for the electronic office. Further, we have suggested certain tasks that may be used as **input**, and **text-editing** changes are listed separately.

INTEGRATED PRODUCTION TYPING Our objective here is to simulate typical office typing, and each project is prefaced by a **typist's log sheet** which gives the name of the organization, the originator's name and department, and the date together with a brief note of the contents of the project. The details given on this **log sheet** need to be referred to constantly by the student while typing the project. Each document is given an approximate target time, the idea being that the whole project should be completed within a maximum of two and a half hours, and at the same time, students are encouraged to make their own decisions and establish work priorities. Further, it is hoped that the thematic approach will develop the student's ability to follow through a project under simulated office conditions, as well as preparing them for examinations. For further details about folders, mailable documents, interruptions (distractions), etc, please see pages 73–74.

PROOFREADING To emphasize the importance of proofreading as part of the typist's training, we have included a greater variety of proofreading exercises on pages 148–154.

KEYBOARDING DISK A keyboarding disk is available to train the individual to operate the keyboard in the shortest possible time. It is based on, and follows the same sequence of drills and exercises as, *Typing First Course, Fifth Edition,* and quickly and easily develops keyboarding skills for the alphabet keys, punctuation, figures and symbols. By the end of this short course, the learner should be capable of typing at 25 words a minute for three minutes with not more than three errors.

DATA STORE Straightforward information about essential aspects of typing display is given in each unit, but other details will be found in the **data store**, which is displayed in alphabetical order on pages 175–197.

Typing Target Practice, Revised Edition and Workguide and Resource Material

In addition to *Typing: Two-in-One Course, Second Edition*, there are two complementary books that will be helpful:

1 *Typing Target Practice, Revised Edition* This book contains further examples of exercises introduced in *Typing: Two-in-One Course, Second Edition*, and is an invaluable addition as extra practice on all topics. It will be extremely useful if success in examinations is to be assured. At the bottom of the pages in *Typing: Two-in-One Course, Second Edition*, reference is made to the relevant pages in *Typing Target Practice, Revised Edition*.

2 *Workguide and Resource Material* This contains:
(a) displayed solutions in what we consider to be an acceptable form and gives sizes of paper used, margins, tab stops, etc. These examples are ideal guides against which students should check their completed work;
(b) a variety of charts, forms and letterhead paper which may be duplicated and used in the class-room—these are referred to in *Typing: Two-in-One Course, Second Edition* and in *Typing Target Practice, Revised Edition*;
(c) the 'interruptions' to be handed to the students during the typing of each of the **integrated production typing** projects.

Typing Three

For those students who wish to progress to a more advanced stage, *Typing Three* provides a completely new, modern and up-to-date approach and follows on smoothly from *Typing: Two-in-One Course, Second Edition*.

Acknowledgements

The contents of this textbook reflect the comments, suggestions and recommendations made to us by students and tutors who have used our previous textbooks, and we attach a great deal of value to their contributions which, over the years, have helped enormously in the effectiveness and popularity of our typing publications.

We also wish to thank our colleagues for their helpful advice and assistance in copying the manuscript exercises.

The authors hope that students will gain experience, satisfaction and fulfilment from working through *Typing: Two-in-One Course, Second Edition*, and the supplementary books and aids and will find pleasure and reward from using *Typing Three*, details of which are given on the back cover of this text.

ARCHIE DRUMMOND
ANNE COLES-MOGFORD

superscript. In the footnote, the sign may be typed either on the same line or as a superscript, and one space is left after the sign and before the start of the typing.

It should be noted that when you use the asterisk on the keyboard (not a combination character of x and hyphen) then the sign will be a superscript and any other footnote signs used in the same exercise must be superscripts. Usually there is no ruled line before a footnote in tabulation.

Telephone index

See page 107.

Typefaces (sizes of)

See page 9.

Variable linespacer

See page 2.

Vertical linespacing

See page 20.

Window envelopes

Some firms use envelopes from which a panel has been cut out at the front. This is known as a 'window' envelope. The object of window envelopes is twofold:

1   It saves time in typing the name and address on both letter and envelope.
2   It avoids the possibility of error in copying the address on the envelope.

When a window envelope is used, the name and address of the addressee must be typed in full on the letter itself, and in such a position that, when the letter is folded, the position of the address will coincide with the cut-out portion on the envelope. To help the typist, the position of the cut-out is sometimes marked on the letter heading either by marks in the corner or by a ruled box. Window envelopes may also be provided with a transparent cover over the cut-out part.

This type of envelope is not normally used for personal letters. It is used, without the transparent cover, mainly for statements, invoices, form letters, etc.

Words and figures

1   Use words instead of figures for:
   1.1   The number one on its own.*
   1.2   Figures at the beginning of a sentence.
2   Use figures in all other cases.

* If number one is part of a list of figures, it should be typed as a figure, eg 'Follow the instructions in 1, 2 and 3'.

NOTE: These are the basic rules, but other methods may be used.

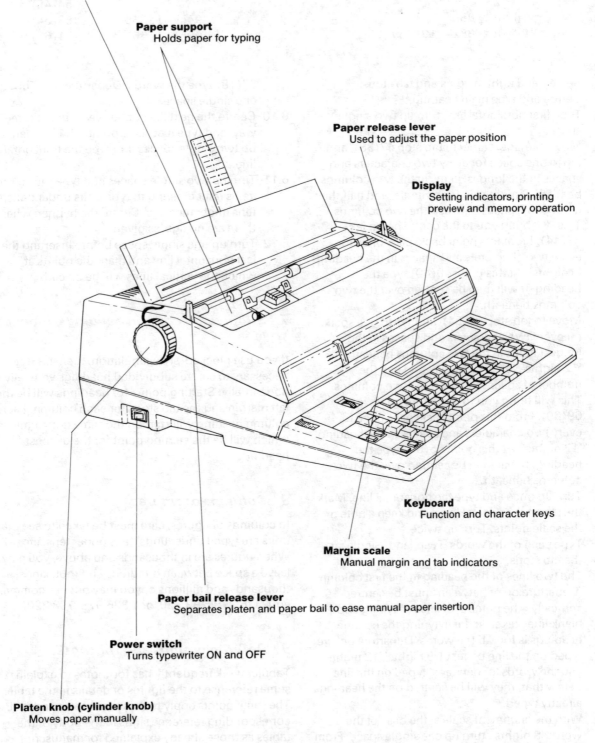

Print carrier
Composed of ribbon cassette, daisywheel, correction tape, carrier adjust lever and printing mechanism

Paper support
Holds paper for typing

Paper release lever
Used to adjust the paper position

Display
Setting indicators, printing preview and memory operation

Keyboard
Function and character keys

Margin scale
Manual margin and tab indicators

Paper bail release lever
Separates platen and paper bail to ease manual paper insertion

Power switch
Turns typewriter ON and OFF

Platen knob (cylinder knob)
Moves paper manually

36(27) CRUISES – PRICES (PER PERSON)

21(12)   78(69)

Left margin: 23(14)   27(18) Departure on or between   49(40) 9 nights   65(56) 12 nights   Right margin: 79(70)   Tab stops: 47(38) 54(45) 63(54) 71(62)

Departure on or between	9 nights		12 nights	
	Twin	Single	Twin	Single
16 Oct 88	–	–	945	1,230
22 Oct 88 – 19 Nov 88	870	1,100	1,025	1,355

6.1   Set left and right margins and tab stops.

6.2   Centre and type main heading.

6.3   Type first horizontal line, turn up two single spaces.

6.4   Move carriage/carrier to tab stop 47(38), and tap in one space for every two characters and spaces in the longest items in the two columns beneath '9 nights', ie Twin Single, and half the number of spaces between the two columns. This will bring you to the centre point, ie 53(44). From this point backspace once for every two characters and spaces in the heading '9 nights'. At this point 49(40) type the heading. It will then be centred over the two columns beneath.

6.5   Move to tab stop 63(54), and tap in one space for every two characters and spaces in the longest items in the two columns beneath '12 nights', ie 1,025 Single, and half the number of spaces between the two columns. This will bring you to the centre point, ie 69(60). From this point backspace once for every two characters and spaces in the heading '12 nights'. At this point 65(56) type the heading. It will then be centred over the two columns beneath.

6.6   Turn up once and type the horizontal line. Mark the top of the vertical lines, and keep a note of the scale points. Turn up twice.

6.7   Type each of the words 'Twin' and 'Single' at the tab stops.

6.8   The two lines of the heading in the first column 'Departure on or between' must be centred vertically. The number of lines of typing and blank lines taken so far in typing the column headings is four. If the words 'Departure on' are typed on the line beneath '9 nights' '12 nights' and the words 'or between' typed on the line below that, they will be centred on the headings already typed.

6.9   With the alignment scale at the base of the words '9 nights', turn up one single space. From the left margin find the centre point of the longest line in the first column. From this point backspace once for every two letters and spaces in the line 'Departure on'. At scale point 27(18) type the words 'Departure on'. Turn up one single space.

6.10   Centre the next line 'or between' in the same way, and type it at scale point 28(19), then turn up two single spaces and type the horizontal line.

6.11   Turn up two single spaces and type the column items remembering to type units under units, tens under tens, etc. Centre the hyphen where there are no figures given.

6.12   Turn up one single space before inserting the last horizontal line and mark the points at which the vertical lines will be placed.

7   Subdivided column headings–blocked style

If you use blocked-style tabulation, then it is not necessary to centre subdivided headings vertically or horizontally. Starting points for headings will be the left margin and the tab stops for each column. Each column heading will start on the same horizontal line which will be the starting point for the deepest heading.

8   Columns of figures

In columns of figures, care must be taken to see that units are typed under units, tens under tens, etc. When figures are in thousands and above, you may leave a space between hundreds and thousands, thousands and millions or you may put in a comma, eg 1,326,978; 793,220; or 1 326 978; 793 220.

9   Reference signs and footnotes

Tabular work frequently has footnotes to explain some reference to the figures or details in the table. The same points apply to these footnotes and their corresponding reference signs in the body of the tables as those already explained for manuscript work, ie the footnotes are typed underneath the table in single spacing with double spacing between each. The reference sign in the body is typed immediately after the item to which it refers and is always a

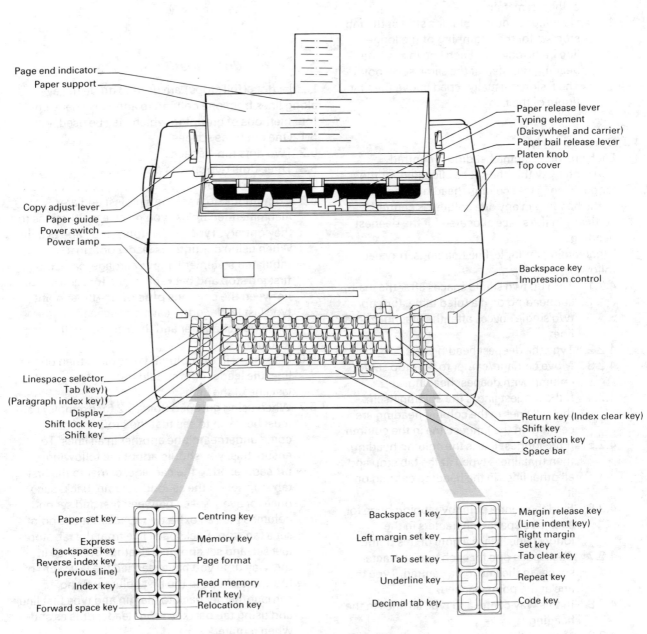

Page end indicator

Paper support

Paper release lever

Typing element
(Daisywheel and carrier)

Paper bail release lever

Platen knob

Top cover

Copy adjust lever

Paper guide

Power switch

Power lamp

Backspace key

Impression control

Linespace selector

Tab (key)

(Paragraph index key)

Display

Shift lock key

Shift key

Return key (Index clear key)

Shift key

Correction key

Space bar

Paper set key — Centring key

Express
backspace key — Memory key

Reverse index key
(previous line) — Page format

Index key — Read memory
(Print key)

Forward space key — Relocation key

Backspace 1 key — Margin release key
(Line indent key)

Left margin set key — Right margin
set key

Tab set key — Tab clear key

Underline key — Repeat key

Decimal tab key — Code key

**The function keys above may be found
on your electronic typewriter/word processor**

4.1 Blocked style

4.1.1 Set margins and tab stops.

4.1.2 All column headings start on the second single space after the main or subheading. However, if the table is ruled, then the column headings will start on the second single space after the first horizontal line.

4.1.3 The heading over the first column is typed at the left margin.

4.1.4 Headings in other columns start at the tab stop set for the beginning of the longest line in the column. Each line in any one heading will start at the same scale point. The £ sign is usually typed above the first figure of the £'s.

4.2 Centred style

Each line of a column heading is centred horizontally within the space allocated for the longest line in that column/heading. The whole of the heading in any one column is centred vertically in the space allocated for the deepest heading.

When typing multiple-line headings, proceed as follows:

4.2.1 Turn up two single spaces after the main/ subheading or, if a ruled table, turn up two single spaces after the first horizontal line.

4.2.2 Type the deepest heading first.

4.2.3 Move carriage/carrier to tab stop set for column with deepest heading.

4.2.4 If the longest line is the column itself, then all lines in the column heading are centred on the longest line in the column.

4.2.5 If the longest line is the column heading, then that line is typed at the tab stop and all other lines in the heading centred on it.

4.2.6 Find the centre point by tapping once for each two spaces/characters in the longest line. Make a note of this point.

4.2.7 Backspace one for each two characters/ spaces in the line to be centred. Type the line at the point reached.

4.2.8 In this way centre and type all lines in the heading.

4.2.9 Move to the next deepest heading.

4.2.10 Count the number of lines in this heading and subtract the number from the number of lines in the deepest heading just typed. Divide the result by two; eg:

Deepest heading	5 lines
Next deepest	2
Difference	3
Divide by two	$1\frac{1}{2}$—turn up one and a half spaces from first line of deepest heading.

4.2.11 Turn the cylinder towards you so that the alignment scale is at the base of the first line of the deepest heading just typed. From this point turn up one and a half spaces and start typing the next deepest heading. Use the same method as in 4.2.6 and 4.2.7.

4.2.12 Continue with other column headings in the same way.

5 Leader dots (*leader lines*)

Leader dots (full stops) are used to guide the eye along lines from one column to another. There are four methods of grouping which may be used, viz:

5.1 One dot three spaces .　　.　　.　　.　　.

5.2 Two dots three spaces ..　　..　　..　　..

5.3 Three dots two spaces ...　　...　　...　　...

5.4 Continuous dots . . . .

5.5 Continuous dots are the simplest and are recommended unless you receive instructions to the contrary. Type leader dots lightly and evenly. When using continuous leader dots in a tabulated statement, move carriage/carrier to first tab stop and backspace one for each space between the columns **plus one**. At that point type last leader dot. Leave one space after the last typed character and then complete the leader dots.

5.6 If any item in the column takes more than one line, the leader dots should be typed only on the last line of the item.

5.7 When using grouped dots (5.2 for example) care must be taken to see that the groups of dots come underneath one another in all lines. To ensure this, you should adopt the following procedure: bring the carriage/carrier to the first tab stop set for the second column; backspace once for every space between first and second columns plus an extra two spaces. At this point set a tab stop. Backspace five from the tab stop just set, and set another tab stop. Continue in this way until you have reached the last word of the shortest line in the first column. Bring carriage/carrier back to margin and type first line, and using tab bar/key insert leader dots as and when required.

6 Subdivided column headings–centred style

Tabular statements may have subdivided columns. A column heading may be further divided into two or three separate items which are displayed beneath the main column heading as three separate columns. See the example on page 196; the following explanatory steps will give you an idea of how to proceed. Paper used is A5 landscape.

Electronic typewriters and word processors

This is the symbol that we will use to draw your attention to information and instructions about word processing concepts and applications. In business today, it is important that you understand how modern machines with the QWERTY keyboard may be employed to format more easily a great variety of documents.

If you are typing on an electronic typewriter, a word processor or a computer with word processing software, study the manufacturer's handbook that accompanies your machine, and practise the functions, movements and settings. You will probably find that there are a number of automatic operations. As it is essential for you to know the types of errors you make and how to overcome errors, **do not** employ the correction key during the keyboard-learning stage or when typing exercises from **skill measurement**, **record your progress** or **skill building** pages.

Cursor

When a VDU (visual display unit) is used in conjunction with an electronic machine, the typing appears on the VDU screen. On the screen there is a movable dot (hyphen) that indicates the typing point at which the next typed character will appear. This movable dot/hyphen is called the cursor. At the end of the typing line the cursor will return to the left margin automatically or when the return key is pressed.

Margins

To save the typist's time, many electronic typewriters and word processors have pre-stored margin settings, tab settings, page length, etc, which may be changed to suit the layout required for a particular document. When any of these pre-stored settings are not appropriate for a particular exercise in this textbook, we suggest that you may wish to change the setting(s) by following the instructions given in the manufacturer's handbook.

Pitch

When only manual typewriters were marketed, the two typefaces available were 10 pitch (pica) or 12 pitch (elite). Then the golf ball electric typewriter brought dual pitch and a choice of 10 or 12 on any one typewriter. Most electronic typewriters and word processors now offer 10, 12 and 15 pitch; however, on the more sophisticated machines there is a wider selection including proportional spacing (PS). The instructions and exercises in this edition of *Typing: Two-in-One Course, Second Edition*, are based on 10 or 12 pitch, and we use the word pitch when referring to margin settings—not pica and elite as in the previous edition.

Single-element typewriters

Nearly all electric and electronic typewriters have single-element heads. These typewriters have no movable carriage, and there are no type bars. Instead, they have a printing head attached to a carrier that moves across the page from left to right, stroke by stroke. When you wish to return the carrier to the left margin, you press the return key as you would with the electric typewriter. On most electronic keyboards, the automatic carrier return is employed.

The printing element is usually a daisywheel which is a rapidly spinning disk with flexible arms. On the tip of each arm there is a typeface character. The required character stops at the printing point and is struck by a small hammer which imprints the image on the paper.

Before typing the **column items**, clear tab stop already set, find centre point of column by tapping space bar once for every two characters and spaces in the heading (this will give you the centre point of the heading) then backspace one for every two characters and spaces in the longest column item. Set a tab stop at point reached. If the column items are words, this scale point will give you the starting point for each item in the column. If the column items are figures, units must be typed under units and tens under tens.

Where the **column heading** is **shorter** than the **longest item** in the column, find the centre point of the longest column item by tapping space bar once for every two characters and spaces in that item. From the point reached, backspace once for every two characters and spaces in the heading. At this point type the heading. If there is more than one line in a column heading, see instructions under **multiple-line** headings.

3 Ruling

Tabulated statements are sometimes made more effective and clearer by ruling horizontal and/or vertical lines. Although it is assumed that you have already learnt how to rule up tabulated work, the following notes will serve as a reminder.

3.1 If horizontal lines only are ruled, use the underscore and let the lines project two spaces beyond the margins on either side.

3.2 Always turn up one single space before a horizontal underscore and two single spaces after.

3.3 If both horizontal and vertical lines are required, rule these (a) either by underscore, in which case the paper has to be removed from the machine after the table has been typed, and reinserted sideways for the ruling of the vertical lines; or (b) by ink; or (c) a combination of the two, eg horizontals by underscore, verticals by ink. See that the ink ruling is the same colour as the underscore line.

3.4 The vertical lines between the columns must be ruled exactly in the middle of each blank space. It is therefore advisable to leave an odd number of spaces between the columns—one for the vertical ruling and an equal number on either side of the ruling. The points on the scale at which the vertical lines are to be ruled should be marked by light pencil marks at the top **and** bottom of the columns.

3.5 To find the point at which to mark the vertical line, proceed as follows: (It is assumed that you have left either three, five or seven spaces between columns.) (a) Move to tab stop following first vertical line. (b) If you have left three spaces between columns, backspace two

and make a pencil mark; if you have left five spaces between, backspace three; if seven spaces between, backspace four.

3.6 Move to second and other columns and repeat 3.5.
NOTE: Do not extend the vertical lines above or below the horizontals—see that they meet precisely.

3.7 **Ink** If horizontal and vertical lines are to be ruled in ink, follow the same procedures as for ruling by underscore, but in this case the beginning and end of each horizontal line must be marked in pencil, as well as the vertical lines. When the table has been completed, remove paper from machine and, with a fine nib, rule lines carefully and neatly to scale points marked. It is essential that vertical and horizontal lines meet exactly.

3.8 **Typewriter** Apart from the use of the underscore, on some typewriters provision is made for the speedy ruling of both horizontal and vertical lines. On the alignment scale/card holder you will find two small notches or round holes. Place the point of a pencil or suitable ball pen in one of these notches or holes and hold it in position against the paper with the right hand. With the left hand on the carriage release, you will obtain a continuous horizontal by running the carriage along. To avoid running the carriage too far, it is advisable to stop about two spaces before the scale point at which the horizontal line is to end, and then tap the space bar until the scale point is reached.

To make a vertical line, instead of running the carriage along, you release the cylinder ratchet by means of the interliner and turn the cylinder up with the left-hand knob. If the vertical lines extend almost to the bottom of the page, it is better to rule these by hand after the paper has been removed from the machine, to avoid the paper slipping when the cylinder is turned down for the start of the next line. After you have had some practice in ruling in this way, you will find that it saves a great deal of time, particularly if carbon copies are being taken. On your electronic typewriter there may be a function key for inserting vertical lines.

3.9 If you wish to make a very clear distinction between sections of a table, the horizontal and vertical lines can be emphasized by double or thicker ruled lines. With electronic keyboards, the **bold** function key may be used.

4 Multiple-line headings

Where column headings consist of more than one line or are of unequal depth, they are always typed in single spacing. They are never underscored in a **ruled** table.

Basic machine parts and adjustments

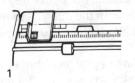

1

1 Paper guide

One of the marks on the paper rest shows where to set the paper guide so that the left edge of the paper will be at '0' on the paper guide scale. Check that the paper guide is set at that mark.

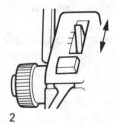

2

2 Linespace selector

The linespace selector has a 1, a 2 and in some cases a 3 printed on or beside it. In addition, many machines are now fitted wtih half-line spacing to give $1\frac{1}{2}$ and $2\frac{1}{2}$ linespaces. Use the manufacturer's handbook and make sure you know how to set the selector. Always adjust the selector so that it is at the required position.

3 Margins

See previous page and manufacturer's handbook.

4

4 Paper bail

Before inserting the paper into the typewriter or printer, pull the paper bail forward, away from the cylinder, so that you may insert the paper without it bumping into the paper bail.

5.1

5 Inserting paper—typewriters and printers

5.1 Hold the sheet in your left hand. Place the paper behind the cylinder, against the raised edge of the paper guide. Turn the right cylinder knob to draw the paper into the machine. Many machines now have a special paper insertion key that should always be used when inserting the paper.

To prevent damage to the cylinder of the typewriter, use a piece of stout paper as a backing sheet.

5.2

5.2 **Check that the paper is straight**
Push the top of the paper back. If the left side of the paper, at top and bottom, fits evenly against the paper guide, your paper is straight. If it is not straight, loosen the paper (use the paper release), straighten it, and return the paper release to its normal position.

5.3 **Place the paper bail against the paper**
Slide the rubber rollers on the bail to the right or left to divide the paper into thirds. Then, position the bail back against the paper.

5.4

5.4 **Top margin**
For most exercises, it is usual to leave 25 mm (1 inch) clear at the top of the page. Many machines now have a pre-stored top margin setting; if necessary, change this so as to leave 25 mm (1 inch) clear. Where an automatic paper insertion key is not provided, turn up seven single spaces which will leave 25 mm (1 inch) clear.

Subscripts

See page 66.

Sums of money in columns

See page 61.

Sums of money in context

See page 36.

Superscripts

See page 66.

Tabulation

There are many kinds of statements and records that the typist may have to set out in tabulated form.

As you gain experience in the different forms of display, you should be able to look at a script and decide what margins are suitable. With tabulation, it is often possible to study a table and decide on a left margin. In other cases, all that will be necessary is to type out the longest line in each column, or tap out the longest line of each column (together with the spaces between columns) and see whether the table will fit in with the margins already set (within a document you are already typing) or whether a 25 mm (1 inch) left margin would be adequate.

In other situations, it will give a better result if you use the backspacing method for the horizontal centring and adopt the following procedure:

1 Main headings and columns without headings

1.1 Clear margin stops and all previous tab stops.

1.2 Insert paper with left edge at 0.

1.3 Calculate number of vertical lines in exercise and subtract this number from number of vertical lines on paper being used. Divide answer by two and add one to this figure: turn up this number from top edge of paper. Example using A5 landscape paper:

Number of vertical lines
in A5 landscape paper   35
Less number of lines in
exercise to be typed, say $\underline{22}$
Divide by two $13 \div 2 = 6$ (ignore
Plus one $\underline{1}$ fractions)
Turn up $\overline{7}$

1.4 Bring carriage to horizontal centre point of paper.

1.5 If **centred** style is being used, from centre point of paper backspace once for every two characters and spaces in the main heading and type heading at point reached. Turn up two single spaces.

1.6 Mark the longest line in each column. From the centre of the paper backspace once for every two characters and spaces in the longest line of each column, carrying any odd letter to the next column.

1.7 Backspace once for every two spaces to be left between the columns, including any odd number left over in step 1.6.

1.8 Set margin stop at point reached.

1.9 From left margin, tap space bar once for each letter and space in the longest line of the first column, and once for each blank space between the first and second columns. Set tab stop at point reached for start of second column.

1.10 From the first tab stop, again tap space bar once for each character and space in the longest item of the second column, and once for each blank space between second and third columns. Set tab stop at point reached for start of third column.

1.11 Continue in the same way for any additional columns.

NOTES: (a) If **blocked** style is being used, follow items 1.6–1.11 and type main heading at left margin.

(b) The number of spaces left between columns depends on the total width of the table. A minimum of three and a maximum of seven are recommended.

2 Column headings

2.1 **Blocked**   Set margins and tab stops. Turn up two single spaces after the main/subheading or, if a ruled table, turn up two single spaces after the first horizontal line. The heading over the first column is typed at the left margin. Headings in the other columns start at the tab stop set for the beginning of the longest line of each column (could be heading or column item). The £ sign is usually typed above the first figure of the £'s.

The column **items** are typed at the tab stops set for the start of the longest item. With figures, remember to type units under units and tens under tens, etc.

2.2 **Centred**   Set margins and tab stops. If the **column heading** is **longer** than the column items and if there is only one line in the heading, type it at the left margin or at the tab stop set. If there is more than one line in a column heading, see instructions under **multiple-line** column headings.

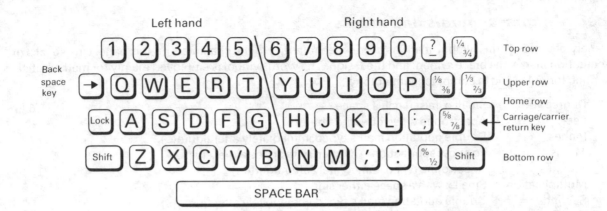

Left hand   Right hand

Back space key

1 2 3 4 5 6 7 8 9 0 ? ¼/¾   Top row

→ Q W E R T Y U I O P ⅛/⅜ ⅓/⅔   Upper row

    Home row

Lock A S D F G H J K L : ⅝/⅞ ←   Carriage/carrier return key

Shift Z X C V B N M / : %/½ Shift   Bottom row

SPACE BAR

Preliminary practice

1 ·Place your book on the right-hand side of your machine, or as indicated by your teacher.
2 Place your finger tips on the home keys. Left finger tips on **A S D F** and right finger tips on **J K L**; Check that you place them correctly.
3 Keep your left thumb close to your left first finger.
4 Extend your right thumb so that it is slightly above the centre of the space bar.
5 Now check your **posture**.
   Your head—hold it erect, facing the book.
   Your shoulders—hold them back and relaxed.
   Your body—centre yourself opposite the J key a hand-span away from the machine.
   Your back—straight, with your body sloping slightly forward from the hips.
   Arms and elbows—let them hang loosely.
   Wrists—keep them low, barely clearing the machine.
   Hands—close together, low, flat across the backs.
   Fingers—slightly curved.
   Waist—sit back in the chair.
   Feet—on the floor, one foot slightly in front of the other.

6 **VDU screen**
Wherever possible:
6.1 Position the body so that you are looking straight ahead at the VDU—avoid looking at the screen sideways.
6.2 Eyes should be level with the top of the screen and between 406 mm (16 inches) and 762 mm (30 inches) from the screen.
6.3 Use adequate lighting and see that there is no glare on the screen from daylight or artificial light.

Finger movement drill

1 Without typing, practise the finger movement for the exercise you are about to type. During this preliminary practice, you may look at your fingers. You will find it helpful to say the letters to yourself. Continue the preliminary practice until your fingers 'know' where to move from the home key. Always return finger to its home key.
2 When you are confident that your fingers have acquired the correct movement, repeat this practice **without looking at your fingers**. Keep your eyes on the copy in your book and do not strike the keys. If you hesitate in making the finger movement, go back and repeat step 1.
3 Practise the finger movement for each new key until your finger moves confidently and crisply to that key.

Special signs, symbols and marks

A variety of words (sign, symbol, mark) is used when referring to the characters on this page. One speaks of punctuation marks, the brace symbol and the £ sign. The word symbol is employed mainly for mathematical and scientific formulae and in computer terminology.

Degree	Small o, raised half a space.	6°
Feet	Apostrophe typed after the figure(s).	8'
Inches	Double quotation marks typed immediately after figure(s).	7"
Minus	To show subtraction—hyphen with space either side.	6 - 4 = 2
Minutes	Apostrophe typed immediately after figure(s).	10'
Multiplication	Small x with a space either side.	4 x 5
Seconds	Double quotation marks typed immediately after figure(s).	9"
To	Hyphen or dash.	21-25

Constructing special signs, symbols and marks

Some characters, not provided on the keyboard, can be typed by combining two characters, ie by typing one character, backspacing and then typing the second character, or by typing one character and then the second immediately afterwards. In a few cases the interliner must be used to allow the characters to be raised or lowered.

Asterisk	Small x and hyphen.	☒
Brace	Continuous brackets typed one underneath the other.	( ) ( ) ( )
Caret	Underscore and oblique.	∠
Cedilla	Small c and comma.	ç
Cent	Small or capital C and oblique.	¢ ¢
Dagger	Capital I and hyphen.	‡
Diaeresis	Quotation marks.	ü
Divide into	Right bracket and underscore on line above.	)
Division	Hyphen, backspace and type colon.	÷
Dollar	Capital S, backspace and type oblique.	$
Double dagger	Capital I raised half a space, backspace and type another capital I slightly below; or capital I and equation sign.	‡
Equation	Two hyphens—one slightly above the other.	=
Exclamation	Apostrophe, backspace and type full stop.	!
Paragraph	Small c and lowered capital I.	¶
Plus	Hyphen and lowered apostrophe.	+
Section	Two capital S's or two small s's.	§ §
Square brackets	Oblique and underscore.	[ ]
Square root	Small v and oblique, followed by underscore on line above.	√
Thousand	Capital K.	£20,000 = £20K
Umlaut	Quotation marks.	ü

On modern typewriters many of the above characters are provided. On others, it is difficult to type the division or plus as combined characters. Where this is the case, it would be wise to insert these in matching-colour ink.

When the **asterisk** has to be typed in the body of the text, it is typed as a superscript (raised character). Before typing the combination asterisk, turn the cylinder one half space towards you, type small x, backspace and type hyphen; then turn back to normal typing line. Where the asterisk is already fitted, **do not** lower the paper before typing, as the sign on the typeface is already raised.

To type a **square bracket** take the following steps:

Left bracket
1 Type oblique sign.
2 Backspace one and type underscore.
3 Turn cylinder back one full linespace and type underscore.
4 Turn cylinder up one full linespace, backspace once and continue with typing up to the right bracket.

Right bracket
1 Type oblique sign.
2 Backspace two and type underscore.
3 Turn cylinder back one full linespace and type underscore.
4 Turn cylinder up one single space, tap space bar once and continue typing.

Practise carriage/carrier/cursor return

1 *MANUAL MACHINES*
See manufacturer's handbook.

2 *ELECTRIC MACHINES*
2.1 Preliminary practice *without returning the carriage/carrier.* Look at the carriage/carrier return key (on the right-hand side of the keyboard) and make the reach with your right-hand little finger from the semicolon to the return key and back to the semicolon.
2.2 All fingers remain just slightly above their HOME KEY except the right-hand little finger.
2.3 With eyes on textbook:
2.3.1 raise the little finger of the right hand and lightly press the return key,
2.3.2 return the little finger to the semicolon key immediately.

3 *ELECTRONIC MACHINES*
With electronic keyboards you can, by depressing a function key, use automatic carrier/cursor return. You will notice that the carrier/cursor returns automatically at the set right margin when the line is full. This is often referred to as word wraparound. Follow the instructions given in the machine handbook or ask your teacher for advice.

Striking the keys

Manual machines—strike keys firmly and sharply.
Electric/electronic machines—stroke keys.

Prepare to type

In order to prepare yourself and your machine for typing, take the following action:
1 Electric/electronic machines—insert plug in socket and switch on machine.
2 Place book on right-hand side of machine or as instructed by your teacher.
3 Place blank typing paper on left-hand side of machine or as instructed by your teacher.
4 Set left margin at 20*.
5 Set linespace selector on '1'.
6 Set paper guide on '0'.
7 Move paper bail out of the way.
8 Insert sheet of A4 paper.
9 If necessary, straighten paper.
10 Return paper bail to normal position.
11 If necessary, turn the paper back, using right cylinder knob, until only a small portion of paper shows above paper bail.
12 Place front of keyboard level with edge of desk so that the J key is opposite the centre of your body.
13 If necessary, adjust chair height so that your forearms are on the same slope as the keyboard.
14 Place chair so that you are about a hand-span away from edge of desk.
15 Feet apart and firmly on floor.
16 See that carriage/carrier/cursor is at left margin.

Computers, word processors and electronic typewriters may be programmed to provide whatever top, bottom and side margins you consistently require.

NOTE: Until you are instructed otherwise, all exercises should be typed line for line as in the text—use return key.

* You may use a pre-stored margin setting if you wish.

Quotation marks

See page 112.

Roman numerals

1   Units I (1)   X (10)   C (100)   M (1000)
    Fives V (5)   L (50)   D (500)

2   The four *unit* symbols can be repeated to express two or three units of the *same* symbol.

    Examples

1 = I	2 = II	3 = III
10 = X	20 = XX	30 = XXX
100 = C	200 = CC	300 = CCC
1000 = M	2000 = MM	3000 = MMM

3   The symbol I may be used or repeated (up to III) *after* any of the above units or fives, in which case it *adds* to the symbol in front.

    Examples

I = 1	VI = 6	XI = 11	LI = 51
II = 2	VII = 7	XII = 12	LII = 52
III = 3	VIII = 8	XIII = 13	LIII = 53

CI = 101	DI = 501	MI = 1001
CII = 102	DII = 502	MII = 1002
CIII = 103	DIII = 503	MIII = 1003

4   To express 4, 9, 40, 400 and 900, take the symbol immediately *above* and put the appropriate unit symbol *in front*, which means that *it is subtracted* from the higher symbol.

4 =	5 −	1 = IV
40 =	50 −	10 = XL
400 =	500 −	100 = CD
9 =	10 −	1 = IX
90 =	100 −	10 = XC
900 =	1000 −	100 = CM.

    NOTE: I can be placed *only* before V or X;
    X can be placed *only* before L or C;
    C can be placed *only* before D or M.

5   To express numbers other than those in point 4, take the unit of five symbol immediately *below* and *add* to it the remaining symbols by putting these *after* the unit or five symbol.

    Examples
    6 = *5* + 1 = VI
    7 = *5* + 2 = VII
    8 = *5* + 3 = VIII
    14 = *10* + 4 = XIV
    15 = *10* + 5 = XV
    16 = *10* + 6 = XVI
    17 = *10* + 7 = XVII
    18 = *10* + 8 = XVIII

    60 = *50* + 10 = LX
    70 = *50* + 20 = LXX
    80 = *50* + 30 = LXXX
    600 = *500* + 100 = DC
    700 = *500* + 200 = DCC
    800 = *500* + 300 = DCCC

6   A horizontal line drawn over the unit symbol means that the unit is multiplied by 1000.

    Example
    $\overline{M}$ = 1000 × 1000 = 1,000,000.

7   To convert arabic figures into roman numerals, take each figure in turn.

    Example
    To convert 467, proceed as follows:
    400 = 500 − 100 = CD; 60 = 50 + 10 = LX;
    7 = 5 + 2 = VII; 467 = CDLXVII.

8   Used as follows:
    For monarchs, form and class numbers, chapters, preface pages, tables or paragraphs. Sometimes to express the year, enumerations, subsections, etc.

Semi-blocked letters

See page 133.

Semi-blocked memos

See page 136.

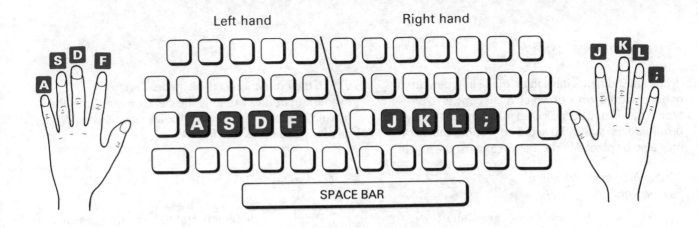

Introduction to home keys

Type the following drills.

Exercise 1

1.1 Curve fingers slightly.
1.2 Look at keyboard and place fingers on HOME KEYS
   —left hand **A S D F**, right hand **J K L ;**
1.3 Type the two lines exactly as they are—**do not look at the keyboard**.

fffjjjfffjjjfffjjjfffjjjfffjjjfff   Return carriage/carrier/cursor
fffjjjfffjjjfffjjjfffjjjfffjjjfff   Return carriage/carrier/cursor
   twice

1.4 Sit back, relax and look at what you have typed.

Exercise 2—operating the space bar

A clear space is left between each group of
letters or words. This is done by tapping the
space bar with the right thumb. Keep your other
fingers on the HOME KEYS as you operate the
space bar. Practise operating the space bar and
returning carriage/carrier/cursor.

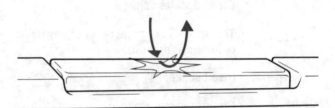

See that carriage/carrier/cursor is at left margin.

Exercise 3

3.1 Curve fingers slightly.
3.2 Look at the keyboard and place your left-hand fingers on **A S D F** and right-hand
   fingers on **J K L ;**
3.3 Type the three lines exactly as they are—**do not look at the keyboard**.

fff   jjj   fff   jjj   fjf   jfj   fff   jjj   fff   fjfj   Return carriage/carrier/cursor
fff   jjj   fff   jjj   fjf   jfj   fff   jjj   fff   fjfj   Return carriage/carrier/cursor
fff   jjj   fff   jjj   fjf   jfj   fff   jjj   fff   fjfj   Return carriage/carrier/cursor
   twice

3.4 Sit back, relax and look at what you have typed.

Exercise 4

Repeat exercises 1, 2 and 3.

Proofreaders' marks

When amendments have to be made in typewritten or handwritten work of which a fair copy is to be typed, these may be indicated in the original copy by proofreaders' marks. To avoid confusion, the mark may also be placed in the margin against the line in which the correction is to be made. Certain examining bodies use only the stet signs, ie ⊘ in the margin, but other examining bodies may use any or all of the examples that follow.

Mark which may be in margin	Meaning		Mark in text
lc	Lower case—small letter(s).	— /	Under letter(s) to be altered or struck through letter(s).
uc or CAPS	Upper case—capital letter(s).	= /	Under letter(s) to be altered or struck through letter(s).
ᴈ	Delete—take out.	/	Through letter(s) or word(s).
NP or //	New paragraph.	// or ⌐	Placed before the first word of a new paragraph.
Stet or ⊘	Let it stand, ie type the word(s) that has been crossed out and has a dotted or broken line underneath.	- - - -	Under word(s) struck out.
Run on	No new paragraph required. Carry straight on.		
⅄	Caret—insert letter, word(s) omitted	⅄	Placed where the omission occurs.
⌒	Close up—less space.	⌒	Between letters or words.
trs	Transpose, ie change order of words or letters as marked.		Between letters or words, sometimes numbered.
#	Insert space.		
//	Straighten margin.		
ital.	Italic	—	(Underscore)
⊙	Insert full stop.		
;/	Insert semi-colon.		
⊙	Insert colon.		
⸴/	Insert comma.		
⸌	Insert apostrophe.		
H	Insert hyphen.		
/−/	Insert dash.		
⸌⸌ ⸌⸌	Insert quotation marks.		
#	Insert space.		
⅄	Insert words.		
(⅄)⅄	Insert brackets.		

If a word is not clear in the text, it may be written in the margin in capitals. The word should be typed in lower case, or as indicated in the original script.

Follow the routine suggested on page 6 under the heading **prepare to type**, then type each line or sentence three times, saying the letters to yourself. If time permits, complete your practice by typing each group of lines as it appears. Keep your eyes on the copy while you type and also when using the return key. The carriage/carrier/cursor must be returned **immediately** after the last character in the line has been typed. Set left margin stop at 20 (or pre-stored margin setting) use single spacing, and turn up two single spaces between exercises.

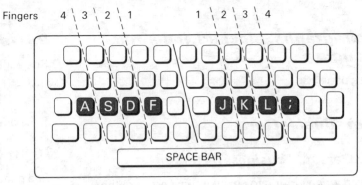

Fingers

Back straight   Feet firmly on floor

New keys **F** *and* **J**
Use first fingers

1   fff jjj fjf jfj fjf jfj fff jjj fjf fjfj

Turn up TWICE between exercises

New keys **D** *and* **K**
Use second fingers

2   ddd kkk dkd kdk dkd kdk ddd kkk dkd dkdk
3   fff jjj ddd kkk fkf kfk jdj djd fjk fdjk

New keys **S** *and* **L**
Use third fingers

4   sss lll sls lsl sls lsl sss lll sls slsl
5   fff jjj ddd kkk sss lll fds jkl fds jklj

New keys **A** *and* **;**
Use little fingers

6   aaa ;;; a;a ;a; a;a ;a; aaa ;;; ;a; a;a;
7   f;f jaj d;d kak a;s lal aaa ;;; a;a a;a;

Word building

8   aaa lll all lll aaa ddd lad ddd aaa dad;
9   fff aaa ddd fad sss aaa ddd sad fad lad;

*Apply the keys
you know*

10 dad fad sad lad ask all dad fad sad lad;
11 lass fall lads fads lass fall dads fads;

ONE space after semicolon

12 all sad lads; a sad lass; a lad asks dad
13 all sad lads ask a dad; a sad lass falls
14 as a lass falls dad falls; all lads fall

*End of typing
period*

Remove paper by using paper release.
If electric, turn off machine and remove plug from socket.
Cover machine.
Remove used and unused paper.
Leave desk tidy.

Paragraphs, blocked, indented, hanging

See page 130.

Personal letters

1 Personal business letters

Used when writing to an unknown person or firm about a personal business matter. The layout is similar to that of a business letter. If your home address is not printed on your stationery, type it about 13 mm ($\frac{1}{2}$ inch) from the top at the left margin, or centred on page, or in such a way that the last line ends flush with the right-hand margin. Date in usual place. Name and address of addressee may be typed in usual place or two spaces below your name at the left margin.

2 Formal personal letters

Used when writing to someone older than yourself or to whom you owe respect. Layout as for personal business letter. Salutation is formal, eg Dear Miss Brown, Dear Mrs Taylor, Dear Mr Emery.

3 Personal letters

Used when writing to a personal friend. Your address and date as in a personal business letter. No name and address of addressee. Salutation is informal, eg Dear Mary, Dear Arthur, Dear Uncle George.

Postcards

See page 105.

Postscript

See page 72.

Pre-stored margins

See pages 6 and 24.

Print (typing from)

See page 128.

Proofreading

The most competent typist makes an error occasionally, but that error does not appear in the letter or document placed on the employer's desk for signature. Why? Because the typist has carefully proofread the work before it has been taken from the machine; the error has been detected and it has been corrected.

While proofreading has always been an integral part of the typist's training, it is now doubly important because if you wish to operate a word processing machine, your ability to check quickly and correct errors in typing, spelling, grammar, etc is even more meaningful. Documents prepared on a word processing machine are often used over and over again and you can well imagine the disastrous results if you typed the wrong figures, were careless in checking your finished work and your original error is then repeated hundreds of times. When checking soft copy on the VDU screen, it can be helpful to use the cursor as a guide as you move it across the screen; a less time-consuming aid is to have the base of the screen for the line you are checking and using the vertical scroll to move the text up one line at a time. Adjusting the brightness of the soft copy can also be helpful.

Follow **prepare to type** on page 6 and instructions given at top of page 8.

Set left margin stop at 20 (or pre-stored margin setting) use single spacing, and turn up two single spaces between exercises.

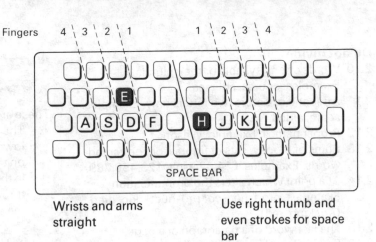

Fingers   4 3 2 1   1 2 3 4

Wrists and arms straight

Use right thumb and even strokes for space bar

Keyboarding review

1 aaa ;;; sss lll ddd kkk fff jjj asd jkl;

2 ask a lad; ask all lads; ask a sad lass;

3 all lads fall; dad falls; dad asks a lad

Turn up TWICE between exercises

New key **E**
Use D finger

4 ddd eee ded ded see ded lee ded fee ded;

5 ded sea ded lea ded led ded fed ded eke;

New key **H**
Use J finger

6 jjj hhh jhj jhj has jhj had jhj she jhj;

7 jhj has jhj had jhj she jhj ash jhj dash

Word building

8 hhh eee lll ddd held jjj aaa fff jaffas;

9 sss hhh aaa lll shall fff eee ddd feeds;

Apply the keys you know

10 see lee fee sea lea led fed eke see lee;

11 ash dash fash sash hash lash; heel shed;

12 a lass has had a salad; dad sees a lake;

13 a jaffa salad; she held a sale; he shall

14 she feeds a lad; dad has a hall; a shed;

Sizes of typefaces

10 pitch   10 characters take up 25 mm (1 inch) of space
12 pitch   12 characters take up 25 mm (1 inch) of space
15 pitch   15 characters take up 25 mm (1 inch) of space

What size of typeface are you using?

Do not divide

2.10 Words of one syllable or their plurals.
Examples: course, courses.

2.11 After one or before two letters only. Examples:
again, aided.

2.12 Proper names. Example: Wilson.

2.13 Sums of money, sets of figures, or contracted
words. Examples: £14.32, isn't, 123,456,789.

2.14 At a point which alters the pronunciation.
Examples: prod-uct (*not* pro-duct), kin-dred
(*not* kind-red).

2.15 The last word of a paragraph or a page.

2.16 Foreign words—unless you know the language
and where to divide.

NOTE: With many electronic keyboards it is not
necessary to press the return key at the end of each
line to move the cursor down to the beginning of the
next line. If the last word does not fit on the line, the
system automatically brings the word down to the
next line. This is known as wraparound or wordwrap.
However, it will be necessary to press the return key
for extra linespacing and after short lines, headings,
etc.

It may also be possible for your machine to
hyphenate a word at the end of the line, but, as the
machine does not know the rules for hyphenation, it
will insert the hyphen after the last character on the
line, whatever it may be, and ask you to make a
decision.

Manuscript (typing from)

See page 44.

Margin-release key

See page 51.

Margins (standard)

If no margin settings are given for an exercise, the
following suggestions will be helpful:

	Typing line	12 pitch	10 pitch
A5 portrait	50 spaces	13–63	6–56
A4 and A5	60 spaces	22–82	12–72
landscape	70 spaces	18–88	—not suitable
Memoranda		13–90	11–75

Measurements (typing of)

See page 53.

Minutes of a meeting

See page 102.

Modification and rearrangement of material

See page 81.

Notice of meeting

See page 100.

Numbers

1 Cardinal numbers

These are arabic numbers—1, 2, 3, etc.

1.1 The figure 1 is expressed either by the
lower-case l or by the figure 1 if this is provided
on the typewriter, but these must not be mixed,
ie the same key must be used for figure 1
throughout an exercise. **Never** use capital I for
the cardinal number 1.

2 Ordinal numbers

Denote order or sequence, eg 1st, 2nd or first,
second.

2.1 These are not abbreviations and must not,
therefore, be followed by a full stop.

2.2 Words or figures may be used: follow the script
and be consistent—either words or figures.

3 Roman numerals

These are formed from seven symbols known as units
and fives, viz:

3.1 Units   I (1)   X (10)   C (100)   M (1,000)
3.2 Fives   V (5)   L (50)   D (500)

4 Figures in columns

4.1 Units under units, tens under tens, etc.

4.2 Thousands, etc, should be marked either by a
comma or space—be consistent.

5 Figures in continuous matter

5.1 Four digits—thousands marked by comma or
typed close up—4,582, 4582; preferable always
to use the comma.

5.2 Five or more digits, thousands **must** be marked
by commas—28,372, 613,924.

5.3 If a task contains groups of five or more digits,
then any four digit figures, in the same task,
must have a comma separating hundreds and
thousands.

5.4 Always be consistent when typing figures; eg
type 20,000 not 20 thousand; type 300 not 3
hundred.
EXCEPTION   It is acceptable to type
£3,000,000 or £3m or £3 million, but it would
seem preferable always to use figures.

5.5 Thousand(s) may be represented by K, eg 24K
equals 24,000.

Open punctuation

See page 22.

Paper sizes

See pages 10–13.

Follow **prepare to type** on page 6 and
instructions given at top of page 8.

Set left margin stop at 20 (or pre-stored margin
setting) use single spacing, and turn up two
single spaces between exercises.

Fingers   4 3 2 1   1 2 3 4

SPACE BAR

Smooth, even strokes   Eyes on copy always

Keyboarding
review

1 asd ;lk ded jhj def khj fed has lee had;

2 add salads; a sea lake; lads feed seals;

3 add leeks; she had leeks; he has a hall;

Turn up TWICE between exercises

New key **G**
Use F finger

4 fff ggg fgf fgf fag fgf lag fgf sag fgf;

5 fgf jag fgf gag fgf hag fgf keg fgf leg;

New key **U**
Use J finger

6 jjj uuu juj juj due juj sue juj hue juj;

7 juj sug juj jug juj dug juj hug juj lug;

Word building

8 uuu sss eee ddd use uses used useful us;

9 jjj uuu ddd ggg eee judge judges judged;

Apply the keys
you know

10 fag sag lag jag gag hag keg leg egg keg;

11 dues hues jugs hugs lugs suds eggs legs;

12 he had a dull glass; a judge has a flag;

13 see she has a full jug; she used jaffas;

14 dad had a full keg; he shall guess; use;

Size of paper
12 pitch

When giving the measurements of paper, always state the width first.
With 12 pitch typeface there are 12 characters to 25 mm (1").
A4 paper 210 × 297 mm ($8\frac{1}{4}$" × $11\frac{3}{4}$")

0   100

centre point 50

Horizontal and vertical display

1 Horizontal display

1.1 Arithmetical calculation—See page 46.

1.2 Headings and displayed items may be centred on the paper or on the typing line. In either case, find the centre point and backspace once for every two letters and spaces that the typed line will occupy (ignore any odd letter) and begin typing at the point to which you have backspaced. To centre THE TOTAL, backspace TH Espace TO TA (ignore the L). Say the letters to yourself as you backspace.

No punctuation is inserted at the end of lines unless the last word is abbreviated and full punctuation is being used.

NOTE: When the paper is inserted so that the left edge is at 0, note the scale point at which the right edge appears; half that number is the centre of the paper. For example: A4 paper extends from 0 to 100 (elite) or 0 to 82 (pica); the centre would be 50 (elite) or 41 (pica). To find the centre point of the typing line, when the margins have already been set, add the margins together and divide by two. For example, with margins of 20 and 85 the centre point of the typing line is, $20 + 85 = 105 \div 2 = 52$ (ignore fraction left over).

1.3 All lines centred—See page 128.

2 Vertical display

2.1 Count the number of lines (including blank ones) that the material will occupy.

2.2 Subtract that figure from the number of line-spaces on your paper. On A4 paper there are approximately 70 single spaces; on A5 portrait paper there are 50 single spaces, and on A5 landscape paper there are 35 single spaces.

2.3 After subtracting, divide the remainder by two (ignoring any fraction) to determine on what line to begin typing. For example, to centre eight lines of double-spaced copy on A5 portrait paper:
you need 15 lines, ie 8 typed, 7 blank.

$50 - 15 = 35$ lines left over.

$35 \div 2 = 17$ (ignore $\frac{1}{2}$). Start to type the matter on the next line (18).

Inset matter (left margin)

See page 56.

Interliner lever

See page 61.

Invitations

It is customary to use formal wording when sending out invitations to weddings, coming of age parties, etc. The invitations are written in the third person with a blank space left for the insertion of names of the guests in ink. The invitation begins with the name(s) of the writer(s) whose address is placed at the bottom left margin. The date and RSVP are at the lower right margin. Invitations are not signed. The invitation should be placed in an envelope addressed to the recipient.

Itinerary

See page 124.

Justified right margin

See page 124.

Line-end division

1 General

1.1 If possible, avoid dividing a word at the end of a line.

1.2 If it is necessary to do so in order to avoid an unsightly right-hand margin, you should not divide on more than two consecutive lines.

1.3 Divide according to syllables *provided that the pronunciation of the word is not thereby changed*.

1.4 Wherever possible, let the portion of the word left at the end of the line indicate what the word is.

2 Specific

Divide

2.1 After a prefix and before a suffix. Examples: inter-sect, absorp-tion.

2.2 *Before* the repeated consonant if the final consonant is doubled (to apply spelling rule). Example: shop-ping.

2.3 *After* the repeated consonant if the root word ends in a double consonant. Example: miss-ing.

2.4 Between the two consonants (usually) when a consonant is doubled medially. Example: bag-gage.

2.5 After a single-letter syllable in the *middle* of a word. Example: manu-script.

2.6 Between two *different* consecutive consonants in the *middle* of a word. Example: desig-nation.

2.7 After the first of three consecutive consonants in the *middle*. Example: magis-trate.

2.8 At the original point of junction in compound words and words already hyphenated. Example: fisher-man, pre-eminent.

2.9 Between two separately sounded vowels. Example: radi-ator.

Follow **prepare to type** on page 6 and instructions given at top of page 8.

Set left margin stop at 20 (or pre-stored margin setting) use single spacing, and turn up two single spaces between exercises.

Fingers   4 3 2 1   1 2 3 4

SPACE BAR

Check your posture   Return carriage/carrier without looking up

Keyboarding review

1 fds jkl ded juj fgf jhj hag jug dug leg;
2 a lass uses a flask; all lads had a jug;
3 sell us a full keg; see she has a glass;

New key R *Use F finger*

4 fff rrr frf frf jar frf far frf rag frf;
5 frf are frf ark frf red frf fur frf rug;

New key I *Use K finger*

6 kkk iii kik kik kid kik lid kik did kik;
7 kik dig kik fig kik rig kik jig kik gig;

Word families

8 fill hill rill drill grill skill frills;
9 ark lark dark hark; air fair hair lairs;

Apply the keys you know

10 fill his flask; he is here; he had a rug
11 her red dress is here; she has fair hair
12 she likes a fair judge; he has dark hair
13 his lad fills a jug; she has rare skills
14 she is sure; ask her here; he likes figs

Size of paper   A4 paper 210 × 297 mm (8¼″ × 11¾″)

10 pitch

0	82
	centre point 41	

15 pitch

0	124
	centre point 62	

Footnotes

1 Footnotes are used

1.1 To identify a reference or person quoted in the body of a report.

1.2 To give the source of a quotation cited in a report.

1.3 For explanations that may help or interest a reader.

2 Each footnote is

2.1 Preceded by the reference mark which corresponds to the reference in the text.

2.2 Typed in single spacing.

The reference mark in the text must be a superscript. In the footnote it is typed either on the same line or as a superscript. In the text **no** space is left between the reference mark and the previous character. In the footnote **one space** is left between the reference mark and the first word. The reference mark may be a number, asterisk, dagger or double dagger, and is placed outside the quotation mark and the punctuation mark.

It is now more popular to use one asterisk for the first footnote, two for the second and three for the third, rather than a dagger or double dagger, as the daggers are not always easy to construct on an electronic keyboard. The use of figures (in brackets) as a reference mark is favoured by printers.

In ordinary typewritten work, the footnote is usually placed at the foot of the page on which the corresponding reference appears in the body, and typed in **single** spacing. Care must be taken to leave enough space at the bottom of the page for the footnote, and, if a continuation page is needed, a clear space of 25 mm (1 inch) should be left after the last line of the footnote. It is usually separated from the main text by a horizontal line from margin to margin, and this line is typed by the underscore one single space after the last line of the text, and the footnote on the second single space below the horizontal line. If there is more than one footnote, turn up two single spaces between each. Where the typed text is short and there is plenty of white space on the sheet of paper, you may wish to make a more attractive display by leaving the clear space after the text and before the footnote, with the last line of the footnote ending 25 mm (1 inch) from the bottom of the page. Some examining bodies do not always insert a horizontal line before the footnote and, in that case, it may be wise for the examination candidate to omit the line, and we suggest that examining bodies should be asked to make the candidate's position clear. There is no horizontal line before footnotes which follow a tabulated statement.

If the typewriter has an asterisk key, the typed character will be raised half a space, but if a small x and the hyphen key are used, then it will be necessary to use the halfspace mechanism of the typewriter, or the interliner, to raise the mark above the line of typing. All footnote signs should be superscripts if the asterisk key on the typewriter is used. On word processors, there will be a superscript facility for raising characters above the typing line.

When typing a draft of a document which contains a footnote(s), it is helpful to type the footnote on the next line after the reference in the text, with a horizontal line **above** and **below** it. When the final copy has to be typed, the amount of space required for the footnote(s) at the bottom of the page will then be obvious. The *Oxford Dictionary for Writers and Editors* says that copy for the printer may have the footnotes at the bottom of the page or on a separate sheet with reference figures for identification.

Form letters

See page 62.

Forms and deletions

See pages 59–60.

Forms of address

See pages 180 and 184.

Fractions

See page 36.

Full punctuation

See page 126.

Half-space corrections

See page 127.

Hard copy (printout)

See page 24.

Headings, blocked:

Main—See page 30.

Paragraph—See page 31.

Shoulder—See page 32.

Side—See page 82.

Sub—See page 30.

Headings, centred (with indented paragraphs)

See pages 130–31.

Follow **prepare to type** on page 6 and instructions given at top of page 8.

Set left margin stop at 20 (or pre-stored margin setting) use single spacing, and turn up two single spaces between exercises.

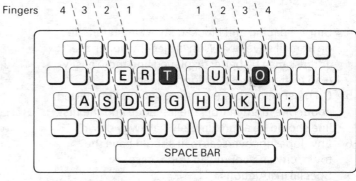

Fingers   4 \ 3 \ 2 \ 1   1 / 2 / 3 / 4

SPACE BAR

Wrists and arms straight

Use right thumb and even stroke for space bar

Keyboarding review

1 fgf jhj frf juj dad kid sid did her rug;
2 his full fees; she likes a dark red rug;
3 his girl is here; he is glad she is sure

New key **T**
Use F finger

4 fff ttt ftf ftf fit ftf kit ftf lit ftf;
5 ftf sit ftf hit ftf sat ftf hat ftf fat;

New key **O**
Use L finger

6 lll ooo lol lol lot lol got lol hot lol;
7 lol rot lol dot lol jot lol tot lol sot;

Word families

8 old hold sold gold; look rook hook took;
9 let set jet get ret; rate late hate date

Homophones

Use your dictionary to check the meaning

10 sea see; here hear; tide tied; aid aide;
11 ail ale; right rite; tare tear; fir fur;

Apply the keys you know

12 get her a set; he took a full jar to her
13 he had sold the gold; at this late date;
14 that old dress looks just right for her;

Size of paper

A5 **landscape** paper measures 210 × 148 mm ($8\frac{1}{4}$″ × $5\frac{7}{8}$″), ie the width is the same as A4 but the length is half A4; therefore, the number of character spaces across a page of A5 landscape paper is 100.

0   100

centre point 50

4 Single spacing and blocked style are preferable on a small envelope. With larger envelopes the address may be better displayed and more easily read by being typed in double spacing.

5 On most envelopes the address should be started about one-third in from the left edge and the first line should be approximately half-way down.

6 Envelopes for overseas mail should have the town/city and country in upper case.

7 Special instructions.

7.1 PERSONAL, CONFIDENTIAL, PRIVATE, URGENT should be typed in capitals, two spaces above the name of the addressee.

7.2 FOR THE ATTENTION OF . . . is typed two spaces above the name and address of the addressee and may be in capitals or lower case with initial capitals when it must be underscored.

7.3 RECORDED DELIVERY, REGISTERED MAIL and SPECIAL DELIVERY are typed in the top left corner in capitals, or immediately below the return address if there is one.

7.4 FREEPOST and POSTE RESTANTE are typed after the name of the addressee.

7.5 The words PAR AVION (BY AIRMAIL) are typed in the top left corner.

7.6 Care of—typed c/o at the beginning of the line containing (a) the name or number of the house, eg Ms R Sharpe, c/o 21 Market Street, or (b) the name of the occupier, eg Ms R Sharpe, c/o Mrs U Needle, 21 Market Street.

7.7 BY HAND is typed in the top right corner in capitals.

8 Remember to type the envelopes for any extra carbon copies which may be sent to the other offices or persons for their information.

9 Forms of address—See page 180.

Financial statements

There are certain accounts which you may be asked to type for your employer, such as balance sheet, income and expenditure account, receipts and payments account.

Guide to typing

1 The financial statement may be divided into two sides and may have a line down the middle of the page.

2 Leave the same number of spaces to the left and right of the centre of the page—say half an inch clear on either side.

2.1 With A5 landscape paper or A4 paper, this would mean the centre of the paper is 50(41) and, to leave half an inch clear, backspace 7(6) from 50(41) plus the number of figures in the longest item in the figure column—set a tab stop for the start of the longest line in the left-hand figure column.

2.2 From 50(41) tap in 7(6) and set a tab stop for the start of the items on the right half of the page.

3 Leave left and right margins of 1 inch clear which means the left margin will be set at 13(11) and a tab stop set at 89(73). To find the starting point for the money column at the far right of the page, backspace from 89(73) one for one in the longest line of the column.

4 All headings, on right and left sides, start on the same lines, including the £ signs.

5 Use double spacing between each item. If any item requires more than one line, type the item in single spacing, indenting two spaces for the second and subsequent lines.

6 The totals on both sides must be typed opposite each other on the same line. This may mean leaving a blank space on the shorter side, before inserting the total and the total lines.

7 The horizontal lines above and below the total itself are typed as explained on page 61.

8 Blocked or centred display may be used with open or full punctuation.

Balance sheets

The method of setting out balance sheets is the same as that already explained above, although in some instances two separate sheets are used, the heading of the balance sheet running right across the two sheets without a break—half being typed on the liabilities side and ending close to the right edge of the paper and the other half typed on the assets side starting close to the left edge of the sheet.

The side containing the larger number of items should be typed first, and, before starting to type the second sheet, you should make a light pencil mark to show the precise point at which the heading is to be continued, to ensure that the two parts of the heading are in line with one another. Also mark lightly in pencil on the second sheet the line on which the £ sign appears, the line on which the first item is to be typed and the exact position for the total, so that the two sides may coincide exactly.

Vertical balance sheets

Decide on the margins. Set left and right margin.

From the right margin backspace one for one for the longest item in the money column and set a tab stop. Where an item runs on to two lines, it is usual to indent the second line two spaces. If there are two columns of figures, leave a minimum of three spaces between each column.

Folded leaflets

See page 108.

Follow **prepare to type** on page 6 and instructions given at top of page 8.

Set left margin stop at 20 (or pre-stored margin setting) use single spacing, and turn up two single spaces between exercises.

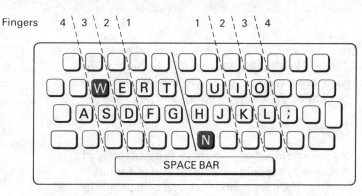

Fingers 4 3 2 1   1 2 3 4

Wrists and arms straight, fingers curved

Return carriage/carrier without looking up

Keyboarding review

1 ftf lol frf juj ded kik tot out rot dot;
2 this is a red jet; the lad took the gold
3 he asked a just fee; the old folk agree;

New key W
Use S finger

4 sss www sws sws low sws sow sws row sws;
5 sws hew sws few sws dew sws sew sws tew;

New key N
Use J finger

6 jjj nnn jnj jnj fan jnj ran jnj tan jnj;
7 jnj sin jnj kin jnj din jnj lin jnj tin;

Word families

8 end send lend tend fend rend wend trend;
9 low sow how row tow saw law daw jaw raw;

Homophones

Use your dictionary to check the meaning

10 sew sow; weak week; wear ware, fair fare
11 oar ore; new knew; knead need; not knot;

Apply the keys you know

12 we saw her look at the new gate; we know
13 he sent us a gift of red jeans last week
14 we had left a jade silk gown and the rug

Size of paper

A5 **portrait** paper measures 148 mm (width) × 210 mm ($5\frac{7}{8}''$ × $8\frac{1}{4}''$); ie the same overall size as A5 landscape paper but with portrait paper the shorter edge is at the top/bottom.

10 pitch	0 ——— 59	centre point 29
12 pitch	0 ——— 70	centre point 35
15 pitch	0 ——— 88	centre point 44

group of words. When used with blocked style, the ditto marks should be blocked at the beginning of each word; with centred style, the ditto marks should be centred under the word(s). See page 124.

Draft

If your employer asks you to type a draft copy of a document, it would be wise for you to enquire whether the document is likely to be radically revised or whether the draft is to show how the document will look when completed.

If the document is likely to be extensively revised after typing, then the draft should be in double or treble spacing with wide margins. On the other hand, if the draft is to show how it will look when finished, then it should be typed in the style required for the finished job.

The word DRAFT should always be typed in capitals at the top left-hand margin at least one clear space above the start of the document.

Elision

This is the omission of a letter (usually a vowel) when pronouncing a word, eg wouldn't, can't, don't. This form of abbreviation is seldom used in business correspondence unless direct speech is quoted, ie using quotation marks, or unless instructions have been given to use it.

Ellipsis

See page 98.

Enumerated items:

Arabic figures—See page 55.

Decimal—See page 103.

Letters—See page 55.

Roman, left—See page 79.

Roman, right—See page 132.

Envelopes and labels

Envelope sizes

C5 162 × 229 mm (6⅜″ × 9″)
takes A5 paper unfolded
and A4 paper folded once

C6 114 × 162 mm (4½″ × 6⅜″)
takes A4 paper folded twice
and A5 paper folded once

DL 110 × 220 mm (4¼″ × 8⅝″)
takes A4 paper folded equally into three

Label sizes

76.2 × 50.8 mm (3″ × 2″)
size preferred by some examining bodies
89 × 63.55 mm (3½″ × 1½″)
101.6 × 76.2 mm (4″ × 3″)

On the smaller labels it is often necessary to take two lines for the ATTENTION LINE, eg

For the attention of
Mr John R J St George-Hamilton

Post Office regulations

1 Post Office regulations require the address to be parallel with the longest side of the envelope.
2 Postal town should be typed in capitals on a fresh line.
3 The postcode should be typed as follows:
   3.1 It is always the last item in the address and should have a line to itself.
   3.2 If it is impossible because of lack of space to put the code on a separate line, type it two to six spaces to the right of the last line.
   3.3 Always type the code in block capitals.
   3.4 Do not use full stops or any punctuation marks between or after the characters in the code.
   3.5 Leave **one** clear space between the two halves of the code.
   3.6 **Never** underline the code.

Example   Open punctuation

Messrs W H Ramsay & Co
Mortimer Street
LONDON
W1N 8BA

Full punctuation

Messrs. W. H. Ramsay & Co.,
Mortimer Street,
LONDON.
W1N 8BA

Addressing envelopes, labels, postcards, etc—See also page 42.

1 Always be sure to use an envelope sufficiently large to take the letter and any enclosure.
2 Many firms have their name and address printed in the top left corner. This ensures the safe and speedy return of the letter if, for any reason, it cannot be delivered.
3 Always type the envelope for each letter immediately after typing the letter.

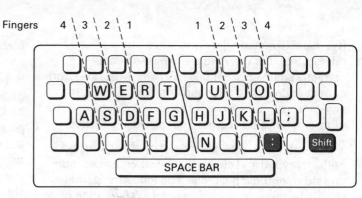

Follow **prepare to type** on page 6 and instructions given at top of page 8.

Set left margin stop at 20 (or pre-stored margin setting) use single spacing, and turn up two single spaces between exercises.

Check your posture   Eyes on copy

Keyboarding review

1   sws jnj ftf lol frf jhj won win new now;

2   we do not like those jars she got for us

3   the red dogs will go for a walk just now

Capital letters

To make capitals for letters typed by the left hand:
1   With right-hand little finger depress and hold right shift key well down.
2   Strike left-hand capital letter.
3   Remove finger from shift key and return all fingers to home keys.

New key **Right Shift**
Use right little finger

4   fF; dD; sS; aA; Ada; Sad; Dad; Fad; Wade

5   Gee; Reg; Ted; Sue; Flo; Ede; Dora; West

New key **:**
Use L finger

6   lll ... l.l f.l j.l Good.   Dear.   Ellis.

TWO spaces after full stop at end of sentence

7   Ask her.   Ted is sad.   Do go.   She will.

Word families

8   Wee; Weed; Feed; Reed; Seed; Deed; Greed

9   And; Sand; Wand; Rand; Send; Tend; Fend;

Homophones

Use your dictionary to check the meaning

10   altar alter; guest guessed; aught ought;

11   dear deer; aloud allowed; threw through;

Apply the keys you know

12   Ask Ed Reid if we should join the Swede.

13   She was right.   Dirk was jealous.   Fine.

14   Flora would like to go; just state when.

Typing errors

If you make a mistake, ignore it until the end of the exercise, then look at the keyboard and study the reach(es) for accurate finger movement—do not type while you look at the keyboard. *Never* overtype, ie type one character on top of another.

It is usual to include the name and address of one referee. See that you give the person's name—correctly spelt—his/her title (Mr/Mrs/Miss/Ms) and correct address and telephone number. **Never**, in any circumstances, give as a reference a person whose permission you have not asked in advance.

Your curriculum vitae/personal data sheet must be perfectly typed and clearly displayed with main, sub, and side/shoulder headings. The following points should be covered: your name and address; date of birth; secondary education/college/university; secretarial/office training; examinations passed; work experience (if any); special interests; name and address of a referee; date on which you are available for employment.

Cursor

When a visual display unit is used in conjunction with an electronic machine, the typing appears on the VDU screen. On the screen there is a movable dot (hyphen) which indicates the typing point at which the next typed character will appear. This movable dot/hyphen is called the cursor.

Data files

As well as being an expert typist, it is essential for you to have practice in finding and using information from various sources. Throughout this textbook, there are exercises where it is necessary for you to refer to another part of the book, or to the data files, for data to enable you to complete an exercise. The **data files** are on pages 173–174.

Dead keys

Some typewriters are provided with keys which, when depressed, do not cause the carriage/carrier to move forward the usual single character space. These are known as 'dead keys'. They are usually fitted for foreign accents so that the accent can be struck first and, without the necessity of backspacing, the letter key is then struck.

Electronic machines may have a few dead keys, eg a key for inserting vertical lines. Refer to the manufacturer's handbook for further details.

Decimals

See page 36.

Degree sign

If the typewriter does not have a special key for the degree sign, it is represented by the small o raised half a space. When typing 20 degrees, type 20° with no space between the figures and the degree sign; but when typing 20 degrees Fahrenheit or 20 degrees Celsius, type 20 °F or 20 °C—note that there is a space between the figures and the degree sign, but no space between the degree sign and the F or C.

Display

1 Horizontal

1.1 **Block-centred**   Centre the longest line which gives the starting point for all lines.
1.2 **Centred**   All lines centred on the paper or on the typing line. To find the centre point of the typing line, add together the points at which the margins are set and divide by two.

2 Vertical

2.1 Find the number of vertical lines on the paper being used.
2.2 Count the number of lines and blank spaces between the lines, in the exercise to be typed.
2.3 Deduct 2.2 from 2.1 and divide by two (ignore fractions).
2.4 Turn up the number of linespaces arrived at in 2.3 **plus one extra**.

Distractions

See page 74.

Distribution lists

See *Business letters, 4.15*, page 179.
Instead of typing cc followed by the names of the persons to whom copies of a document should be sent, your boss may require you to type a distribution/circulation list. An example is given on page 136.

Ditto marks

When the same word is repeated in consecutive lines of display matter, double quotation marks may be used under the repeated word. If there is more than one word repeated, the quotation marks must be typed under each word. The abbreviation 'do' (with the full stop in full punctuation) may be used under a

Follow **prepare to type** on page 6 and
instructions given at top of page 8.

Set left margin stop at 20 (or pre-stored margin
setting) use single spacing, and turn up two
single spaces between exercises.

Fingers 4 3 2 1   1 2 3 4

Leave TWO spaces after
full stop at end of
sentence

Feet firmly on
floor

Keyboarding review	1	aA; sS; dD; fF; wW; eE; rR; Red; Gee; As
	2	Ask Flo. See Roger. Tell Fred. Go in.
	3	Ede had gone. Write to us. A fake jug.

Capital letters

To make capitals for letters typed by the right hand:
1 With left-hand little finger depress and hold left shift key well down.
2 Strike right-hand capital letter.
3 Remove finger from shift key and return all fingers to home keys.

New key Left Shift
Use left little finger

4 jJa kKa lLa jUj kIk Judd Kidd Lode Hoad;
5 Ida Ken Len Jude Owen Hilda Oakes Usual;

New key B
Use F finger

6 fff bbb fbf fbf bud fbf bus fbf but fbf;
7 fbf rob fbf sob fbf fob fbf hob fbf job;

Word families

8 Nib Jib Lib Job Lob Hob Hail Jail Nails;
9 Jill Hill Kill Lill Tall Ball Fall Wall;

Homophones

Use your dictionary to check the meaning

10 break brake; bare bear; blue blew; suite
11 sweet; whether weather; road rode rowed;

Apply the keys you know

12 She will be taking those salads to Jane.
13 Jill knows. Kit had to bluff Bob Green.
14 *Fred will ask us to do those jobs again.*

Typing from manuscript

You may have to type business documents from handwritten drafts. Take
particular care to produce a correct copy. **Before typing**, read the
manuscript through to see that you understand it. Some words or letters, not
very clear in one part, may be repeated in another part more clearly.

Correction of errors

Correct the error as soon as you know you have made a mistake and read through the whole exercise when you have finished typing it and while the paper is still in the machine, in case there is an error you had not noticed before.

There are various methods which may be used to correct errors:

1 Rubber

1.1 Turn up the paper so that the error is on top of the platen or paper table.

1.2 Press the paper tightly against the cylinder or paper table to prevent slipping.

1.3 Erase the error by rubbing gently up and down, blowing away rubber dust as you do so. (Too much pressure may cause a hole.)

1.4 If you are using a new or heavily inked ribbon, erase first with a soft rubber and then with a typewriter eraser.

1.5 Turn paper back to writing line and insert correct letter or letters.

1.6 Always use a clean rubber.

NOTE: If the typewriter has a carriage, move it to the extreme right or left to prevent rubber dust from falling into the mechanism of the machine.

2 Correction paper

These specially coated strips of paper are placed in front of the printing point over the error on the original and between the carbon paper(s) and the copy sheet(s). The incorrect character(s) is (are) typed again through the correction paper(s) which will cover up or lift off the incorrect character(s). Remove the coated strips and type the correct character(s).

3 Correction fluid

Correction fluid is produced in various shades to match the typing paper and is applied with a small brush. The incorrect letter is obliterated and when the fluid is dry, the correct letter may be typed over the top. The liquid may be spirit- or water-based. If the spirit-based liquid is used, it is necessary to add thinner to the bottle as, after a time, the original liquid tends to thicken. Spirit-based liquid dries more quickly than water-based. Avoid unsightly blobs. Use tissue paper to wipe the brush.

4 Correction ribbon

Some electric typewriters and most electronic typewriters are fitted with a correction ribbon. When making a correction with a correction ribbon, it is necessary to:

4.1 Backspace to the error.

4.2 Press the correction key—the error is then removed.

4.3 Type the correct letter(s).

5 Correction on electronic typewriters

Electronic typewriters are equipped with a memory and may have a thin window display so that automatic corrections can be made—from a few characters to ten or more lines. The correction is made by backspacing the delete key and then typing in the correct character(s). Electronic typewriters may be fitted with a relocate key which, when depressed, returns the carrier to the last character typed before the correction was made.

NOTE: The latest electronic typewriters have visual display units and corrections are made by use of the automatic overstrike, delete or erase functions. They also have a disk drive and diskettes.

6 Corrections on word processors/computers

To make a correction on a word processor/computer, one would use the automatic overstrike, delete or erase functions.

Credit note

See page 65.

Curriculum vitae: a brief account of one's career

When you apply for a job, your prospective employer will require a summary of your education and training. He or she will want to know what academic qualifications you have, what specialist qualifications you have, what your main interests are, what recreational activities and hobbies you have, etc. Sometimes this information is referred to as a personal data sheet or a curriculum vitae.

No two people are alike and no two personal data sheets should be exactly the same. It is possible that you will arrange your personal record of your career in a somewhat different way when applying for different jobs. You will always wish to emphasize the qualities and qualifications that would make you valuable in the particular job for which you are applying.

If you have worked—for a salary or as a volunteer—you should mention this. Your work need not have been closely related to the work for which you are applying, but it may indicate to your prospective employer a measure of your intelligent thinking, dependability, resourcefulness, etc. Always list temporary or part-time work (holidays and Saturdays only).

Follow **prepare to type** on page 6 and instructions given at top of page 8.

Set left margin stop at 20 (or pre-stored margin setting) use single spacing, and turn up two single spaces between exercises.

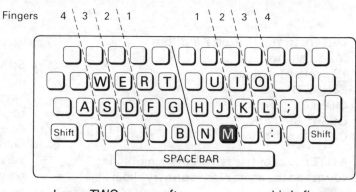

SPACE BAR

Leave TWO spaces after full stop at end of sentence

Little fingers for shift keys

Keyboarding review	1	fbf sws jnj ftf lol frf jhj Len Ken Hen Ian Win Go
	2	*Dan and Rob left. He will go just now. Ask Nell.*
	3	Lois and Earl will see June. Go with Fred Bolton.

New key **M**
Use J finger

4 jjj mmm jmj jmj jam jmj ham jmj dam jmj ram jmjmj;
5 jmj rum jmj hum jmj sum jmj mum jmj gum jmj strum;

Left and right shift keys

6 Ada Ben Dan East Fred Green Hilda Irwin James King
7 Lil Mark Nell Owen Rene Sara Todd Usher Wills Watt

Word families

8 arm farm harm warm alarm art hart tart darts mart;
9 game name dame fame same lame home dome some foam;

Homophones   Use your dictionary to check the meaning

10 there their; moan mown; air heir; eminent imminent
11 missed mist; mail male; aid aide; morning mourning

Practise shift keys 12 Nan Owen Miss Browne Mrs Watts Mr Usher Ms Rhodes.

13 Most of the fame goes to John who had been working
    hard for his father but he has now left the works.
    I think he is now at home.

Apply the keys you know

14 *I will see Fred tomorrow when he is in London. He will not attend the tennis meeting, but Mark will.*

7.4 Letters to the United Kingdom

Ms A Halcrow
12 Scotland Avenue
PENRITH
Cumbria
GREAT BRITAIN
CA11 7AA

NOTE: For overseas mail, the name of the **town** and the name of the **country** should be in capitals.

Cards

The typist will have to type cards for a variety of purposes such as a mailing list, telephone index, credit sales index, etc.

When cards are to be filed in alphabetical order, then the filing 'word' must start near the top edge of the card, say, half an inch down. Other information on the card should be suitably displayed with at least half an inch margins all round, unless the contents are such that it is not possible to leave margins.

A fair amount of practice in typing cards is essential and a great deal of care is necessary in order to see that the card does not slip, or become out of alignment, when turned up/down. A backing sheet will help; otherwise, fold over about half an inch/one inch at the top of a sheet of A4 paper, place the card underneath the fold and feed into the machine.

Catchword

See page 98.

Circular letters

Circulars, or circular letters, are letters of same contents which are sent to a number of customers or clients. The original is usually typed on a master sheet (stencil or offset litho) and a quantity is 'run off'.

Where individually typed circular letters are required, they may be prepared on a word processor or electronic typewriter and then printed.

1   Reference
In usual position.

2   Date
Typed in various ways, eg:
21 October 1989
October 1989 (month and year only)
Date as postmark. (These words are typed where you normally type the date.)

3   Name and address of addressee

3.1 Space may be left for this, and in that case the details are typed on individual sheets after they have been 'run off'. When preparing the master (or draft), turn up eight single spaces after the date (leaving seven clear) before typing the salutation.

3.2 Very often the name and address of addressee are not inserted and, if this is so, no space need be left when the master is prepared. Turn up two single spaces after the date.

4   Salutation

4.1 Dear   , the remainder of the salutation is typed in when the name and address are inserted.

4.2 Dear Sir, Dear Madam, Dear Sir(s), Dear Sir/Madam.

5   Signature

The person writing the letter may or may not sign it. If the writer is signing, type the complimentary close, etc, in the usual way. If the writer is not signing, type Yours faithfully and company's name* in the usual position, turn up two single spaces and type the name of the person writing the letter, then turn up two spaces and type the designation.

* If the company's name is not being inserted, turn up two single spaces after Yours faithfully and type the name of the writer, then turn up two spaces and type the writer's designation.

6   Tear-off portion

See page 85.

Clean and uncreased work

Typed work that is accurate and quickly produced can be spoilt by dirty finger marks, smudges and, particularly on the carbon copy, creases. It is important to be organized and methodical. Keep your workstation neat and tidy with everything within easy reach; this will aid you in producing neat and clean documents.

Continuous stationery

Invoice sets are usually in continuous form with perforations between the sets which may be NCR (no carbons required) paper or one-time only carbon paper. Paper for word processing printouts may also be in continuous form edged by sprocket holes for use on the tractor-feed device. The paper may be letterheads, invoice forms, payslips, etc.

Check your work after each exercise

After returning the carriage/carrier/cursor at the end of an exercise, check your typescript carefully and circle any errors. ALWAYS check BEFORE removing the paper from the machine.

They have to leave early.

1 Each incorrect character is one error.
2 Each incorrect punctuation is one error.
3 An extra space is one error.
4 Omitting a space is one error.

5 A raised/lowered capital is one error.
6 An uneven left margin is one error.

7 Omitting a word is one error.
8 Inserting an extra word is one error.
9 Inserting an extra letter is one error.
10 Omitting a letter is one error.

1 The(u) have to leave early.
2 They have to leave early(?)
3 They() have to leave early.
4 They have(to leave early.
5 (T)hey have to leave early.
6 ()They have to leave early.
7 They have()leave early.
8 They have to (to) leave early.
9 They have to leave(s) early.
10 They have to (l)ve early.

Half- or one-minute goals

1 Type the exercise. If any word causes you to hesitate, type that word three times.
2 Take a half- or one-minute timing.
3 If you reach the goal, or beyond, take another timing and see if you can type the same number of words but with fewer mistakes.
4 If you do not reach the goal after three attempts, you need a little more practice on the key drills. Choose the previous exercise(s) that give(s) intensive practice on the keys that caused difficulty.

NOTES:
1 There is little to be gained by typing any one drill more than three times consecutively. When you have typed it three times, go on to another drill; then, if necessary, go back to the original drill.
2 At present, techniques (operating the keys evenly, good posture, eyes on copy, returning the carriage/carrier/cursor without looking up) are very important and you should concentrate on good techniques. If your techniques are right, then accuracy will follow. However, if you have more than two errors for each minute typed, it could mean that you have not practised the new keys sufficiently and that you should go back and do further intensive practice on certain key drills.

Measure your speed

Five strokes count as one 'standard' word. In a typing line of 50 spaces there are 10 'standard' words. The figures to the right of each exercise indicate the number of 'standard' words in the complete line, and the scale below indicates the number across the page. If in the exercise below you reach the word 'we' in one minute, your speed is 10 + 6 = 16

words per minute. You will now be able to measure and record your speed.

Type the following exercise as instructed under Nos 1–4 of **half- or one-minute goals**. Set left margin at 20.

Goal—8 words in half a minute   16 words in 1 minute

We will take her to see our new house on the north   10

side of the new estates and we shall ask George to   20

join us at that time. (SI 1.04)   24

1 | 2 | 3 | 4 | 5 | 6 | 7 | 8 | 9 | 10 |

complimentary close in this case would be:

Yours faithfully
J R BLACK & CO LTD

Helen M Grant

John Black
Director

or

Yours faithfully,
J. R. BLACK & CO. LTD.

Helen M Grant

Dictated by Mr. Black
and signed in his absence

4.18.2 Your employer may ask you to write a letter on his behalf and sign it, or circumstances may necessitate your writing on behalf of your employer, eg 'Mr Black has asked me to thank you for your letter dated 21 June, etc'. The complimentary close would be:

Yours faithfully
J R BLACK & CO LTD

Helen M Grant

Helen M Grant (Mrs)
Secretary to J Black, Director

or

Yours sincerely,

Helen M. Grant

Mrs. Helen M. Grant
Secretary to J. Black, Director

4.19 Titled persons The less formal wording is now generally used, eg the salutation: Dear Lord Newton; complimentary close: I am, Sir, Yours sincerely/respectfully/faithfully, etc.

5 Folding letters

Letters and documents should be neatly folded to fit the particular size of envelope used. It is important to make sure that the envelope is of a suitable size for any enclosures that may be attached.

6 Forms of address

OPEN PUNCTUATION

6.1 Degrees and qualifications Do not use punctuation. No spaces between the letters representing a degree or qualification, but one clear space between each group of letters, eg:
Mr (space) F (space) Eastwood (space) MA (space) BSc
Mr F Eastwood MA BSc

6.2 Courtesy titles

6.2.1 Must always be used with a person's name, eg:
Miss M K Green   J Bishop Esq
Mr W P Stevens   Mrs G Hill
Ms S G Matthews.

6.2.2 Use either Mr or Esq when addressing a man, never both.

6.2.3 Rev replaces Mr or Esq, eg Rev R S Smith.

6.2.4 Partnerships—the word Messrs is used before the name of a partnership, eg:
Messsrs Martin & Sons
Messrs Johnson & Co
Messrs Bowron & Jones.

6.2.5 Courtesy titles are not used in the following cases:

6.2.5.1 Before the name of a limited company, eg:
P Yates & Co Ltd   W Robertson & Sons Ltd.

6.2.5.2 With impersonal names, eg:
The British Non-ferrous Co.

6.2.5.3 When the title is included in a name, eg:
Sir John Brown & Co   Sir Arthur Hamilton-Grey

Forms of address

FULL PUNCTUATION

See page 127.

7 Overseas mail

7.1 Airmail—countries outside Europe In the letter, the word AIRMAIL is typed two single spaces after the last line of the reference or the date if the date is typed at the left margin. On the envelope the words PAR AVION (BY AIRMAIL) are typed in the top left corner, eg:
PAR AVION (BY AIRMAIL)

Mr J de Munck
88–86 West Street
Elmhurst
NEW YORK
NY 11373
UNITED STATES OF AMERICA

7.2 The All-up European Service Letters (including letter packets) and postcards for countries in Europe are sent by air whenever this will mean quicker delivery. It is not necessary to type the words BY AIRMAIL on the envelope.

7.3 Letters to the Irish Republic
R. O'Connor, Esq.,
24 Kenmore Road,
KILLARNEY,
Co. Kerry,
IRISH REPUBLIC.

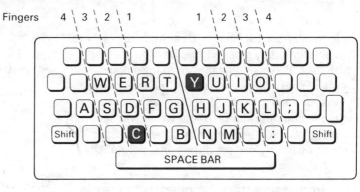

Follow **prepare to type** on page 6 and instructions given at top of page 8.

Set left margin stop at 20 (or pre-stored margin setting) use single spacing, and turn up two single spaces between exercises.

Eyes on copy   Even strokes

Keyboarding review

1   jmj fmj kmk fmf lml am; Mat Tom Ham Sam Lamb Farm;

2   *Mrs Lamb would like to take on the job we offered.*

3   None of them would go with Job down the long road.

New key C
Use D finger

4   ddd ccc dcd dcd cod dcd cot dcd cob dcd cog dcdcd;

5   dcd cut dcd cub dcd cur dcd cud dcd cab dcd cat cd

New key Y
Use J finger

6   jjj yyy jyj jyj jay jyj hay jyj lay jyj bay jyjyj;

7   jyj say jyj day jyj ray jyj may jyj gay jyj way jj

Word families

8   sty try fry dry cry wry dice rice mice nice trice;

9   shy sky sly try sty slay stay fray gray dray stray

Left and right shift keys

10 He Ask Jon Sara Kite Dale Lord Ford Hall Iris Tait

11 Ask Miss Ford if she will see Mrs Tait in an hour.

Homophones

Use your dictionary to check the meaning

12 sealing ceiling; council counsel; cent sent scent;

13 stationery stationary; creak creek; cereal serial;

Apply the keys you know

14 Goal—8 words in half a minute   16 words in 1 minute

NOTE: Leave TWO spaces after full stop

He is not able to find a nice jacket which⁸ he says 10

he lost on the way to your farm.¹⁶ *He will send you* 20

his bill in a week or so. (SI 1.08)   25

1 | 2 | 3 | 4 | 5 | 6 | 7 | 8 | 9 | 10 |

---

letter starts 'Dear Mr . . .', 'Dear Miss . . .', etc, the complimentary close should be 'Yours sincerely'. Never type the company's name after 'Yours sincerely', unless there are special instructions to do so. Whether you type the name and designation of the writer will depend on how well the writer knows the addressee. Follow the style in previous correspondence or ask the writer.

4.11 Name of signatory   In business letters a male person does not append the word 'Mr', before his name. However, it is common practice for ladies to put 'Miss', 'Mrs' or 'Ms' before their name or in brackets after.

4.12 Enclosures   After the last line of typing, turn up a minimum of two spaces, and type Enc at left margin. If there is more than one enclosure, then type Encs. Some organizations list the enclosures. A few employers, and some examining bodies, prefer the abbreviation Att when the word 'attached' is used in the body of the letter, eg 'We attach a copy of our price-list.' If there is more than one attachment, a note must be made of the number, eg Att 3. Another method of indicating an enclosure, or enclosures, is to type three unspaced dots in the left margin opposite the line(s) in which the enclosure(s) is mentioned. This may not be possible with a word processor.

4.13 Postscripts   Sometimes a postscript has to be typed at the foot of a letter, either because the writer has omitted something he wished to say in the body of the letter, or because he wishes to draw special attention to a certain point. The postscript should be started two single spaces below the last line of the complete letter and should be in single spacing. Leave two character spaces after the abbreviation. PS has no punctuation with open punctuation, but a full stop after the S with full punctuation.

4.14 Carbon copies   It is necessary to keep in the office for filing purposes at least one carbon copy of each letter or document typed. To produce a carbon copy, take the following steps:

4.14.1 Place face downwards on a flat surface the sheet on which the typing is to be done.

4.14.2 On top of this place a sheet of carbon paper with the coated surface upwards.

4.14.3 On top of these place the sheet of paper on which the carbon copy is to be made. Pick up all sheets together and insert in machine with coated surface of carbon paper facing the cylinder.

4.14.4 All carbon copies must be a **true copy** of the original, ie any handwritten alterations made on an original must also be made on the carbon copies.

4.14.5 Many organizations do not take carbon copies; instead the originals are photocopied. When **photocopies** have to be made, it is usual to type on the original: pc or p/c followed by the number of copies required, eg pc 6.

4.15 Additional carbon copies   In addition to the carbon copy required for filing, many business letters are typed with extra carbon copies, which are sent to any persons who may be concerned. If a copy of a letter is sent to someone other than the addressee, the letters cc (carbon copy) are typed at the left margin (usually at the foot) followed by the name of the recipient. Where a copy is being sent to more than one person, the names are typed after cc one underneath the other, and the name of the person for whom the copy is intended is either ticked at the side or underlined on individual carbon copies, eg:

(First copy)   (Second copy)
cc Mr Jones   cc Mr Jones
   Mrs Stone   Mrs Stone
   Mr French   Mr French
   File   File

(Third copy)   (Fourth copy)
cc Mr Jones   cc Mr Jones
   Mrs Stone   Mrs Stone
   Mr French   Mr French
   File   File

4.16 Blind carbon copies   It sometimes happens that the writer does not want the addressee to know that copies have been distributed, in which case the typist types bcc (blind carbon copy). When the letter is finished, the carbon copies are reinserted into the machine. At the foot of these copies the typist then types the bcc note at the left margin, as follows:

bcc Mr Jones
    Mrs Stone
    Mr French
    File

marking the name of the recipient(s) as before. The bottom copy on which all the cc or bcc notes appear is the one kept for filing.

4.17 Continuation sheets
   Blocked—See page 110.
   Semi-blocked—See page 134.

4.18 Signing letters on behalf of the writer
4.18.1 Your employer may ask you to type and sign a letter on his behalf. The

Follow **prepare to type** on page 6 and instructions given at top of page 8.

Set left margin stop at 20 (or pre-stored margin setting) use single spacing, and turn up two single spaces between exercises.

TWO spaces after full stop at end of sentence

ONE space after semicolon

Keyboarding review

1 dcd jyj dcd fbf jhj fgf lol yet coy yes call come.

2 *Her mother had bought a new kind of jersey cloth.*

3 He sent us a ticket for the jumble sale on Monday.

New key P
Use ; finger

4 ;;; ppp ;p; ;p; cap ;p; lap ;p; rap ;p; jap p;p;p;

5 ;p; pip ;p; dip ;p; sip ;p; hip ;p; lip ;p; nip p;

New key V
Use F finger

6 fff vvv fvf fvf vow fvf van fvf vat fvf vet fvfvf;

7 fvf eve fvf vie fvf via fvf very fvf give fvf live

Word families

8 tup cup pup sup lop pop fop hop cop top tops mops;

9 live jive hive dive give rave pave save wave gave;

Homophones

Use your dictionary to check the meaning

10 canvas canvass; reviews revues; patients patience;

11 principle principal; presents presence; site sight

Apply the keys you know

NOTE: Leave TWO spaces after full stop

12   Goal—9 words in half a minute   17 words in 1 minute

She moved a pink jug away from the very back ⁹shelf 10

where it had been hidden from sight.¹⁷ *It now shows* 20

up better on that top shelf.   (SI 1.15)   26

1 | 2 | 3 | 4 | 5 | 6 | 7 | 8 | 9 | 10 |

items are separated by a comma, or two character spaces.

3 Printed heading

If you are using paper with a printed heading, turn up at least two single spaces after the last line of the printed heading before starting to type. If you are using plain A5 portrait paper, or A4 paper, turn up seven single spaces.

4 Parts of a business letter

4.1 **Reference** If the words 'Our Ref' are already printed on the letterhead, type the reference in alignment with the print and leave at least **one** clear character space before typing the reference. If 'Our Ref' is not printed, turn up two single spaces after the printed letter heading and type at left margin. Turn up two single spaces and type 'Your Ref' if it is needed.

4.2 **Special marks applying to letters** The words PRIVATE, CONFIDENTIAL, PERSONAL, URGENT, RECORDED DELIVERY, REGISTERED, SPECIAL DELIVERY, BY HAND or AIRMAIL are typed at the left margin at least two single spaces after the last line of the reference, or the date, if the date is typed at the left margin. FREEPOST is typed after the name of the addressee. POSTE RESTANTE means **to be called for**. The words are typed after the name of the addressee who will collect from the post office named in the address.

4.3 **Date** Typed at least two single spaces after the reference, blocked at left margin, or typed on the same line as the reference and blocked at right margin.

4.4 **For the attention of** It is the custom with some firms to have all correspondence addressed to the firm and not to individuals. If, therefore, the writer of a letter wishes it to reach a particular person or department, the words, 'FOR THE ATTENTION OF . . .', are typed at the left margin on the second single space after the reference, date or any special instructions. The wording is also typed on the envelope two single spaces above the name and address. (**NOTE:** The salutation will, of course, be in the plural, ie Dear Sirs.)

4.5 **Name and address of addressee and alternate placement** Typed in single spacing usually on the second/third single space below the reference, date, any special instructions, or 'For the attention of'.

    4.5.1 May be typed in single spacing at the foot of the page at the left margin.

    4.5.2 If the letter finishes with the complimentary close, turn up nine single

spaces before typing the name and address of the addressee.

    4.5.3 If the letter finishes with the name and designation of signatory, turn up two single spaces before typing the name and address of the addressee.

    4.5.4 If you are using a continuation sheet and the name and address of addressee has not been typed before the salutation, then it may be typed at the bottom of the **first** page, two single spaces after the last typed line and ending 25 mm (1 inch) from the bottom of the page.

    4.5.5 If you type the name and address of the addressee at the bottom of the page and the letter is marked for the attention of a particular person, the attention line is typed before the salutation. Similarly, any special instructions must be typed in the usual place and not at the bottom of the page.

    4.5.6 In a one-page letter with the name and address of the addressee at the bottom, the enclosure notation should be placed two spaces after the last line of the address.

4.6 **Salutation** Typed on the second single space below the last line of the address and blocked at the left margin. If the correspondent wishes to write the salutation in ink, leave plenty of space. It is suggested that you turn up nine single spaces after the last line of the address before starting the body of the letter.

4.7 **Subject heading** In fully-blocked letters, the subject heading is typed at the left margin, preferably in capitals without underscore. If lower case letters are used, the heading should be underscored. The heading must be centred if the indented style of display is being used.

4.8 **Body of letter** Start on the second single space after the salutation or the subject heading.

4.9 **Displayed matter** When matter is to be displayed in a fully-blocked letter, all the lines usually start at the left margin, one clear space left above and below the matter. If the display is in columns, it is usual to leave three spaces between each column. If definite instructions are given for the matter to be inset, then it must be inset, even in a fully-blocked letter. The matter is usually centred in a semi-blocked letter.

4.10 **Complimentary close** Typed on second single space below the last line of the body of the letter. A letter with the salutation 'Dear Sir(s), Madam', should end 'Yours faithfully' which may be followed by the company's name. Sometimes the name of the company is typed after the signatory/designation. When a

Follow **prepare to type** on page 6 and instructions given at top of page 8.

Set left margin stop at 20 (or pre-stored margin setting) use single spacing, and turn up two single spaces between exercises.

Back straight   Feet firmly on floor

Keyboarding review	1	;p; fvf ftf jhj dpf apf kpf pot van cop map eve p;
	2	*Jack was glad my family all moved to North Avenue.*
	3	Daniel may have to give back a few paper journals.

New key X
Use S finger

4 sss xxx sxs sxs tax sxs lax sxs pax sxs wax sxsxs;

5 sxs sex sxs hex sxs vex sxs rex sxs cox sxs vox sx

New key Q
Use A finger

6 aaa qqq aqa aqa quad aqa aqua aqa equal aqa quick;

7 aqa quin aqa quit aqa quite aqa equal aqa query qa

Word families

8 qua quad squad quit quip quins quill quint quilts;

9 fox cox mix fix nix axe lax pax wax tax taxi taxed

Homophones

Use your dictionary to check the meaning

10 accede exceed; accept except; access excess; stake

11 steak; checks cheques; choir quire; coarse course;

Apply the keys you know

12 Goal—9 words in half a minute   17 words in 1 minute

Joe quickly moved the gross of new boxes for which 10

you had paid and then took an extra box of the red 20

quilts and sheets you wanted. **(SI 1.15)**   25

1 | 2 | 3 | 4 | 5 | 6 | 7 | 8 | 9 | 10 |

Vertical spacing

6 single lines = 25 mm (1 inch)
Number of single-spaced lines in full length of:
A4 portrait paper—70
A5 landscape paper—35
A5 portrait paper—50

heavy, as this will detract from the general appearance.

```
* * * * * *     0: 0: 0: 0: 0: 0     ***      ***
*           *   :            :      *        *
* * * * * *     :            :      *        *
                0: 0: 0: 0: 0: 0     *        *
                                    *        *
                                    ***      ***
```

Brace (*brackets*)

See page 67.

Brackets (*handwritten or printer's bracket*)

See page 68.

Bring forward reminders

Very often it is important for a person to ascertain by a particular date that a certain action has been taken. The action may be the result of outgoing correspondence, incoming correspondence, a telephone call, etc. A special file, which has a variety of names such as bring-forward file, bring-up file, tickler file, follow-up file, etc, is kept for this purpose.

As a typist it may be one of your duties to keep a bring-forward file, and for that purpose you may have a concertina file with a space for each month of the year and, at the front, pockets for each day of the current month. In the various sections you will keep papers, documents and notes, that require attention on a particular date. At the end of each month, you should transfer the contents of the next month's pocket into the daily pockets. You must train yourself to look in the bring-up file each morning and take out that day's reminders so that action may be taken.

Business letters

1 Layout

Letters can be displayed in various ways, the styles most commonly used being illustrated below.

Fully-blocked (sometimes called 'blocked').

Begin every line at the left margin.

Semi-blocked (sometimes called 'indented').

Date and complimentary close as shown, with first line of each paragraph indented.

2 Punctuation

2.1 **Full punctuation** When typing a letter with full punctuation, punctuation marks are inserted in the appropriate places in the reference, date, name and address of addressee, salutation, complimentary close and after all abbreviations.

2.2 **Open punctuation** When typing a letter with open punctuation, no punctuation marks are inserted in the reference, date, name and address of addressee, salutation, complimentary close or abbreviations. The grammatical punctuation in the body of the letter must be inserted. If a name and address appear in continuous matter, the

Follow **prepare to type** on page 6 and instructions given at top of page 8.

Set left margin stop at 20 (or pre-stored margin setting) use single spacing, and turn up two single spaces between exercises.

Fingers   4 \ 3 \ 2 \ 1   1 / 2 / 3 / 4

Wrists and arms straight   ONE space after a comma

| *Keyboarding review* | 1 | axs aqa fxf fcf axs saj sex vex tax quit aqua quad |

2 *Just have one box of new grey mats packed quickly.*

3 With extra help Clive found many quite black jugs.

New key **Z**
Use A finger

4 aaa zzz aza aza zoo aza zinc aza zeal aza azure za

5 aza zip aza zero aza size aza gaze aza jazz aza za

New key **,**
Use K finger

6 kkk ,,, k,k k,k l,k a,k s,k j,k d,k f,k hj,k g,f,k

ONE space after a comma

7 at, it, is, or, if, one, can, yes, may, for, cross

Word families

8 daze haze gaze laze maze, lazy hazy crazy, puzzle.

9 zeal zero zest zone, size prize, buzz fuzz, azure.

Homophones   Use your dictionary to check the meaning

10 affect effect; style stile; deference difference;

11 born borne; complement compliment; miners minors;

Apply the keys you know

12 Goal—9 words in half a minute   18 words in 1 minute

We do hope the right size is in stock; yes, it is;   10

we have just a few boxes, but the colour, although   20

quite pretty, is not the same. **(SI 1.15)**   26

1 | 2 | 3 | 4 | 5 | 6 | 7 | 8 | 9 | 10 |

4.3 Used with figures only

am (a.m.)	= *ante meridiem* = before noon	
HP (H.P.)	= hire purchase	
No, Nos (No., Nos.)	= number, numbers	
pm (p.m.)	= *post meridiem* = after noon	
% (%)	= per centum	
v, vol (v., vol.)	= volume	
*in (in.)	= inch or inches	
ft (ft.)	= foot or feet	
*oz (oz.)	= ounce or ounces	
*lb (lb.)	= pound or pounds (weight)	
*cwt (cwt.)	= hundredweight or hundredweights	
*m	= metre, metres	
*mm	= millimetre, millimetres	
*cm	= centimetre, centimetres	
*g	= gram, grams	
*kg	= kilogram, kilograms	

* These do not require an s in the plural.

NOTE: It would seem preferable to add an s for the plural of yd and qr (yds/yds. qrs/qrs.). This style is recommended by the *Oxford Dictionary for Writers and Editors*; however, the British Standards Institution gives both examples without the s. Follow the author's copy and/or house style.

4.4 Used in cases indicated

& (&)	= ampersand = and. Used in names of firms and numbers [Nos 25 & 26 (Nos. 25 & 26)] never in ordinary matter.
BA (B.A.)	= Bachelor of Arts. Degree after a person's name.
Bros (Bros.)	= Brothers. In names of firms or companies only.
bf (b.f.)	= brought forward (accounting) *or* boldface (word processing)
c/o (c/o)	= care of. Used only in addresses. (Sometimes the word 'at' is used instead of c/o.)
Co (Co.)	= Company. Used in names of companies.
cod (c.o.d.) COD (C.O.D.)	= Cash on delivery. Used on invoices.
DSc (D.Sc.)	= Doctor of Science. Degree after person's name.
E & OE (E. & O.E.)	= Errors and omissions excepted. Used in invoices.
Junr (Junr.)	= Junior. Used in addresses after a man's name to distinguish from senior [Snr (Snr.)].
Ltd (Ltd.)	= Limited. Used in the name of a private limited company.
PS (PS.)	= Postscript. Abbreviated form

used at end of letter and memo only.

PLC (P.L.C.) plc (p.l.c.)	= Public Limited Company. Used after the name of public limited company.
pro tem (pro tem)	= *pro tempore* (for the time being). Used after a designation, eg Secretary pro tem.
Ref (Ref.)	= Reference. Used in letters and memos.
SERPS	= State Earnings Related Pension Scheme. (May be in full or abbreviated.)

Accents

See page 67.

Agenda

See page 100.

Aligned right margin

Programmes, display, financial statements, etc, sometimes have a right column and the last character of each line of this column may have to end at the same scale point. To do this:

Decide on the exact scale point at which you wish the last character to be typed and set a tab stop one space to the right of that point. From the tab stop, backspace once for each character and space in the line to be aligned; from the point reached, type the word(s)/figure(s). This is sometimes referred to as justifying, but justifying really means inserting extra spaces between words so that the lines of the text all end at the same scale point. Electronic machines may have a 'flush right' facility to allow the information to be typed so that it will end automatically at the right margin.

Allocating space

See page 96.

Blocked paragraphs, double spacing

See page 31.

Borders (*ornamental*)

Display work, such as programmes, menus, etc, can be made more artistic by the use of a suitable ornamental border or corners, such as the following. You should be able to make up other artistic borders, but in doing so, take care not to make the border too

Open punctuation

Many businesses and most examining bodies prefer this style for business documents. It means that the full stop is omitted from an abbreviated word (except at the end of a sentence) and is replaced by a space. Example: Mr (space) J (space) Smith, of W M Smith & Co Ltd, will discuss the terms of payment, etc, with Mrs U E St John-Browne.

Where an abbreviation consists of two or more letters with a full stop after each letter, the full stops are omitted and no space is left between the letters, but one space (or comma) after each group of letters. Example: Mrs G L Hunt, 21 South Road, will call at 7 pm today. She requires past examination papers from several bodies, eg LCCI, RSA and PEI.

Grammatical punctuation must still be used.

The major part of this book is written in open punctuation, ie no full stops are given in or after abbreviations.

Improve your typing technique

If a technique is faulty, check with the following list and carry out the remedial drill.

Faulty technique		*Remedy*

Manual machines

Raised capitals caused by releasing shift key too soon.	`I may go.`	Drills 4–9 page 14; drills 4–9, page 15.
Uneven left margin, caused by faulty carriage return.	`I may go.`	Return carriage without looking up. Any **apply the keys you know**.
Heavy strokes, caused by not releasing keys quickly.	`I mmay go.`	Practise finger movement drills. Any **apply the keys you know**.
Light strokes, caused by not striking the keys hard enough.	`I ay go.`	Practise finger movement drills. Any **apply the keys you know**.

Manual, electric and electronic machines

Omitting or inserting words (looked up from the copy).	`may` `I go`	Eyes on copy always. Page 21—lines 1–3.
Extra spaces, caused by your leaning on the space bar.	`I  may go.`	Right thumb slightly above space bar. Drills 10–14, page 8.
Omitting spaces, caused by poor wrist position.	`I maygo.`	Say 'space' to yourself each time you tap space bar. Drills 10–14, page 8.
Fingers out of position.	`I ,au go.`	Return fingers to home keys. Any **apply the keys you know**.
Turning letters around—eyes get ahead of fingers.	`I may og.`	Eyes on copy always. Say each letter and space to yourself as you type. Any preceding drills.
Extra or wrong characters caused by accidentally depressing keys.	`KKK may go.`	Keep all fingers slightly above home keys—especially with electronic machines.

Skill measurement

*Practice routine for all **skill measurement** exercises:*

1 Type a copy of the exercise.
2 Check and circle all errors.
3 Compare your errors with those shown above.
4 Practise the remedial drills.
5 Type as much of the exercise as you can in the time suggested.
6 Check and circle any errors.

7 On your **skill measurement table** record actual number of words typed in a minute and number of errors, if any.
8 If you made more than the stipulated number of errors, continue with the timed practice and aim for accuracy.
9 If your errors were below the tolerance given, type the exercise again (timed) and endeavour to type a little faster.

Set left margin at 20 or use pre-stored margin
Skill measurement   19 wpm   1 minute   Not more than 1 error

SM1   `As those shoes are too small, you should take them`   10

`back and have them changed for the right size.` **(SI 1.00)** 19

    1 | 2 | 3 | 4 | 5 | 6 | 7 | 8 | 9 | 10 |

UNIT 16   ***Open punctuation, Typing techniques,***
Skill measurement—1 minute at 19 wpm   **22**

DATA STORE

In addition to suggestions for the layout of documents given in the text, this **data store** (in alphabetic order) gives further information about typewriting conventions and display.

Abbreviations

In typewritten work, abbreviations should not, as a rule, be used. There are, however, a few which are **never** typed in full, and others which may be used in certain circumstances.

1 Open and full punctuation

When using **open** punctuation, no full stops are inserted after initials or in abbreviations, eg Mrs Y W T St George-Stevens is Managing Director of Y W T Stevens & Co Ltd. With **full** punctuation, full stops are inserted after initials and in abbreviations, eg Mrs. Y. W. T. St. George-Stevens is Managing Director of Y. W. T. Stevens & Co. Ltd.

Notice the spacing in the following:

Open punctuation   Mrs S J Hudson MA BSc— where an abbreviation consists of two or more letters, there is no space between the letters but one space between each group of letters. **Full** punctuation   Mrs. S. J. Hudson, M. A., B.Sc.— space between the groups is replaced by a comma, followed by a clear space.

1.1 However, with **full** punctuation, full stops need not be inserted in the following cases:

1.1.1 **Acronyms** (words formed from initials): VAT, PAYE, UNESCO, NATO, BUPA, OPEC, NUPE, ACAS, etc.

1.1.2 **Names** of **well-known** companies, states, countries, radio and television broadcasting stations, unions and many government departments: ICI, GKN, USA, UK, RSA, EEC, BBC, IBS, DES, etc.

1.1.3 In metric measurements: 12 mm, 4 m, 6 kg, 30 km, etc.

2 Imperial measurements

No punctuation is inserted with open punctuation, but with full punctuation the full stops are inserted, eg 2 lb., 2 ft. 4 in.

3 Longhand abbreviations

These are used in handwriting, but the words must be typed in full. Examples: dept = department; st = street; shd = should; sh = shall; w = will; wh = which; th = that; etc. Great care must be taken to verify the correct spelling when typing abbreviations in full, eg accom = accommodation; gntee(s) = guarantee(s); recd = received; def = definitely; sep = separate; rec(s) = receipt(s); temp = temporary; etc. Days of the week and months of the year, eg Wed, Fri, Jan, Sept, etc, **must** be typed in full. Where the names of persons, towns, countries, associations, etc, are repeated in any group of tasks, the author may write only the initial(s) or use the initial(s) followed by a long dash to represent the word(s). For example: in a letter addressed to Mrs R Green, the handwritten salutation may read, Dear Mrs G———, and the typist would be expected to type Dear Mrs Green.

4 Standard abbreviations

Lists of standard abbreviations, with their uses, are given below. Study the lists so that you will know when and when not to use the abbreviations. Full punctuation is given in brackets, although the tendency today is to use open punctuation.

4.1 **Common abbreviations**   Usually abbreviated, but may be typed in full. It is wise to follow the style used by the author and/or house style. **Be consistent.**

DSO (D.S.O.)	= Distinguished Service Order
Hon Sec (Hon. Sec.)	= Honorary Secretary. Typed in full.
IQPS (I.Q.P.S.)	= Institute of Qualified Private Secretaries
MEP (M.E.P.)	= Member of the European Parliament
MoD (M.o.D.)	= Ministry of Defence
mph (m.p.h.)	= miles per hour
RMO (R.M.O.)	= Resident Medical Officer
RNLI (R.N.L.I.)	= Royal National Lifeboat Institution
SCF (S.C.F.)	= Save the Children Fund
WCT (W.C.T.)	= World Championship Tennis

4.2 **Always used**

ad lib (ad lib.)	= *ad libitum*	= at pleasure
eg (e.g.)	= *exempli gratia*	= for example
Esq (Esq.)	= Esquire	= courtesy title
etc (etc.)	= et cetera	= and others
et seq (et seq.)	= *et sequentes*	= and the following
ie (i.e.)	= *id est*	= that is
Messrs (Messrs.)	= Messieurs	= courtesy title
Mr (Mr.)	= Mister	= courtesy title
Mrs (Mrs.)		= courtesy title
Ms	= courtesy title used instead of Mrs or Miss	
NB (N.B.)	= *Nota bene*	= note well

Each line or sentence should be typed three times and, if time permits, type each complete exercise once. Use single spacing with double between exercises. For **skill measurement** follow instructions on page 22, and for **record your progress** follow instructions on page 24. Set left margin at 20 or use pre-stored margin.

Keyboarding review– alphabet keys

1 Five excellent school prizes were awarded and Jamy qualified for the best work in his group.

Placement of certain characters

The location of the hyphen, question mark, underscore, etc may vary with the make of machine. This also applies to a few of the signs, symbols and marks keys such as the oblique and quotation marks. When practising these keys, make sure you know whether or not you have to use the shift key, decide on the correct finger, and then practise the reach from the home key; then type the drills given.

New key hyphen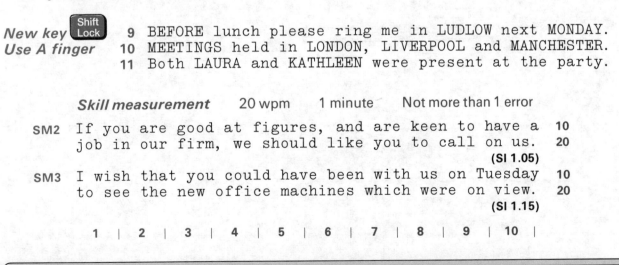

NO space before or after hyphen

2 blue-grey, one-fifth, part-time, left-hand, in-out
3 Over one-third are part-time day-release students.
4 Her father-in-law asked for all-wool yellow socks.

New key question mark

TWO spaces after ? at end of sentence

5 How? When? Where? May she? Must we? Will you?
6 Who said so? What is the time? Is it late? Why?

New key Use ; finger

7 ;;; ::: ;;; a:; l:; s:; k:; d:; j:; f:; h:; gf:; a;

Leave ONE space after colon

8 Delivery Period: one month. Prices: net ex works.

Shift-lock key

When you need to type several capital letters one after the other, the shift lock must be used. When it is depressed, the shift key remains engaged until the lock is released, and you will be able to type capitals without using the shift key. The following steps should be practised:

1 Depress shift lock, using 'A' finger of left hand.
2 Type capital letters.
3 Depress left-hand shift key to release shift lock.

New key Use A finger

9 BEFORE lunch please ring me in LUDLOW next MONDAY.
10 MEETINGS held in LONDON, LIVERPOOL and MANCHESTER.
11 Both LAURA and KATHLEEN were present at the party.

Skill measurement 20 wpm 1 minute Not more than 1 error

SM2 If you are good at figures, and are keen to have a   10
job in our firm, we should like you to call on us.   20
(SI 1.05)

SM3 I wish that you could have been with us on Tuesday   10
to see the new office machines which were on view.   20
(SI 1.15)

1 | 2 | 3 | 4 | 5 | 6 | 7 | 8 | 9 | 10 |

NOTE

Send a credit note (No 3076) to:
Mrs S P Baker, 23 The Broadway, FOLKESTONE,
Kent, CT17 2PY. The invoice (No 10298) was sent
10 days ago (insert date) but one blouse was the
incorrect size £15.00 (plus VAT £2.25).

OFFER

The investment must be in by Friday, 7 September
1990.

ORDER

1 automatic electronic shredder—catalogue No
3141.

PRICE

Mrs A Stewart, 18 The Holt, CROWBOROUGH, East
Sussex, TN6 2QH

PROP

Rateable value—£111
PRICE—£85,999 (freehold)

SALE

2nd Floor
Jonquil   Faces west; balcony   £74,550
Daisy   Faces south; balcony £74,550

STAFF

Colin Skelley is working as Manager of the
Purchasing Department. His telephone extension
number is 3567.

TRAV

3. *Vaccination advice.* Full details of individual
vaccinations, requirements for vaccination
certificates and other precautions are given on pages
7 to 12 of the attached addendum.

UNITS

Ms Chloe Anders
(address in previous task)
Policy No: 328-0089356C
Life assured: Ms Chloe Anders
Sum assured: £15,000
Declaration date: 31.12.90
Bonus allocation: £355.00
Total bonus to date: £3,450.00

USSR

The size of the photograph is 4 cm × 4 cm
($1\frac{1}{2}$″ × $1\frac{1}{2}$″). Please add the following sentence.
Photographs to be taken full face without hat or dark
glasses.

WALK

Snowdrops and Aconites

Record your progress exercises

In this edition of *Typing: Two-in-One Course*, EACH **record your progress** exercise will contain ALL the letters of the alphabet.

Instructions for all **record your progress** exercises:
1 Type the exercise **once** as practice.
2 Check and circle any error.
3 With the assistance of your teacher, analyse your errors and carry out remedial work where necessary.
4 Return to your **record your progress** exercise and type as much of the passage as you can in the time allotted.
5 Check and circle any errors.
6 Record the number of words typed and the number of errors in the second typing—see *Workguide and Resource Material* for the **record your progress chart**.

Record your progress   1 minute

```
R1  I know you will be pleased to hear that Zola Coles  10

    joined this firm on a part-time basis.  Chris said  20

    I must give her a quick test next week.            28
     1  |  2  |  3  |  4  |  5  |  6  |  7  |  8  |  9  |  10  |
```

Typewriting theory and conventions

Over the years certain conventions with regard to display and layout of typewritten documents have become accepted practice. While some examining bodies and employers do not worry unduly about layout as long as the document is clean, attractive and correct (no typing, spelling or grammatical errors), we do suggest that you use the 'theory'/conventions given in this textbook as a guide. In exercise 4 on page 31, it is necessary to leave at least two clear spaces between paragraphs typed in double spacing; however, it would not be 'wrong' if you left three clear, but it would be ridiculous if you left six. When you are familiar with the conventions and standards suggested in this textbook, then you can adjust the layout of a document to suit the contents, your employer or the examiner.

Pre-stored margins

We do not always suggest what left and right margins should be used, and you must decide what margins will suit the particular exercise you are typing. If you wish to use the pre-stored margins on your electronic machine, you may do so provided they are appropriate.

Hard copy printout

When we refer to the insertion of paper, the instructions will also apply to typists using a printer and VDU.

DATA FILES

The following office files contain information that you will need when typing certain documents.

COMP

The page number in the catalogue is 5.

CV

Mr Brian Evans, Personnel Officer,
Glyn James Manufacturing Company,
Gwynfa Street, Swansea, SA5 2RG
Telephone: 0792 59601

DRCT

The page number in the catalogue is 52.

ELEC

Miss Bashire has an appointment at
2 pm. She will be available at 3.30 pm.

EXPEN

The 1989 figures are as follows:

Grant £10,500	Interest £4
Halls £9,456	Groups £723
Publications £6	Events £255
Films £24	

Excess expenditure over income
£1,555
(Please insert the total figure)

FINAN

The Financial section figures should read as follows:

£877K   £978K   £340K   £221K

HEAT

2 **Room thermostat.** This simply turns the radiator
valve on or off to keep the room at the desired
temperature.

HOLS

Travel Guide worth up to £10.95.

ITIN

Secure Building Society, 7 Temple Street.

JOBS

IV SECRETARIAL AGENCY, BOND STREET
CODE: SEC 3807

College leaver; no shorthand; 45 wpm typing. This is
not a normal 9–5 job, but requires someone, resilient,
flexible and with a good memory. £8,500 pa.

LEYS

Item. One acoustic PC workstation—
Code No 5028
Price: £484.50

MORTGAGE

TP/EP

22 January 1990

Mr W Davies
10 Victoria Road
CHELMSFORD
Essex   CM1 1FD

Dear Mr Davies

I am enclosing your Annual Mortgage Statement for
this year.

Because of the changes in interest rates, it has been
necessary to alter the amount of your monthly
repayment. The revised figure is given on your
Statement.

If you have any queries, please do contact me. I shall
be available for help and advice at any time.

Yours sincerely

BENJAMIN CADBY
Chief Executive

Enc

Keyboarding review— alphabet keys

1 *The taxi ranks were busy because of a sizeable jam which caused very long queues of cars up the hill.*

New key
dash

The hyphen key is used for the dash with ONE space **before** and ONE space **after**. There is no space before or after the hyphen.

2 ; - ; ; - ; Call today - no, tomorrow - after tea.
3 The book - it was his first - was a great success.
4 It is their choice - we are sure it will be yours.

Upper and lower case letters

Characters requiring use of shift key are called UPPER CASE characters. Characters not requiring use of the shift key are called LOWER CASE characters.

NOTE: If your typewriter does not have a figure 1 key, use small 'L'.

New key 1
Use A finger

5 We require 11 pairs size 11; also 11 pairs size 1.
6 Add up 11 plus 11 plus 11 plus 11 plus 11 plus 11.
7 On 11 August 11 girls and 11 boys hope to join us.
8 After 11 years, 11 of them will leave on 11 March.

New key 2
Use S finger

9   sw2s sw2s s2ws s2ws s2s2s s2s2s s2sws s2sws 2s2ws.
10 22 sips 22 seas 22 skis 22 sons 22 spas 22 sets 2.
11 We need 2 grey, 2 blue, 2 red, and 22 orange ties.
12 The 12 girls and 12 boys won 122 games out of 212.

New key 3
Use D finger

13 de3d de3d d3ed d3ed d3d3d d3d3d d3ded d3ded 3d3ed.
14 33 dots 33 dips 33 dogs 33 dads 33 dyes 33 duds 3.
15 Send 313 only to 33 Green Road and to 3 West Road.
16 Type the numbers: 3, 2, 1, 11, 12, 13, 32, 31, 23.

Skill measurement   21 wpm   1 minute   Not more than 1 error

SM4 We trust that the hints we gave for the removal of 10
stains will be found to be of great help to all of 20
you. (SI 1.09)   21

1 | 2 | 3 | 4 | 5 | 6 | 7 | 8 | 9 | 10 |

Record your progress   1 minute

R2 At what time does the Zurich bus arrive? You must 10
equip yourself with: extra shoes, raincoats, brown 20
socks, a warm jumper, a large torch, and the maps. 30
                                          (SI 1.23)

1 | 2 | 3 | 4 | 5 | 6 | 7 | 8 | 9 | 10 |

Page 109

Recall the document stored under filename WALK.

Page one—Delete '1990/1991' and insert 'Sunday 29 July 1990—Sunday 3 February 1991'.

Page two—First paragraph—change' 1–2 hours' to '$1\frac{1}{2}$–$2\frac{1}{2}$ hours'. Change the margins to half an inch on both sides on this page and page three.

Proofread soft copy and, if necessary, correct. Print out an original in 10 pitch.

Page 111

Recall the document stored under filename DRCT. Delete the shoulder heading 'ORDERING IS EASY' and close up the space. Underline any words typed in capitals in the body of the letter.

Proofread soft copy and, if necessary, correct. Print out an original in 12 pitch and take two carbon copies.

Page 113

Recall the document stored under filename ELEC. Perform global search and change 'PC' in each case to 'personal computer'. Arrange the subject heading on one line and close up space. Change the inset portion to 25 mm (1 inch) both sides.

Proofread soft copy and, if necessary, correct. Print out an original in 10 pitch and take two carbon copies.

Page 122

Recall the document stored under filename SHEET. Alter the figure for 'General reserve' to '238,989'; and the figure for 'Other assets' to '2,134'. The totals will also need to be changed. Proofread soft copy and, if necessary, correct. Print out original in 10 pitch.

Page 123

Recall the document stored under filename EXPEN. Transpose the '1989' and '1990' columns. Proofread soft copy and, if necessary, correct. Print out original in 12 pitch.

Page 125

Recall the document stored under filename ITIN. Insert the following for 'Wednesday 21st November' in the correct time order.

'1400 hours   Bristol Air Corporation, Filton House
                        Tel 0272 314769—correspondence in file No 3'

Mr Bromley's train will not now be arriving at New Street Station, Birmingham until 1245 hours on Thursday 22nd November.

Proofread soft copy and, if necessary, correct. Print out original in 15 pitch.

Page 135

Recall the document stored under filename HOLS. Add the following sentences after the paragraph headed 'Check-list'.

'Please note that the USSR and Polish visas will *not* be returned with your passport; these visas will both be held on your behalf by the Tour Escort. Please remember that your passport is a valuable document; it should not be sent other than by Registered Mail.'

Proofread soft copy and, if necessary, correct. Print out an original in 15 pitch and take two carbon copies.

Page 139

Recall the document stored under filename FINAN. Delete the line about 'Education expenditure' and add the following in correct alphabetical order.

'Computer Bureaux   £623K   £987K   £333K   £420K'

Proofread soft copy and, if necessary, correct. Print out original in 10 pitch.

Please follow instructions at top of page 23.

Keyboarding review— alphabet keys

1 The jam that he bought tasted of exotic fruit like quince, guava and pomegranate, and May ate it with zeal.

New key **4**
Use F finger

2 fr4f fr4f f4rf f4rf f4f4f f4f4f f4frf f4frf 4f4rf.
3 44 furs 44 fish 44 firs 44 feet 44 figs 44 fans 4.
4 The 4 men, 4 women, 24 boys and 4 girls go by car.
5 We ordered 434 sets and received 124 on 14 August.

New key **7**
Use J finger

6 ju7j ju7j j7uj j7uj j7j7j j7j7j j7juj j7juj 7j7uj.
7 77 jugs 77 jars 77 jigs 77 jets 77 jags 77 jaws 7.
8 The 7 boys and 77 girls sent 77 gifts to the fund.
9 Take 4 from 47, then add 27 plus 7 and you get 77.

New key **8**
Use K finger

10 ki8k ki8k k8ik k8ik k8k8k k8k8k k8kik kik8k 8k8ik.
11 88 keys 88 kits 88 kids 88 kinds 88 kilts 88 kings
12 Type 38, 83, 28, 848 and 482 with alternate hands.
13 The 8 men, 28 women, 8 boys and 78 girls are here.

New key **9**
Use L finger

14 lo9l lo9l 19ol 19ol 19l9l 99 laws 99 logs 99 lids.
15 Type 29, 39, 49, 927 and 939 with alternate hands.
16 Joe is 99, Bob is 89, Jim is 79, and George is 49.

If your machine does not have a 0 key, use capital 'O' and 'L' finger.

New key **0**
Use right little finger

17 101 201 301 401 701 801 901 10 left 10 look 10 lie
18 The 40 men, 70 women, 80 boys and 90 girls remain.
19 See the dates: 10 March, 20 July, 30 June, 10 May.

Skill measurement   22 wpm   1 minute   Not more than 1 error

SM5 We want a first-class employee: one who has a good 10
knowledge of accounts. She must be able to manage 20
a section. **(SI 1.32)**   22

1 | 2 | 3 | 4 | 5 | 6 | 7 | 8 | 9 | 10 |

Record your progress   1 minute

R3 No charge will be made for any extra copies of the 10
GAZETTE: but their account must be paid at the end 20
of the quarter. Will this suit Kate? James would 30
like to have your reply. **(SI 1.20)**   35

1 | 2 | 3 | 4 | 5 | 6 | 7 | 8 | 9 | 10 |

UNIT 20   **Keys: 4, 7, 8, 9, 0**   **26**
             SM5—22 wpm   R3—1 minute

Word processor operators—text editing instructions

Page 41

Recall the document stored under filename POST. To save retyping this letter for exercise 5, alter John Frazer's name and address to that of Dr Ann James. Close up the extra linespace and change the salutation to 'Dear Madam'. Proofread soft copy and, if necessary, correct. Print out original only in 12 pitch.

Page 43

Recall the document stored under filename POLICY. Add the following sentence to the end of the second paragraph.
'Tuesday, 17 April at 1430 hours would be a suitable date and time for me.'
Proofread soft copy and, if necessary, correct. Print out original in 12 pitch.

Page 71

Recall the document stored under filename LEASE. Change the 1990 figure for 'Provision for major repairs' to '£232.00', and alter the total accordingly.
Proofread soft copy and, if necessary, correct. Print out an original and one copy in 12 pitch.

Page 72

Recall the document stored under filename HEAT. Add the following as item number two (change the numbers of the following items accordingly).
'*Appliance thermostat*. This type of control is often fitted to a room heater and will sense the temperature of the appliance.'
Proofread soft copy and, if necessary, correct. Print out an original in 10 pitch and take one carbon copy.

Page 80

Recall the document stored under filename TV. Add an extra item number V as follows:
'British Satellite Broadcasting distributed three million of its special square dishes ('squarials') free before its launch in 1990.'
Proofread soft copy and, if necessary, correct. Print out an original in 10 pitch.

Page 86

Recall the document stored under filename HOLS. Delete the sentence that starts—'And we know that you, ...'; in its place type—'Whether you have travelled abroad before or not, we are sure you will find something to suit you.'
Proofread soft copy and, if necessary, correct. Print out an original in 12 pitch and take one carbon copy.

Page 88

Recall the document stored under filename CLEAN. Delete the item on 'Upholstery'. Add two items under 'Curtains':
'Full length (lined) £28.00   £14.00
Half length (lined) .... £18.00   £9.00'
Proofread soft copy and, if necessary, correct. Print out an original in 10 pitch.

Page 91

Recall the document stored under filename INS. Insert the following sentence after the words '... living with you, can be included.'
'If you decide to take out an 'All Risks' Insurance, your personal possessions, including valuables, cameras, money, credit cards and even bicycles can be covered for accidental loss or damage.'
Alter the first footnote to read: 'See attached for a complete list of areas.'
Proofread soft copy and, if necessary, correct. Print out an original in 12 pitch.

Page 97

Recall the document stored under filename NURSE. Start a fourth paragraph with the words 'Florence Nightingale will always be remembered ...'. Add the following to the footnote:
'She is buried in a simple family grave in Hampshire.'
Proofread soft copy and, if necessary, correct. Print out an original in 12 pitch.

Page 99

Recall the document stored under filename CHARGE. Perform a global search and change the word 'council/s' back to 'authority/ies'. Justify the right margin.
Proofread soft copy and, if necessary, correct. Print in single spacing and 10 pitch. (Keep double between the enumerated items.)

Please follow instructions at top of page 23.

Keyboarding review— alphabet keys

1 *The brightly coloured liquid was mixed in the jug and given to the lazy patients for sickness.*

New key **5**
Use F finger

2 fr5f fr5f f5rf f5rf 55 fill 55 flit 55 fled 55 fit
3 5 firs, 15 furs, 25 fish, 35 figs, 45 fewer, 515 5
4 25 January 1525; 15 August 1535; 15 December 1545.

New key **6**
Use J finger

5 jy6j jy6j j6yj j6yj 66 jump 66 jerk 66 jest 66 jam
6 6 jars, 16 jets, 26 jabs, 36 jots, 46 jolts, 616 6
7 We need 656 green and 566 red by 16 February 1986.

NO space after initial " NO space before closing "

New key **"**
quotation marks

8 "Go for 30 days." "Call at 12 noon." "Ring now."
9 "I am going," he said. "It is already very late."
10 Mary said, "Mr Bell is here." "Ring me tomorrow."

(ONE space before NO space after
) NO space before ONE space after

New keys **( )**
brackets

11 (1 (2 (3 (4 (5 (6 (7 (8 (9) 10) 11) 12) 13) 14) 8)
12 (22) (23) (24) (25) (26) (27) (28) (29) (30) (31).
13 Mail: (a) 2 pens; (b) 3 pins; (c) 1 tie; (d) 1 hat

NO space before or after the apostrophe in the MIDDLE of a word

New key **'**
apostrophe

14 It's Joe's job to clean Mary's car. Joe's unwell.
15 Don't do that; it's bad for Mary's dog; he's nice.
16 Bill's 2 vans are with John's 8 trucks at Reading.

Skill measurement 23 wpm 1 minute Not more than 1 error

SM6 If you feel some day that you would like a trip in 10
the country, perhaps you could drive out to a farm 20
to pick fruit. **(SI 1.09)** 23

SM7 Do you wish to take a holiday? Now is the time to 10
take one of our out-of-season vacations. Send for 20
our brochure. **(SI 1.26)** 23

1 | 2 | 3 | 4 | 5 | 6 | 7 | 8 | 9 | 10 |

Record your progress 1 minute

R4 The gavels which Liz Max saw last July are now out 10
of stock, and we would not be able to replace them 20
for some weeks - perhaps a month - when we hope to 30
receive a further quota. **(SI 1.23)** 35

1 | 2 | 3 | 4 | 5 | 6 | 7 | 8 | 9 | 10 |

Keys to proofreading exercises

Page 148—exercise 1
Line 1—program; line 2—visual; 3—100; line 4—a daisy-wheel printer; line 5—stock; line 6—Spreadsheet.

Page 148—exercise 2
Line 1—your; line 2—top and bottom; line 3—interrupt; line 4—dictation.; line 5—omit the word 'the';
line 6—omit comma after 'pencil'.

Page 148—exercise 3
Line 1—GARDENING; line 2—month; line 3—or; line 4—lettuces; line 5—spring-flowering; line 6—line not at left margin;
line 7—omit the word 'ANY'.

Page 149—exercise 4
Line 1—definite; line 2—two spaces after full stop; line 3—handling; line 4—index cards; line 5—loose-leaf; line 6—omit
'they may'.

Page 149—exercise 5
Line 1—retrieval; line 2—accessed; line 3—insert 'an' before annual; line 4—varied,; line 5—retrieve; line 6—a telephone
line; line 7—adapted; line 8—insert full stop after 'use'.

Page 150—exercise 6
FIELD WALK; 10 April; Shân; Mow'; A4057; Route; reference; SU637856).; hear; binoculars; 3¾ miles. (two spaces before)
Suitable.

Page 150—exercise 7
GCSE; General Certificate of Secondary Education; Visual Display Unit (without the semicolon); RSA; Cultural;
Organization; Beginners'; Telegraphy; Errors and Omissions Excepted.

Page 151—exercise 8
Brook-Little; PB-L/TSEv; SEPTEMBER 1989 TO DECEMBER 1989; enrolment; run,; follows–; underline column headings;
type the whole line 'Audio Typing' before 'Beginners' Typing'; 25.9.90; 20.9.90.; B207; I shall be glad; dates and times.

Page 152—exercise 9
Address; Installed; Due; Treatments; Tel: (0603) 623091; postcode on the same line as Norwich; Computer; November;
(0272); BS16 1RP; 10A; Felton; Peterborough (without the full stop); April (without the comma).

Page 153—exercise 10
countryside; town. (2 spaces after full stop, s omitted); obedient; dog-training; know; told,; which is hard to break; line space
between each numbered item; dog's lead; when there are farm; and (not the ampersand).

Page 153—exercise 11
manufacturers; Their furniture; companies; e.g.,; executive's; approximately; £981.50; The colours; yellows, (2 errors—
delete apostrophe, add comma); inset 5 spaces for second paragraph; year's; breaking; 27.7%.

Page 154—exercise 12
Prestel; and (in full, not the ampersand); British; world's; service. (2 spaces); computers; you are given; modem; device; do
not indent the third paragraph; stories; advertisements; information,; etc.; goods,.

Page 154—exercise 13
all day; headaches,; miscarriages; worries; stress comes highest; that not 'than'; breaks; possible; detachable; swivel; screen;
(one space); adjust; processor; typewriter.

Language arts—apostrophe

Page 155—Lines 1 and 3	Singular (one only) noun not ending in **s**, add an apostrophe **s**.
Lines 2 and 4	Plural noun ending in **s**, add an apostrophe.
Lines 5 and 6	If the singular noun ends in **s**, or an **s** sound, and the addition of an apostrophe **s** makes the word **difficult to pronounce**, add the apostrophe only. What one considers difficult to pronounce is debatable.
Lines 7 and 8	Plural nouns (children, men) **not** ending in **s**, add an apostrophe **s**.
Line 9	The contractions **don't** and **it's** require the apostrophe to show the omission of **o** and **i**. The pronoun **its** (The dog chased its tail.) does not require an apostrophe.
Line 10	The apostrophe is sometimes used in place of quotation marks to indicate the exact words of a speaker or writer.
Line 11	Used as the sign for feet. Is also the sign for minutes: 1' equals 60".
Line 12	To avoid confusing the reader, the apostrophe is used around the word 'embarrass' and between the single letter and the **s** that follows. Electronic typewriters usually have an emboldening facility and one would then embolden the word(s)/letter(s) instead of using the apostrophe.

Language arts—agreement of subject and verb

Page 155—Line 1	**daisywheel** (singular noun) requires singular verb **is**.
Line 2	**disks** (plural noun) requires plural verb **are**.
Line 3	A plural verb is always necessary after **you**.
Line 4	Although **s** or **es** added to a noun indicates the plural, **s** or **es** added to a verb indicates the third person **singular**.
Line 5	When singular subjects are joined by **nor**, the verb must be singular.
Line 6	Singular subjects joined by **and** require a plural verb.

Please follow instructions at top of page 23.

Keyboarding review— alphabet keys

1 *A small quiet boy who lives next door to Jack came out of the gate and went down the zigzag path.*

Backspace key

Locate the backspace key on your machine. This is usually on either the top left or top right of the keyboard. When the backspace key is depressed, the carriage/carrier/cursor will move back one space at a time. On most electric and electronic machines the carriage/carrier/cursor will continue to move for as long as the backspace key is depressed.

Underscore key—underline function

Before underscoring a short word, backspace once for each letter and space in the word to be underscored. For longer words, or several words, use carriage release lever. After you finish underscoring, always tap space bar. Use shift lock when underscoring more than one character. A final punctuation mark may or may not be underscored. If you are using an electronic keyboard, follow instructions given for underscoring (underlining) in manufacturer's handbook. With word processors, it is not possible (on most systems) to underscore a heading, or words, in the normal way because a special underline function is available. If you need to rule a horizontal line on a word processor, depress the underscore key in the usual way. In offices today, there is a tendency to use the word **underline** instead of the word **underscore**.

New key underscore

2 Please send them 29 only - not 9 - by air-freight.
3 John Brown, Mary Adams and Janet Kelly are coming.

ONE space before £ but NO space after . Some word processors and computers do not have a £ sign. Where this occurs, the hash sign should be used. However, it is preferable to write in the £ sign.

New key pound sign

4 Buy 5 at £15, 8 at £68, 17 at £415 and 30 at £270.
5 £1, £2, £3, £4, £5, £6, £7, £8, £9, £10, £20, £30.

ONE space before and after &

New key ampersand

6 Jones & Cutler Ltd, 67 & 68 North Street, Falkirk.
7 Mr & Mrs Weston, 18 & 19 Main Street, Cirencester.

NO space before or after oblique

New key oblique or slash

8 I can/cannot be present. I do/do not require tea.
9 Jim Minett will take an aural and/or written test.

Skill measurement   24 wpm   1 minute   Not more than 1 error

SM8 The account for May should now be paid, and I must   10
     ask you to let me have your cheque for the sum due   20
     as soon as you can. **(SI 1.04)**   24

SM9 When you leave the office at night you should make   10
     sure that your machine is covered up and that your   20
     desk is quite clear. **(SI 1.12)**   24

     1 | 2 | 3 | 4 | 5 | 6 | 7 | 8 | 9 | 10 |

Record your progress   1 minute

R5   Our parents are fond of telling us that, when they   10
     were quite young they were expected to work harder   20
     than we do today; however, we will, no doubt, tell   30
     our lazy children the same joyful tale. **(SI 1.29)** 38

     1 | 2 | 3 | 4 | 5 | 6 | 7 | 8 | 9 | 10 |

R32 For the better-paid typist's job you should have appropriate 12
qualifications: a Stage III in Typing, Stage II/III in Audio 24
Transcription, and a good knowledge of English. This job 35
usually demands common sense, initiative, and tact. However 47
rushed you may be, you will have to be pleasant to the bore 58
who will often deviate from the topic and perhaps waste your 70
time. If you have a question, ask for advice - there may be 82
a maze of regulations that you will not understand. 92

You may be required to deal with internal and external tele- 104
phone calls and to make certain decisions. The typist often 116
has to operate a filing system. Typing is also a means of 127
providing input for word processors and computers and it may 139
be that you will have extra pay for using these machines. 150
Employment prospects for typists are excellent. Thousands 161
of typists are added to the work-force each year, and the 172
typist who is familiar with processing equipment has an even 184
better chance. **(SI 1.45)** 187

1 | 2 | 3 | 4 | 5 | 6 | 7 | 8 | 9 | 10 | 11 | 12 |

R33 A FAX or facsimile machine is a copier which will transmit 11
a document by electronic means usually over telephone lines 22
from one location to another. At the distant end it appears 34
as a printed copy, or facsimile, of the original. 44

Almost anything that can be put on paper can be transmitted 55
by facsimile - text, graphs, charts, etc, can be sent and 66
also received. Quotations, orders, price-lists, delivery 77
schedules, specifications, etc, are just a few examples. 88
As originally planned it was slow and only small sizes of 99
paper could be used. The equipment used today takes advan- 110
tage of today's technology which means that it is much 121
faster. 122

One of the great advantages of facsimile is the reduction of 134
keyboarding errors because if the original copy is correctly 146
prepared, no further typing or checking is necessary, and no 158
carbon copies, envelopes, postage, etc, are required. Also, 170
you will know that the document cannot get lost in the post. 182
These machines have answering devices and other automatic 193
mechanism which means they can receive documents without an 204
individual being present, and documents may be sent when 215
phone prices are at a lower rate, such as in the evening. 226

(SI 1.54)

1 | 2 | 3 | 4 | 5 | 6 | 7 | 8 | 9 | 10 | 11 | 12 |

Please follow instructions at top of page 23.

Keyboarding review— alphabet keys

1 *In spite of the likely hazard, a decision was made to grant their request and give him the extra job.*

New key at @

ONE space before and after, in continuous text

2 f@f f@f d@d j@j 9 @ 10p; 8 @ 11p; 7 @ 12p; 3 @ 8p.
3 Please send 44 @ £5; 6 @ £7; 13 @ £8; and 28 @ £9.
4 Order 420 @ £12, 50 @ £5, 40 @ £6 and 5 @ £8 each.

Numeric keypad

Some machines with electronic keyboards have a numeric keypad, usually placed to the right of, and separate from, the alphabet keyboard. This keypad may be used in addition to, or instead of, the figure keys on the top row of the keyboard. When using the 10-key pad, employ the **456** as the home keys on which you place the **J K L** fingers. The fingers and thumb will then operate the keypad as follows:

J = 1 4 7   **K** = 2 5 8   **L** = decimal point 3 6 9
Thumb = 0   **Little finger** = enter, comma, minus

The layout of the keypad will differ from one machine to another. Study your keyboard and, if you have a keypad, note any differences from the layout above and the characters to which the suggested fingering applies.

Practise on numeric keypad

5 456 654 147 258 369 041 520 306 470 508 906 159 02
6 417 528 639 159 350 256 107 369 164 059 378 904 38
7 4.5 6.9 4.1 4.7 5.2 5.8 4,655 3,987 2,541 8,465 79

Skill measurement   25 wpm   1 minute   Not more than 1 error

SM10 I have just moved to my new house and, when I have   10
      put it straight, I would be glad if you could then   20
      spend a few days with me. **(SI 1.00)**   25

SM11 I am delighted to tell you that we have now joined   10
      the team. We had hoped to do so last year, but we   20
      were then not old enough. **(SI 1.12)**   25

  1 | 2 | 3 | 4 | 5 | 6 | 7 | 8 | 9 | 10 |

Record your progress   1 minute

R6 I was sorry to find that my cheque - sent to Suzie   10
    on Monday - had not been received. I think it has   20
    just gone astray in the post. Shall I ask my bank   30
    to stop it now? Please excuse the delay. **(SI 1.18)** 38

  1 | 2 | 3 | 4 | 5 | 6 | 7 | 8 | 9 | 10 |

R28 A typed document which is not 'mailable' is not acceptable.   11
By mailable copy we mean: the contents must make sense; no   22
omissions; no uncorrected errors (misspellings, incorrect   33
punctuation, typing errors, etc); no careless corrections   44
(if part of the wrong letter(s) is showing, the correction   55
is not acceptable); no smudges; no creases.   63

When using the VDU screen, it is fairly easy to text edit a   74
document that has been amended by the author. The data is   85
retrieved from the file and displayed on the screen. The   96
backspace-strikeover method is normally used to correct typ-   108
ing errors and, with the use of the function keys, text-   119
editing techniques are used to change information in the   130
text. If the text on the VDU looks hazy, you should clean   141
the screen or adjust the luminous intensity.   149

Whilst corrections and amendments are easily made on the   160
VDU screen, these changes may take up a lot of time which   171
could better be spent on other work. Try to produce a   182
correct copy on the first printout. **(SI 1.43)**   189

1 | 2 | 3 | 4 | 5 | 6 | 7 | 8 | 9 | 10 | 11 | 12 |

R29 All of you will be glad to hear that I now have a scheme for   12
refunding to staff the part of their expenses for travelling   24
long distances to work. Just details of local conditions,   35
the grades of staff, and travel zones, will help settle your   47
queries. **(SI 1.31)**   48

1 | 2 | 3 | 4 | 5 | 6 | 7 | 8 | 9 | 10 | 11 | 12 |

R30 Electronic mail will justify its use because of the speed   11
with which it is known to deliver large amounts of infor-   22
mation: it offers immediate delivery if this is required.   33
There are one or 2 points you should remember about this   44
means of communication. We were amazed to find that dif-   55
ferent kinds of equipment can communicate with each other -   66
telephone lines, telegraph lines, satellites are good   77
examples. The message is communicated in the form of elec-   89
tronic signals, not a copy on paper. **(SI 1.35)**   96

1 | 2 | 3 | 4 | 5 | 6 | 7 | 8 | 9 | 10 | 11 | 12 |

R31 Zodiac Travel, our branch in High Street, can help you in a   11
number of ways to solve your travel and transport queries.   22
In these days, when time seems to be the most important com-   33
modity of all, you can depend on Zodiac Travel to deal with   44
all your problems. Just telephone Karen Gallagher and she   55
will use both her own and her staff's time in dealing with   66
the hundred and one irritating little things that crop up,   77
but which are so easily overcome by the expert who has made   88
the whole subject her own intimate profession. Should you   99
wish to do business with a country with which you are not   110
in touch, our agents will be pleased to help you. **(SI 1.31)**   119

1 | 2 | 3 | 4 | 5 | 6 | 7 | 8 | 9 | 10 | 11 | 12 |

KEYBOARDING SKILLS

Before proceeding to the exercises below, you should type the following skill building exercises:

improve your spelling Nos 1 and 2, page 155.　　**alphabetic sentence** No 1, page 156.
skill measurement No 12, page 158.　　　　　　**record your progress** No 7, page 164.

PRODUCTION DEVELOPMENT

Types of display headings

Main headings

The main heading, the title of a passage, is blocked at the left margin when using blocked display. Unless otherwise instructed, turn up seven single spaces, 25 mm (1 inch), from the top edge of the paper before starting the main heading. It may be typed in:

1　closed capitals—leave one space between each word;
2　spaced letters—leave one space between each letter and three spaces between each word;

3　lower case with initial capitals;
4　bold print.

Any of these headings may be underlined. Generally it is wise to follow the display indicated in the exercise to be copied. Lower case headings, particularly, can be given greater emphasis by the use of underlining. The underline must not extend beyond the typing.

1　Type the following on A5 landscape paper. (a) Single spacing. (b) Suggested margins: 12 pitch 22–82, 10 pitch 12–72, or pre-stored margins where appropriate.

Turn up 7 single spaces

ELECTRIC AND ELECTRONIC TYPEWRITERS

Turn up 2 single spaces

On most of these machines the keyboard slopes only slightly (although some have adjustable keyboards) and, by and large, the less slope there is, the lower the typewriter should be placed - the palms of the hands should be parallel to the slope of the keyboard.

Turn up 2 single spaces

Because the keys need only a touch to activate them, the fingers should <u>hover</u> over the home keys, <u>not touch</u> them. You should stroke the keys very lightly.

Subheadings

The main heading may be followed by a subheading which further clarifies the contents of the passage. Turn up two single spaces after typing the main heading and then type the subheading.

2　Type the following on A5 landscape paper. (a) Single spacing. (b) Suggested margins: 12 pitch 22–82, 10 pitch 12–72, or pre-stored margins where appropriate.

Turn up 7 single spaces

BANKING FACILITIES

Turn up 2 single spaces

Safe Custody of Valuables

Turn up 2 single spaces

It is wise to leave jewellery and other valuable items with your bank for safekeeping when you go on holiday.

Turn up 2 single spaces

The bank do not charge for this service but require you to insure the articles deposited with them.

R25 The number of guide cards used and their arrangement depend 12
on the filing system; however, the purpose of the guide card 24
is the same in all systems: to guide the eye when filing and 36
finding papers, and to support the folders. Guide cards can 48
be bought in all standard sizes, as well as for special sys- 60
tems such as fingerprint, medical, and insurance classifica- 72
tions. Most guide cards have a tab along the top edge, and 83
the space contains a plain and clear reference to the folder 95
behind. It is important that this reference should be easy 106
to read, and the marker show the exact order of the folders. 117
These cards, quite rightly, justify their existence. (SI1.36) 127

    1 | 2 | 3 | 4 | 5 | 6 | 7 | 8 | 9 | 10 | 11 | 12 |

R26 We were very glad to learn from your letter of 16 April that 12
the prospects we discussed when you visited us some 3 months 24
ago are now materializing. You inform us that you have pur- 36
chased a new truck for business purposes and that you intend 48
saving storage charges by housing it in your factory; doubt- 60
less you have calculated well and the truck will cut down on 72
your expenses. 75

Have your insurance brokers reviewed your policies since you 87
bought the truck? We do venture to suggest that you go over 99
your insurance cover with your brokers to make sure that you 111
have comprehensive protection. The fact that you have this 122
truck in your works may change the rates and may invalidate 133
the policies. (SI1.39) 135

    1 | 2 | 3 | 4 | 5 | 6 | 7 | 8 | 9 | 10 | 11 | 12 |

R27 The storage medium used on a word processor (and some elec- 12
tronic typewriters) is referred to as a floppy disk or disk- 24
ette because it is made from flexible materials, as distinct 36
from hard disks which are much larger and used more in com- 48
puter memories. Floppy disks are usually 8 inch or 5¼ inch 60
in size (adequate for 120 and 75 A4 pages) and you can even 72
buy smaller ones known as minidisks. There are also single- 84
and double-density disks - the double-density disk will hold 96
more data. Disks are in a jacket-type cover. 105

When using a floppy disk, you will have a disk drive into 116
which you insert the disk. Inside the drive, the disk spins 128
at high speed and when keying in information, the data will 139
be transferred to the disk by a device called a head. This 150
head will also read data from the disk and transfer it to a 161
screen or thin window display. (SI1.38) 167

    1 | 2 | 3 | 4 | 5 | 6 | 7 | 8 | 9 | 10 | 11 | 12 |

Paragraph headings

Apart from the main heading and the subheading at the beginning of a passage, paragraph headings are used to give emphasis to the first few words of a paragraph. In blocked style the paragraph heading starts at the left margin as in exercise 3 below. They may be typed:

1 in upper case, with or without underlining;
2 in lower case with underlining;
3 with a full stop and two spaces, or just the two spaces without the full stop;
4 running straight on into the following words of the paragraph, but may be emphasized by using capitals, underlining and/or bold print.

3 Type the following on A5 portrait paper. (a) Single spacing. (b) Suggested margins: 12 pitch 13–63, 10 pitch 6–56, or pre-stored margins where appropriate.
   NB The coloured figures after the paragraph headings indicate the number of character spaces to be left and should not be typed.

Turn up 7 single spaces

FLEMING & COX PLC

Turn up 2 single spaces

Terms and Conditions of Sale

Turn up 2 single spaces

GUARANTEE^2 All workmanship and equipment supplied by us will be guaranteed for a period of 12 months from the date of completion.

TERMS^2 The prices quoted are nett and are due for payment on completion of the contract.

Blocked exercises typed in double spacing

If the text is typed in double spacing it is wise and easier for the reader, if an extra space, or spaces, is left after the headings. It may be easier for you to return twice on double, but three single spaces are equally acceptable.

4 Type the following on A5 portrait paper. (a) Double spacing. (b) Suggested margins: 12 pitch 13–63, 10 pitch 6–56, or pre-stored margins where appropriate.

Turn up 7 single spaces

I T I N E R A R Y

Turn up 2 single spaces

MAKING TRAVEL ARRANGEMENTS

Turn up 3 single spaces

An itinerary is a programme listing arrangements

made for travel and/or appointments.

Turn up 3 single spaces

Dates and times of arrival and departure are given

with the names and addresses and telephone numbers

of the places to be visited.

R19 Many people who pay rent are entitled to a rent allowance or | 12
rebate - an allowance if a private tenant or a rebate if you | 24
are a council tenant. | 28

You should write to your local council. Then they will need | 40
to know your income, and the larger your family the more you | 52
are justified in seizing the chance of getting help, and the | 64
more quickly you may expect help. **(SI 1.36)** | 70

1 | 2 | 3 | 4 | 5 | 6 | 7 | 8 | 9 | 10 | 11 | 12 |

R20 If you are asked to compile a business letter, you must: (a) | 12
use short words if they express clearly what you want to say | 24
and (b) also keep your sentences short. Tackle the job with | 36
zeal, acquire a good style, and avoid vague statements. **(SI 1.25)** | 47

1 | 2 | 3 | 4 | 5 | 6 | 7 | 8 | 9 | 10 | 11 | 12 |

R21 Dear Ms Knight, Since July 1987 we have had your name on our | 12
mailing lists, and although we have, from time to time, sent | 24
you details of many exclusive properties, you have not tele- | 36
phoned as you said you would. We are now anxious to know if | 48
you have any queries and still wish to buy a desirable resi- | 60
dence at an amazingly low price. **(SI 1.33)** | 66

1 | 2 | 3 | 4 | 5 | 6 | 7 | 8 | 9 | 10 | 11 | 12 |

R22 In September 1985, 9,000 people were killed in an earthquake | 12
in Mexico City. Also, in June 1986 slight damage was caused | 24
by a weak tremor which recorded as 5.4 on the Richter scale. | 36
In March 1986, an earthquake struck southern Turkey and some | 48
14 people were injured in 4 villages as houses fell. We are | 60
lucky in Great Britain as there are only one or 2 zones that | 72
have slight earth tremors. **(SI 1.32)** | 77

1 | 2 | 3 | 4 | 5 | 6 | 7 | 8 | 9 | 10 | 11 | 12 |

R23 When you arrive, you should follow the clearly marked black- | 12
on-yellow 'arrivals' signs to immigration. If you are going | 24
to take an onward flight, follow the signs to the 'Transfer | 36
Desk'. After clearing immigration, wait in the lounge until | 48
your flight number appears on the TV screen indicating which | 60
carousel in the Baggage Hall to go to. Just place your bag- | 72
gage on one of the unique, free-of-charge trolleys and go on | 84
through customs to the exit zone on the terminal concourse. | 96

(SI 1.35)

1 | 2 | 3 | 4 | 5 | 6 | 7 | 8 | 9 | 10 | 11 | 12 |

R24 A wide range of tax-free goods is available on the aircraft, | 12
and a list of the products, with prices and comparative UK | 24
retail prices, will be found in the seat pocket. Your cabin | 36
staff will let you know in good time as to when the tax-free | 48
products will be on sale. For your guidance a list of items | 60
you can hear on the audio channels is in the pocket - adjust | 72
the sound to suit your needs, but keep the volume low. Some | 84
flights have a film and you should select a suitable channel | 96
to listen to the sound-track and channel 2 for quality jazz. | 108
Your headset should be placed in the seat pocket before you | 120
leave the aircraft. **(SI 1.27)** | 124

1 | 2 | 3 | 4 | 5 | 6 | 7 | 8 | 9 | 10 | 11 | 12 |

Shoulder headings

When this form of heading is used, it is typed at the left margin and may be in closed capitals or in lower case with initial capitals, with or without the underscore, and/or in bold print. It is preceded and followed by one blank line when using single spacing. When using double spacing, it is preceded by two or three blank lines and followed by one.

5 Type the following on A5 landscape paper. (a) Single spacing. (b) Suggested margins: 12 pitch 22–82, 10 pitch 12–72, or pre-stored margins where appropriate.

C o m p u t e r   H a r d w a r e

Turn up 2 single spaces

Output Devices

Turn up 2 single spaces

There is a wide variety of printers that create output on paper. They fall into 2 categories - impact and non-impact.

Turn up 2 single spaces

IMPACT PRINTERS

Turn up 2 single spaces

These create an image by having a print element which actually strikes the paper through a ribbon.

Turn up 2 single spaces

NON-IMPACT PRINTERS

Turn up 2 single spaces

These produce images without any physical impact being made on the paper.

6 Type the following on A5 portrait paper. (a) Double spacing. (b) Suggested margins: 12 pitch 13–63, 10 pitch 6–56, or pre-stored margins where appropriate.

OVERSEAS TELEPHONE CALLS

Turn up 2 single spaces

International Direct Dialling

Turn up 3 single spaces

CHARGES

Turn up 2 single spaces

On IDD calls you pay only for the length of time

you are connected.

Turn up 3 single spaces

OPERATOR CALLS

Turn up 2 single spaces

Operator calls abroad are more expensive with a

3-minute minimum charge.

1 minute

R13 A thick haze covered the headland, and the wind, now at gale   12
force, was sharp and biting. I walked on and in a long time   24
I judged I had done only 3 miles. Anxious and quite worried   36
I sat down for a short time. **(SI 1.12)**   41

1 | 2 | 3 | 4 | 5 | 6 | 7 | 8 | 9 | 10 | 11 | 12 |

1½ minutes

R14 Have you ever been to a large airport just to watch the end-   12
less movement of people and planes? You can see hundreds of   24
folk getting on and off these exciting jets, and it makes me   36
wonder how such unique planes zoom so gently into the air or   48
land without skidding. **(SI 1.27)**   52

1 | 2 | 3 | 4 | 5 | 6 | 7 | 8 | 9 | 10 | 11 | 12 |

2 minutes

R15 She exhaled deeply as they crossed the frozen lake and moved   12
swiftly past the hole lined with jagged ice. The sleds were   24
light and the 6 dogs well rested; consequently, there was no   36
need to think about a stop until we were in the next hamlet.   48
Then a sudden squall brought more snow and the track's mark-   60
ings were lost. **(SI 1.22)**   63

1 | 2 | 3 | 4 | 5 | 6 | 7 | 8 | 9 | 10 | 11 | 12 |

1 minute

R16 From our magazine you will see that we have spent many years   12
fitting all kinds of carpets - all our staff are specialists   24
and quietly complete their jobs. In truth, they are experts   36
who have spent their lives in this trade. **(SI 1.25)**   44

1 | 2 | 3 | 4 | 5 | 6 | 7 | 8 | 9 | 10 | 11 | 12 |

2 minutes

R17 Different kinds of wild plants do not grow in the same place   12
because they need the soil and conditions to suit them, just   24
as you have your likes and dislikes. If you acquire a plant   36
which excels in a warm, dry place, it is prone to die if you   48
move it to a zone which is cold and damp. It is possible to   60
alter its habits over a period of time. **(SI 1.20)**   68

1 | 2 | 3 | 4 | 5 | 6 | 7 | 8 | 9 | 10 | 11 | 12 |

1 minute

R18 It may be next June before I can be certain of the number of   12
folk who may be present at the Market Square for this year's   24
Fair. Four years ago our efforts added up to zero, but I am   36
sure we have already sold more tickets than in 1987. **(SI 1.22)**   46

1 | 2 | 3 | 4 | 5 | 6 | 7 | 8 | 9 | 10 | 11 | 12 |

KEYBOARDING SKILLS

Before proceeding to the exercises below, you should type the following skill building exercises:

proofreading No 1, page 148.   **techniques and reviews** No 1, page 157.
skill measurement No 13, page 158.   **record your progress** No 8, page 164.

PRODUCTION DEVELOPMENT

- *Standard sizes of paper*—See, pages 10–13.
- *Vertical linespacing*—See, page 20.
- *Horizontal linespacing*—See, pages 9–13.

Display

Some types of matter such as notices, menus and advertisements are much more attractive if items are displayed on separate lines and good use is made of capital letters, small letters, the underscore and bold print. In its simplest form, and to save time, decide on a *suitable* left and top margin depending on the length of the longest line and the actual number of lines to be typed. Then type each line at the left margin, leaving extra lines between items, as required, for emphasis.

Spaced letters

Important lines may be given prominence by using spaced capitals, or lower case spaced letters, ie leave one space between each letter and three spaces between each word. NB When using closed capitals, it is usual to leave one space between each word.

Notice the use of spaced letters, both capitals and lower case, closed capitals and lower case, and a variation in linespacing to place emphasis and stress on individual lines, in the exercises that follow. Examining bodies use the word emphasize or highlight when they wish the typist to give prominence to a particular word, words or lines of text.

Electronic machines

If you are using an electronic machine, you may be able to make use of the bold function key. This key is depressed before typing the chosen line, eg POST OFFICE. The line will then appear in a heavier print than the others in the exercise, and so be given prominence.

1   Display the following on A5 portrait paper. (a) Leave 51 mm (2 inches) at the top of the page, ie turn up 13 single spaces. (b) Suggested left margin: 12 pitch 13, 10 pitch 11, or pre-stored margins where appropriate. (c) Copy the exercise line for line.

			Turn up 13 single spaces
1	Line 1	USE YOUR	Turn up 2 single spaces
2	Space	↓	
3	Line 2	P O S T O F F I C E	Turn up 2 single spaces
4	Space	↓	
5	Line 3	f o r	Turn up 2 single spaces
6	Space	↓	
7	Line 4	Pensions	Type the last 5 lines in
8	Line 5	Giro Bank	single spacing
9	Line 6	Postal Orders	
10	Line 7	Motor Vehicle Licences	
11	Line 8	Savings Stamps (TV, Telephone, Car)	

2   Display the following on A5 landscape paper. (a) Leave 51 mm (2 inches) at the top of the page. (b) Suggested left margin: 12 pitch 25, 10 pitch 21, or pre-stored margins where appropriate. (c) Copy the exercise line for line.

			Turn up 13 single spaces
1	Line 1	JOIN OUR TEMPORARY STAFF TEAM	Turn up 2 single spaces
2	Space	↓	
3	Line 2	Summer work for students	Turn up 3 single spaces
4	Space	↓	
5	Space	↓	
6	Line 3	S E C R E T A R I A L V A C A N C I E S	Turn up 2 single spaces
7	Space	↓	
8	Line 4	Shorthand secretaries	Type the last 4 lines in
9	Line 5	Word processing secretaries	single spacing
10	Line 6	VDU operators	
11	Line 7	Audio secretaries	

Record your progress

Follow instructions on page 24.

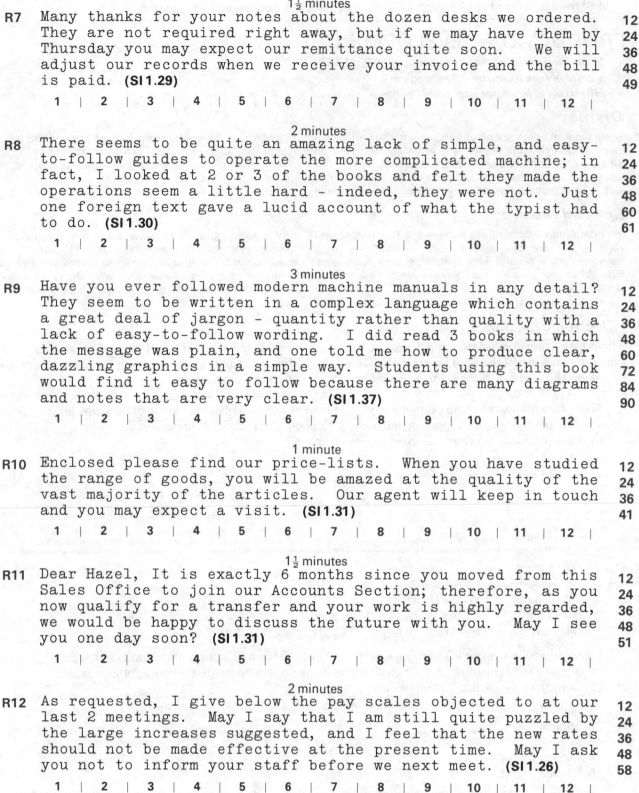

1½ minutes

R7   Many thanks for your notes about the dozen desks we ordered.   12
They are not required right away, but if we may have them by   24
Thursday you may expect our remittance quite soon.   We will   36
adjust our records when we receive your invoice and the bill   48
is paid. **(SI 1.29)**   49

`1 | 2 | 3 | 4 | 5 | 6 | 7 | 8 | 9 | 10 | 11 | 12 |`

2 minutes

R8   There seems to be quite an amazing lack of simple, and easy-   12
to-follow guides to operate the more complicated machine; in   24
fact, I looked at 2 or 3 of the books and felt they made the   36
operations seem a little hard - indeed, they were not.   Just   48
one foreign text gave a lucid account of what the typist had   60
to do. **(SI 1.30)**   61

`1 | 2 | 3 | 4 | 5 | 6 | 7 | 8 | 9 | 10 | 11 | 12 |`

3 minutes

R9   Have you ever followed modern machine manuals in any detail?   12
They seem to be written in a complex language which contains   24
a great deal of jargon - quantity rather than quality with a   36
lack of easy-to-follow wording.   I did read 3 books in which   48
the message was plain, and one told me how to produce clear,   60
dazzling graphics in a simple way.   Students using this book   72
would find it easy to follow because there are many diagrams   84
and notes that are very clear. **(SI 1.37)**   90

`1 | 2 | 3 | 4 | 5 | 6 | 7 | 8 | 9 | 10 | 11 | 12 |`

1 minute

R10   Enclosed please find our price-lists.   When you have studied   12
the range of goods, you will be amazed at the quality of the   24
vast majority of the articles.   Our agent will keep in touch   36
and you may expect a visit. **(SI 1.31)**   41

`1 | 2 | 3 | 4 | 5 | 6 | 7 | 8 | 9 | 10 | 11 | 12 |`

1½ minutes

R11   Dear Hazel, It is exactly 6 months since you moved from this   12
Sales Office to join our Accounts Section; therefore, as you   24
now qualify for a transfer and your work is highly regarded,   36
we would be happy to discuss the future with you.   May I see   48
you one day soon? **(SI 1.31)**   51

`1 | 2 | 3 | 4 | 5 | 6 | 7 | 8 | 9 | 10 | 11 | 12 |`

2 minutes

R12   As requested, I give below the pay scales objected to at our   12
last 2 meetings.   May I say that I am still quite puzzled by   24
the large increases suggested, and I feel that the new rates   36
should not be made effective at the present time.   May I ask   48
you not to inform your staff before we next meet. **(SI 1.26)**   58

`1 | 2 | 3 | 4 | 5 | 6 | 7 | 8 | 9 | 10 | 11 | 12 |`

Effective display

Displayed work looks more effective when it is centred on the page. The underscore, closed capitals, spaced capitals or bold type may be used to emphasize or highlight important lines.

Backspace key

Refer to page 2 and locate the backspace key on your machine.

Horizontal centring—blocked style

When centring a piece of display in the full width of the paper, take the following steps:

1 See that the left edge of the paper is at 0 on the paper guide scale.
2 Move margin stops to extreme left and right.
3 Divide by two the total number of spaces between 0 and the scale point reached by the right edge of the page; this gives the centre point of the paper.
4 Bring carriage, carrier or cursor to the centre point.
5 Locate the backspace key and backspace once for every two characters and spaces in the longest line. Ignore any odd letter left over.
6 Set the left margin at the point reached.
7 All lines in the exercise start at the left margin.

Electronic machines

On electronic keyboards there are usually:

1 An automatic centring function which will centre the typed line when you press the appropriate key(s), but on most machines this is only satisfactory when each line of the exercise is centred.

2 An automatic underline feature; and
3 A bold function key. This key is depressed before typing the chosen line, or word(s), eg **post office**. The line/word(s) will then appear in a heavier print than the others in the exercise, and so give it prominence.

3 Display the following on A5 landscape paper. (a) Leave 25 mm (1 inch) at the top of the page. (b) Centre the longest line horizontally. (c) Set the left margin and start all lines at this point.

		Turn up
		6 single spaces
	FILING AND INDEXING	2 single spaces
	↓	
	<u>CLASSIFICATIONS</u>	3 single spaces
	↓	
NOTE: The left	Alphabetical	Use single
margin will be	Chronological	spacing for the
set at	Geographical	last five items
12 pitch 41	Numerical	
10 pitch 32	Subject	

4 Display the following on A5 portrait paper. (a) Leave 25 mm (1 inch) at the top of the page. (b) Centre the longest line horizontally. (c) Set the left margin and start all lines at this point.

	Turn up
	6 single spaces
L U N C H M E N U	2 single spaces
↓	
<u>Saturday, 3 February 1990</u>	3 single spaces
↓	
Soup of the day	2 single spaces
↓	
Steak and kidney pie	1 space
Lasagne	1 space
Cold buffet from the bar	2 spaces
↓	
Apple crumble and cream	1 space
Various ices	

SM40 Have you ever 'met' a person for the very first time over   11
the telephone? How did you know what kind of person she/he   23
was? By the voice, of course! Was it gruff or pleasant,   35
calm or excited? How do you sound over the telephone? You   46
cannot be seen, only heard, and your voice will convey your   58
personality.   61

You should speak clearly and distinctly, and be very tactful   73
and logical in expressing your thoughts. The good telephon-   85
ist will handle all telephone calls courteously and intelli-   97
gently by speaking in a well-modulated voice, enunciating   108
distinctly, choosing words that convey her thoughts clearly,   120
and expressing through her tone sincere interest in the per-   132
son calling. How well you represent your employer on the   143
telephone will depend on your telephone technique.   153

Answer all calls promptly. Make a habit of having pen and   165
paper ready so that you can record any messages.   **(SI 1.46)** 175

1 | 2 | 3 | 4 | 5 | 6 | 7 | 8 | 9 | 10 | 11 | 12 |

SM41 Input is the information prepared by the author and entered   12
into the system by means of the keyboard. The input may be   24
in the form of typed or handwritten drafts, or shorthand/   36
audio dictation. Whatever kind of input you work from,   47
typing letters and reports will always predominate. You   58
must use: the correct paper for the printout - letterhead,   70
memo, plain bond, and, of course, bank paper for the carbon   81
copies; the preferred house style; accurate spelling, gram-   93
mar, and punctuation. You must proofread thoroughly, mak-   105
ing correction on the soft copy before printout.   115

Converting the input to usable form requires processing.   126
You should follow instructions precisely, use your time   137
wisely, apply common sense and initiative, and type mail-   149
able copy, within a given time, ready for approval, sign-   160
ing and/or comment. Processed input in its final form is   171
known as 'output'.   **(SI 1.51)**   175

1 | 2 | 3 | 4 | 5 | 6 | 7 | 8 | 9 | 10 | 11 | 12 |

5 Display the following on A5 landscape paper. (a) Leave 25 mm (1 inch) at the top of the page. (b) Centre the longest line horizontally.

	Turn up
O F F I C E E Q U I P M E N T	2 single spaces
Text Processing	3 single spaces
Electronic typewriters	1 space
Memory typewriters	1 space
Text editing and text processing machines	1 space
Word processors	1 space
Computers	

Spaced capitals

To centre words that are to be typed in spaced capitals:

1 Say the letters and spaces in pairs.
2 Backspace once for each complete pair, including the two extra spaces between the words, eg S space P space A space C space E space D space space space C space A space, etc.

3 Do NOT backspace for the last letter in the final word and remember to leave three spaces between each word. Practise centring the following two words.

$$S \cap P \cap A \cap C \cap E \cap D \cap \cap C \cap A \cap P \cap I \cap T \cap A \cap L \cap s$$

6 Display the following on A5 portrait paper. (a) Leave 25 mm (1 inch) at the top of the page. (b) Centre the longest line horizontally.

	Turn up
Q U E S T I O N T I M E	2 single spaces
for	2 single spaces
G a r d e n e r s	2 single spaces
ROCKLEIGH VILLAGE HALL	3 single spaces
Friday, 2 February 1990	4 single spaces
THE TEAM - Bill Davis	1 space
May Jones	1 space
Don Aldis	

The left margin will be set at 12 pitch 23, 10 pitch 17.

7 Display the following exercise on paper of a suitable size.

THE   SINGLE   MARKET

PLAN AHEAD

for

1992

Europe — open for business

SM34   If the new shop is to be ready in June, there are a few jobs 12
that must be done at once.   First, we must find a person who 24
will make some effort to put the business on its feet. **(SI 1.14)** 35

SM35   My brothers and I were terrors when we were boys, but I do 12
not believe we were really bad.   In those days there were no 24
movies or radio, and television was a thing of the future, 35
                                        (SI 1.31)

   1 | 2 | 3 | 4 | 5 | 6 | 7 | 8 | 9 | 10 | 11 | 12 |

SM36   A dozen climbers, roped together, had struggled for hours 12
up one of the Swiss heights, and the summit lay only half a 23
mile ahead.   Behind them a snow slope fell steeply away for 35
more than a third of a mile.   The group was nearly across 46
the slope when they heard a deep tearing noise, and a crack 59
appeared in the snow and ice just five yards above them. 70
                                        (SI 1.23)

SM37   There has always been a great deal of good advice available 12
for the person seeking a job.   Much of this excellent advice 24
lays stress on making a good first impression, and I do feel 36
that the first few minutes are critical to your chances of 47
being selected for a job.   This means that you should carry 59
out some careful planning before you attend an interview. 70
                                        (SI 1.31)

   1 | 2 | 3 | 4 | 5 | 6 | 7 | 8 | 9 | 10 | 11 | 12 |

SM38   We understand that you will be leaving this country shortly 12
to take a job overseas, and we thought that your friends and 24
family might like an up-to-date photograph of you before you 36
leave.   We can supply large prints, and we should be pleased 48
to arrange a sitting at short notice when convenient to you. 60
May we also mention that we offer a service for business men 72
which is both efficient and complete in every way.   We will 84
be pleased to show you numerous pictures which show clearly 96
the eye-catching style presented by our cameraman. **(SI 1.35)** 106

   1 | 2 | 3 | 4 | 5 | 6 | 7 | 8 | 9 | 10 | 11 | 12 |

SM39   Yes, they should call here to see the goods which I spoke to 12
you about last Monday.   I do not send stock out on approval. 24
I shall be very pleased to do business with you and to allow 36
you monthly credit of £10,000.   In the late autumn I hope to 48
offer some first-class quality goods, and in the meantime I 60
can let you have the best value in woollens, with a special 72
line in sweaters.   I am sorry that I am unable to suggest a 84
reliable house for socks: this is part of the trade in which 96
I have not done business, and it would not be fair of me to 108
pass an opinion on the firms whose names you mention in your 120
letter.   I have always kept my prices low, and will write to 132
you when next I have some special offers. **(SI 1.23)** 140

   1 | 2 | 3 | 4 | 5 | 6 | 7 | 8 | 9 | 10 | 11 | 12 |

Fractions

8 Find the $\frac{1}{2}$ key and the % key on your keyboard and make certain you know whether or not you have to use the shift key. Type each of the following lines three times. Margins: 12 pitch 22–82, 10 pitch 12–72, or pre-stored margins where appropriate.

```
; ; ;   1̲1̲1̲   ; ; ;   1̲1̲1̲   ;1̲;   ;1̲;   1½;  2½;   3½;   4½;   5½;   6½;   7½;   8½;   90½;
        2 2 2         2 2 2    2    2
; ; ;   %%%   ; ; ;   %%%   ;%;   ;%;   ½%;   2%;   3%;   4%;   5%;   6%;   7%;   9%;   19%;
```

NOTE: In addition to the $\frac{1}{2}$, most typewriters have keys with other fractions. Examine your machine to find what fractions it has. These are all typed with the ; finger. Some will require the use of the shift key. Practise the reaching movement from the home key to the fraction key you wish to type. Remember ALWAYS return your finger quickly to the home key.

Sloping fractions

When fractions are not provided on the typewriter, these should be typed by using ordinary figures with the oblique, eg 2 fifteenths = 2/15; 3 sixteenths = 3/16. Where a whole number comes before a 'made-up' fraction, leave a clear space (NOT a full stop) between the whole number and the fraction. Fractions already on the keyboard and sloping fractions may both be used in the same exercise.

9 Type the following on A5 landscape paper. (a) Double spacing. (b) Margins: 12 pitch 22–82, 10 pitch 12–72.

```
2½,  3¼,  6 2/5,  2 5/16,  3 7/8,  4 8/9,  8 2/9,  17 3/7,  16 3/10.
The following widths are in inches:  7½,  5 3/8,  16¾,  17 1/10.
```

Decimals

1 Use full stop for decimal point. This is usually typed in the normal position of the full stop.

2 Leave NO space before or after decimal point.

3 No punctuation required at the end of figures except at the end of a sentence.

4 Always insert the number of decimal places required by using zero.
Examples: Two decimal places: type 86.40 not 86.4.
  Three decimal places: type 95.010 not 95.01.

10 Type the following sentences three times.

```
Add up 12.54, 13.02, 24.60, 6.75 and 0.20 and you get 57.11.
The sheet measures 1.200 × 5.810 × 2.540 m; the gross weight
is approximately 50.802 kg and the net weight is 38.102 kg.
```

Sums of money in context

1 If the sum comprises only pounds, type as follows: £5, £10 or £5.00, £10.00.

2 If only pence, type: 10p, 97p.
NOTE: No space between figures and letter p and no full stop after p (unless, of course, it ends a sentence).

3 With mixed amounts, ie sums comprising pounds and pence, the decimal point and the £ symbol should always be used, but NOT the abbreviation p.
Example: £7.05.

4 If the sum contains a decimal point but no whole pounds, a nought should be typed after the £ symbol and before the point.
Example: £0.97.

11 Type the following exercise in double spacing.

```
We have purchased goods to the value of £200.50, and we must

send our cheque for this amount; however, we still await a

credit note for £61.49 which means the cheque should be for

£139.01.  The latest discount we were offered was 2½% and

not 3½% as stated in their letter.
```

UNIT 25   See Typing Target Practice, R/E, page 8, for further exercises on
Fractions, Decimals, Sums of money in context

36

SM31 Please note that as from 2 October there will be an increase   12
of 9% in air fares because of higher landing charges, a drop   24
in the value of sterling, and a surge in the price of fuel.   36

May we again remind you that you must comply with police and   48
immigration regulations at the points of arrival and depar-   60
ture and at any place along the route. Your journey may be   72
broken at most stops (except on package tours) with no extra   84
charge, provided you complete your journey within the dates   96
stated. As there are a number of formalities, the check-in   107
time quoted is the time you must register at the check-in   118
desk. **(SI 1.37)**   119

1 | 2 | 3 | 4 | 5 | 6 | 7 | 8 | 9 | 10 | 11 | 12 |

SM32 Before your employer leaves on a business trip, obtain from   12
her/him instructions as to what business or private letters   24
may be opened and what correspondence should be forwarded by   36
mail. If you decide to send on the actual letters, make a   47
copy of each as a safeguard against loss or damage in the   58
post. When posting, make sure that the envelope used is of   70
a suitable size and that it is addressed to the town your   81
employer will have reached by the time the letter arrives.   92

Mark the letter/package clearly TO AWAIT ARRIVAL, and state   104
your business address to which the letter should be returned 116
if not claimed within a certain time. You must also record   127
the date of posting mail. **(SI 1.35)**   132

1 | 2 | 3 | 4 | 5 | 6 | 7 | 8 | 9 | 10 | 11 | 12 |

SM33 When you apply for your first post, how should you look? Is   12
the prospective employer going to say to himself, "This per-   24
son is smart looking and I will be pleased to introduce her   36
to the office staff." Or will he feel that your clothes are   48
'way out', your hair is too startling and unkempt, and your   60
finger nails look dirty. Make certain that your appearance   72
is suitable for the job you are seeking, and forget about it   84
until after the interview.   89

At an interview you will be required to answer and ask ques-   101
tions. The interviewer will have your application form and   113
will perhaps ask you questions that you have answered on   124
paper; however, he wishes to have the information repeated   135
orally. When answering questions, speak clearly and do not   147
bite your words. **(SI 1.37)**   150

1 | 2 | 3 | 4 | 5 | 6 | 7 | 8 | 9 | 10 | 11 | 12 |

KEYBOARDING SKILLS

Before proceeding to the exercises below, you should type the following skill building exercises:

improve your spelling Nos 3 and 4, page 155   **alphabetic sentence** No 2, page 156.
skill measurement No 14, page 158.   **record your progress** No 9, page 164.

PRODUCTION DEVELOPMENT

- *Personal letters*—See **data store**, page 189.

1   Type the following formal personal letter on plain A5 portrait paper. (a) Suggested margins: 12 pitch 13–63, 10 pitch 6–56. (b) Follow the layout and capitalization exactly. NB Leave one clear character space between the two parts of the postcode.

Turn up
4 single spaces

Sender's home
address

    27 George Road
    CORBY
    Northants
    NN18 8BR

2 single spaces

    26 February 1990

2 single spaces

    Dear Mrs Elford

2 single spaces

    I am sorry to tell you that I will not be able to attend the committee meeting to be held on Friday, 9 March. Unfortunately, my mother is ill in hospital, and I shall be going to Birmingham to visit her on that day.

2 single spaces

    However, I shall be able to come to the coffee morning on Monday, 12 March, and I look forward to seeing you then.

2 single spaces

    Yours sincerely

5 single spaces

    Jane Mortimore

2   Type the following letter on a sheet of plain A5 portrait paper. (a) Suggested margins: 12 pitch 13–63, 10 pitch 6–56. (b) The letter is from Jane Mortimore to Mrs Elford; therefore, apart from the date, which is 2 March 1990, follow layout and wording in the letter above, as far as the salutation, then type the following.

Many thanks for your letter informing me that the date for the committee meeting has been changed.

All being well, I shall be able to attend on that day.

Type the complimentary close and Mrs Mortimore's name as in the letter displayed in exercise 1.

SM26 You will be pleased to learn that we have made more machines 12
this year than we did last year, and that we are also making 24
all vital spare parts. Over the next 2 months we shall take 36
orders only for the new models we are producing. **(SI 1.22)** 45

1 | 2 | 3 | 4 | 5 | 6 | 7 | 8 | 9 | 10 | 11 | 12 |

SM27 Some large offices have a pool of typists who share the work 12
to be done, but we do not know whether or not this is a good 24
plan. It is a matter upon which each firm should make a de- 36
cision based on the pressure of work and the number of staff 48
employed as typists. You may prefer a job in a typing pool. 60
                              (SI 1.22)

1 | 2 | 3 | 4 | 5 | 6 | 7 | 8 | 9 | 10 | 11 | 12 |

SM28 The Chairman of the Board tells me that Tom Younger has been 12
badly hurt in an accident on the M5, and points out that Tom 24
will not be at work for at least 18 months. You are aware, 36
no doubt, of the fact that he has a large number of speaking 48
engagements in many different cities, and these will have to 60
be cancelled at once unless we are able to engage someone to 72
take over from him. **(SI 1.25)** 76

1 | 2 | 3 | 4 | 5 | 6 | 7 | 8 | 9 | 10 | 11 | 12 |

Speed building

Speed is built up more easily on short, simple exercises and, as we have now reached 2½ minutes at 30 wpm, and will continue at 30 wpm with increased lengths of timing, we suggest that you use the earlier **skill measurement** exercises as practice material for speed building. For example, to increase your speed from 30 wpm to 35 wpm, use SM12 on page 158. As a guide, we suggest that if have more than one error for each minute typed, then should strive for greater accuracy. With less than one for each minute typed, you may wish to build your spee using short exercises of low syllabic intensity.

SM29 When travelling in an aeroplane, make sure that none of your 12
hand luggage obstructs the aisle or seat areas. It should 24
be stored in the overhead lockers or under the seat in front 36
of you. Enjoy your flight! Sit back, relax, and make your- 48
self comfortable - the cabin staff will be pleased to attend 60
to your needs. Hot or cold meals will be served during the 72
flight, depending on the time of day and length of flight. 83
Radio and tape players may be used. **(SI 1.27)** 90

1 | 2 | 3 | 4 | 5 | 6 | 7 | 8 | 9 | 10 | 11 | 12 |

SM30 You get basic tax relief on most mortgages by paying less to 12
the society who lent you the money, so no allowance is made 24
in your code. If you pay higher rate tax, your code will be 36
adjusted to give the extra relief due. If you pay interest 48
in full on mortgages or other loans for such things as home 60
improvements, an estimate of the amount of interest payable 72
will be given in your code. If you have a mortgage on prop- 84
erty that you let for a commercial rent (during 6 months of 95
each year) interest will be allowed as a deduction. **(SI 1.33)** 105

1 | 2 | 3 | 4 | 5 | 6 | 7 | 8 | 9 | 10 | 11 | 12 |

Keyboarding skills—skill measurement   SM26–SM30   **160**
1½, 2, 2½, 3 and 3½ minutes at 30 wpm
Speed building

- *Personal business letters*—See **data store**, page 189.

3 Type the following personal business letter on plain A5 portrait paper. (a) Suggested margins: 12 pitch 13–63, 10 pitch 6–56. (b) Type the letter in fully-blocked style with open punctuation. (c) Follow the layout and capitalization precisely.

Turn up
4 single spaces

Sender's home
address

39 Amphlett Road
BICESTER
Oxon
OX6 8HX

2 single spaces

6 March 1990

2 single spaces

Name and address
of addressee

J P Roache & Sons
Dove House
High Street
BICESTER
Oxon
OX6 6PR

2 single spaces

Dear Sirs

2 single spaces

I settle my account with you by Banker's Order, and received your letter, reference RC/BT, which stated that last month's instalment was directed to an incorrect account number.

Unfortunately, my bank forwarded the instalment for this month to the incorrect account number before I had the opportunity to inform them of the error. I hope that you will be able to rectify this.

I can assure you that the instalment for April will quote the correct number, which is NM24601/9.

2 single spaces

Yours faithfully

5 single spaces

Nicholas Logan

4 Type the following letter on a sheet of plain A5 portrait paper. (a) Use margins of 12 pitch 13–63, 10 pitch 6–56. (b) The letter is from Nicholas Logan to J P Roache & Sons; therefore, apart from the date, which is 14 March 1990, follow layout and wording in the letter above, as far as the salutation, then type the following:

Thank you for your letter of 12 March in which you state that my account, number NM24601/9, is now correct and up to date.

I apologize for the inconvenience caused.

Type the complimentary close and Mr Logan's name as in the letter displayed in exercise 3.

SM19 27 wpm 1½ minutes Not more than 2 errors

At the moment, there is no guide to help us to judge how far 12
we are from the roadside or from the car in front of us. We 24
know that a device is being made that will help us gauge how 36
far away we may be. (SI 1.22) 40

1 | 2 | 3 | 4 | 5 | 6 | 7 | 8 | 9 | 10 | 11 | 12 |

SM20 27 wpm 2 minutes Not more than 2 errors

He said that if you want a garden then you will have to do a 12
great deal of work, but in these days you can buy many tools 24
which will be helpful for the heavy work, and thus save time 36
and effort. You would not need to employ hired help, and so 48
you could then save some money. (SI 1.13) 54

1 | 2 | 3 | 4 | 5 | 6 | 7 | 8 | 9 | 10 | 11 | 12 |

SM21 28 wpm 1 minute Not more than 1 error

A computer is now being made that will store voice patterns. 12
It will know your voice when you speak to it, and it will be 24
able to reply to you. (SI 1.21) 28

1 | 2 | 3 | 4 | 5 | 6 | 7 | 8 | 9 | 10 | 11 | 12 |

SM22 28 wpm 2 minutes Not more than 2 errors

When you eat your Brazil nuts at Christmas do you ever think 12
of the men who pick them and of the risks they run to do so? 24
One of the risks is the falling of nuts from the trees which 36
grow to a very great height. What we usually call nuts are, 48
in fact, really the seeds from the tree. (SI 1.20) 56

1 | 2 | 3 | 4 | 5 | 6 | 7 | 8 | 9 | 10 | 11 | 12 |

SM23 29 wpm 1 minute Not more than 1 error

Against the clear blue morning sky, the white sails of their 12
graceful yachts made an ever-changing pattern as they danced 24
and swayed in the breeze. (SI 1.21) 29

1 | 2 | 3 | 4 | 5 | 6 | 7 | 8 | 9 | 10 | 11 | 12 |

SM24 29 wpm 2 minutes Not more than 2 errors

One of the great problems of today is the pressure of noise: 12
noise in the streets, in the home, by day, and sometimes far 24
into the night. Are buses and lorries the chief cause? No. 36
As we hear these all day, we get used to them. So it is the 48
infrequent sounds, such as those made by jet planes. (SI 1.16) 58

1 | 2 | 3 | 4 | 5 | 6 | 7 | 8 | 9 | 10 | 11 | 12 |

SM25 30 wpm 1 minute Not more than 1 error

The weather is likely to remain mild in the south, with some 12
light rain, but in the north there may be ground frost which 24
could cause ice on some roads. (SI 1.10) 30

1 | 2 | 3 | 4 | 5 | 6 | 7 | 8 | 9 | 10 | 11 | 12 |

Keyboarding skills—skill measurement SM19–SM25 **159**
1½ and 2 minutes at 27 wpm   1 and 2 minutes at 28 wpm   1 and 2 minutes at 29 wpm
1 minute at 30 wpm

KEYBOARDING SKILLS

Before proceeding to the exercises below, you should type the following skill building exercises:

proofreading No 2, page 148.   **techniques and reviews** No 2, page 157.
skill measurement No 15, page 158.   **record your progress** No 10, page 164.

PRODUCTION DEVELOPMENT

Business letters—open punctuation—fully-blocked—see also data store, page 177.

Letters are ambassadors and advertisements for the organization that sends them; therefore, you must ensure that your letters are well displayed and faultlessly typed. Businesses have a variety of forms of display, and the examples that follow are in fully-blocked style with open punctuation, which you used in the letters in unit 26.

A business organization will always have paper with a printed letterhead and you should turn up a minimum of two single-line spaces after the last line of the printed heading before starting to type. The originator (writer or author) of a business letter will also have a reference at the top and this, in its simplest form, consists of the initials of the dictator followed by an oblique and the typist's initials. Many organizations today use the dictator's initials, followed by the disk number, the document number and the typist's initials, eg PD/15/22/AH. It is also accepted practice, but by no means essential, to type the dictator's name five single spaces after the complimentary close with her/his designation (official position) typed underneath.

1   Type the following letter on A4 letterhead paper which will be found in the *Workguide and Resource Material*. (a) Suggested margins: 12 pitch 22–82, 10 pitch 12–72. (b) Follow the layout and capitalization given.

Printed
heading

LEYS ENTERPRISES

Registered No 241199 (England) Freefone 0270 700014 Telex 76335 Fax 0270 709822	Registered Office 6-9 Druce Road Cox Bank CREWE CW3 2AF Telephone 0270 701387

Turn up
2 single spaces

Ref   PD/15/22/AH

2 single spaces

21 March 1990

2 single spaces

Mr Jeremy Cartwright
20 Herrings Lane
Cranage
CREWE
CW4 3PR

2 single spaces

Dear Mr Cartwright

2 single spaces

Thank you for the completed application form which we received today. We will contact you again as soon as we have any details.

In the meantime, if you would like any further information or advice on investment matters, please do not hesitate to let me know.

2 single spaces

Yours sincerely

5 single spaces

Paul Durndell
INVESTMENT MANAGER

Skill measurement

Follow instructions on page 23.   Margins: 12 pitch 22–82, 10 pitch 12–72

25 wpm   1½ minutes   Not more than 2 errors

SM12 Just a year ago I said that you should be given a trial as a   12
clerk in our sales section, and, as one of the staff will be   24
leaving a week today, I would like you to take her job. Let   36
me know. **(SI 1.16)**   38

    1 | 2 | 3 | 4 | 5 | 6 | 7 | 8 | 9 | 10 | 11 | 12 |

25 wpm   2 minutes   Not more than 2 errors

SM13 There must be little imps who sleep until we start to do our   12
work, and then they visit our office and begin to harass us.   24
We must all try to keep our minds on the work that has to be   36
done, and avoid letting our line of thought be broken by any   48
visitors. **(SI 1.24)**   50

    1 | 2 | 3 | 4 | 5 | 6 | 7 | 8 | 9 | 10 | 11 | 12 |

25 wpm   3 minutes   Not more than 3 errors

SM14 We have not yet been able to send the goods you ordered last   12
week as they are not stock lines, but we shall do all we can   24
to let you have some of the goods, if not all, by Tuesday of   36
next week. We trust that you will excuse the delay in send-   48
ing your requirements, and that we may look forward to meet-   60
ing your requests more promptly in the future. We enclose a   72
new price list. **(SI 1.21)**   75

    1 | 2 | 3 | 4 | 5 | 6 | 7 | 8 | 9 | 10 | 11 | 12 |

26 wpm   1 minute   Not more than 1 error

SM15 In spite of the rain all of us thought it had been an excel-   12
lent evening; but the guests could not travel till the storm   24
had passed. **(SI 1.15)**   26

    1 | 2 | 3 | 4 | 5 | 6 | 7 | 8 | 9 | 10 | 11 | 12 |

26 wpm   1½ minutes   Not more than 2 errors

SM16 As a good typist you must be fast, accurate, and able to set   12
out all kinds of documents. In your first post there may be   24
some forms of layout that are not clear. If that is so, you   36
may need help. **(SI 1.18)**   39

    1 | 2 | 3 | 4 | 5 | 6 | 7 | 8 | 9 | 10 | 11 | 12 |

26 wpm   2 minutes   Not more than 2 errors

SM17 Last May we had a chance to buy a large stock of fine cotton   12
sheets, and we are now selling these at a reduced price. If   24
your own stock of sheets is low, now is the chance to obtain   36
some of these goods at half price or less. Send an order by   48
July at the latest. **(SI 1.13)**   52

    1 | 2 | 3 | 4 | 5 | 6 | 7 | 8 | 9 | 10 | 11 | 12 |

27 wpm   1 minute   Not more than 1 error

SM18 The day was sunny but cool. After we had rested and had our   12
snack, we packed our bags and set out for the distant cliffs   24
some 2 miles off. **(SI 1.15)**   27

    1 | 2 | 3 | 4 | 5 | 6 | 7 | 8 | 9 | 10 | 11 | 12 |

2 Type the following fully-blocked letter in open punctuation, from Leys Enterprises, on A4 letterhead paper. (See *Workguide and Resource Material*.) (a) Suggested margins: 12 pitch 22–82, 10 pitch 12–72. (b) Keep to the spacing and layout indicated at this elementary stage of your learning process.

● For an explanation of the different parts of the letter, see **data store**, page 178.

Reference	Our ref KW/23/29/PR	Turn up 2 single spaces
Date	26 March 1990	
		2 single spaces
Name and address of addressee	Mr and Mrs J F Simister 57 Meadow Way BOURNEMOUTH BH8 8AL	
		2 single spaces
Salutation	Dear Mr and Mrs Simister	
		2 single spaces
Body of letter	Thank you for your cheque for £15.90 in respect of the out- standing premium for policy number 230-006193C.	
	So that future premiums may be collected by us on a regular monthly basis, would you please complete and return to us the enclosed Direct Debit Mandate.	
	We look forward to receiving your reply.	
		2 single spaces
Complimentary close	Yours sincerely	
		5 single spaces
Signatory Designation	KATRINA WAINE Broker Administration Division	1 single space
		Minimum of 2 single spaces
Enclosure	Enc	

3 Type the following fully-blocked letter in open punctuation, from Leys Enterprises, on A4 letterhead paper. (a) Suggested margins: 12 pitch 22–82, 10 pitch 12–72. (b) The details as far as the salutation are exactly as those given in the letter above. (c) After typing the salutation, turn up two single spaces and type the following paragraphs.

I refer to my letter mailed to you this morning.

I do apologize most sincerely for omitting to enclose the Direct Debit Mandate form. I am now enclosing this form and should be most grateful if you would complete it, sign it, and return it to me as soon as possible.

I am sorry for any inconvenience I may have caused.

(d) The complimentary close etc, is the same as in the letter above.

Techniques and reviews

Knowledge of display, of word division and of tabulation are useless if you cannot operate the machine efficiently. Therefore, the basic need of all typing courses is the development and consolidation of good techniques. Technique and review drills may be used as 'warming-up' exercises or for remedial work. Type each line or sentence three times, and then type the complete exercise.   Left margin 15

1   *Improve control of space bar*
    as is so or be in am if an me go my do he by us ask may you.
    It is so.   Ask me to go.   You must be in time.   I may do so.
    Who is she? He can go home on 6 May.   It is a 65-page book.

2   *Improve control of down reaches*
    Ac lack back rack hack jack track crack brace vacant accents
    Ab cabs dabs tabs jabs able table gable sable labels enables
    Ask Jack to bring back the labels for that one vacant table.

3   *Build speed on fluency drills*
    Did for the key all dog why see you put car ask new her site
    She did not see the new bus.   Ask her for all the old shoes.
    I will talk to him as soon as he is ready to go to the play.

4   *Improve control of up reaches*
    Ki kick kirk kite kind king skim skips taking asking napkin.
    Aw awed laws saws paws yawn Shaw shawl crawls brawls straws.
    He is taking the skips of straw to Crawley on Monday 3 June.

5   *Review hyphen key*
    full-time, up-to-date, blue-grey, 48-page, re-cover, co-opt.
    Full-time students wore pin-striped blue-grey ties.   He con-
    sidered that the up-to-date 248-page document was now ready.

6   *Build accuracy on punctuation review*
    "Is John - John Mann, not John Green - here, please?" "No."
    Send me the documents immediately; I cannot wait any longer.
    Call on me today.   I require: 2 books, 3 ribbons, 4 pencils.

7   *Improve control of out reaches*
    Ga game gape gave gates gales garlic galley baggage Algarve.
    Up upon sups cups upset soups couple duplex couplet superior
    The superior baggage belongs to the couple going to Reigate.

8   *Improve control of shift keys*
    Dear Sir, Yours faithfully, Mr J Brown, New York, Hong Kong.
    Dear Mr Brown, Dear Mrs Green, Miss R Grey, Miss Jean R Dua.
    The book Advanced Word Processing is by J and D Stananought.

9   *Improve control of figures*
    ewe 323 woe 293 our 974 rye 463 you 697 tour 5974 writ 2486.
    Drill: 10, 29, 38, 47, 56, 123, 456, 789, 010, 343, 678, 86.
    Accounts: 00-11-2345, 00-12-6789, 00-13-5858, 00-14-2679-80.

10 *Improve control of jump reaches*
    Ve five live jive dive even vain pave have rave valve events
    On loan zone cone tone hone bone fond only once bonus lesson
    Five of these events have a once only bonus for the winners.

11 *Improve control of in reaches*
    Ar are art ark lark dark park arch larch tartar barter March
    Ou out our sour dour pour tour ounce pounce bounced trounced
    It was dark in the park and the rain poured on the tourists.

12 *Improve control of adjacent keys*
    Oi toil boil soil foil join voice noise coins choice adjoins
    Rt tart part dart cart sort forts sport mirth berths sported
    The many voices joined in cheering the sporting darts teams.

---

4 Type the following fully-blocked letter in open punctuation from Leys Enterprises, on A5 letterhead paper. (a) Suggested margins: 12 pitch 13–63, 10 pitch 6–56. (b) Insert today's date.

● For an explanation of **subject heading** see **data store**, page 178.

```
              Ref JR/20/64/FT

              Mr John W Frazer MP
              The Coach House
              Church Lane
              NANTWICH
              Cheshire
              CW5 2RF                                    Turn up
                                                         2 single spaces
              Dear Sir
                                                         2 single spaces
Subject heading   SIMON PATRICK HATT
                                                         2 single spaces
              The above-named has applied to us for the position
              of Chief Accountant in our Accounts Department.

              As your name has been given as a referee, it would
              be appreciated if you would give me your opinion of
              the applicant's skills and abilities and general
              suitability for the post.

              I should be most grateful if you could let me have
              a reply by the end of next week at the latest.  A
              stamped addressed envelope is enclosed.

              Yours faithfully



              Jennifer Ripley (Mrs)
              PERSONNEL OFFICER

              Enc
```

Key in document 4 (filename POST) for 12-pitch printout. Use the word wraparound function and embolden the subject heading. When you have completed this task, save under filename POST and print out one original. Recall the document and follow the instructions for text editing on page 171.

5 Type an identical letter to the one given in exercise 4, but address it to the other referee—Dr Ann James, 26 Juniper Way, Nantwich, Cheshire, CW5 30T. Except for the name and address of the addressee and the salutation, the wording will be exactly as that given above.

KEYBOARDING SKILLS

Alphabetic sentences

It is very important that you start each typing period with a 'warm-up' drill, and the alphabetic sentence is excellent material because it gives intensive practice on the alphabet keys and, therefore, improves accuracy. Type each sentence three times.   Left margin 15

1 The pretty girl gave a cry of terror as those ravens quickly seized the jewels from the box.

2 The fox came quietly into the open, and enjoyed walking over the field which was bathed in hazy sunshine.

3 The bold pilot was unable to land the jet owing to extremely thick fog which quite covered the whole zone.

4 The thick haze over the lake meant that Jacques would not be expected to visit his good friends living nearby.

5 I saw the grey squirrel relax by the very old trees and then jump with zest from one piece of bark to another.

6 The breakfast Jackson requested was excellent even though it was cooked for him in a frying pan over a brazier.

7 The male patient lay back quietly in the oxygen tent dozing, just after his operation for a broken hip was over.

8 Flexible working is generally favoured and requested by most employees as they can just avoid the crazy traffic.

9 When we walked among the foxgloves and bluebells on that hot day in June, the crazy paving looked quite attractive.

10 The exquisite butterflies flew past, and Kathy could see the amazing colours of jade, blue, and mauve on their wings.

11 Mike was so full of zeal for the project but exaggerated his abilities very much, and they were not quite up to the task.

12 An extract from the magazine on the technique of painting in oils was requested by the majority of folk who were revising art.

13 The dozens of climbers were frequently exhausted when trying to complete the fantastic job of climbing the very high rock mountain.

14 With maximum efficiency vivacious Eliza completed the formal tests, was judged to be the best candidate, and acquired the highest marks.

15 Then we saw the five models at the waxworks, which were just amazing, as the exact resemblances to folks in the past were quite remarkable.

16 The executive was next in line for the position of editor on the Gazette as the skills required for the job were just the ones possessed by him.

17 The examination was very difficult for the lazy boy who just managed to complete the first question; but unfortunately he did not gain many marks.

18 The azure blue sky was quite a breathtaking event for Trixie to see, but it lasted just a few moments as the storm clouds blew up and covered the sun.

- *Forms of address*—See **data store**, page 180.

- *Envelopes and labels*—See **data store**, page 184.

Addressing envelopes and labels

Approximately one-third from top edge

First line half way down ⟶ Mrs Margot Lawden BSc JP
Moorend   Each item on a
177 Barry Avenue   separate line
Sedgebrook
Post town in capitals ⟶ GRANTHAM
Lincs
One space between the two halves of ⟶ NG32 2EL
postcode

DL envelope—110 × 220 mm (4¼″ × 8⅝″)

```
FOR THE ATTENTION OF MR DAVID MRAMBA

Grosvenor Studios
Grosvenor House
Watlington Trading Estate
Bletchley
MILTON KEYNES
Bucks
MK2 3EY
```

6 Type the above addresses, given as examples, on DL envelopes or labels. Type the following addresses on envelopes or labels. Mark the first one URGENT and the second one PERSONAL. Start a new line where two blank spaces have been left between items.

```
Sir Joseph Bliss JP  Oak Lodge  Four Oaks  SUTTON COLDFIELD  West Midlands  B74 4EH
Dr Jeremy Brooker  1 St Julian's Avenue  St Peter Port  GUERNSEY  Channel Islands
Mr & Mrs Harold Hunter  Orchard Cottage  Webb Way  GREAT DUNMOW  Essex  CM6 2BR
Miss Gwyneth Jones  26 Ely Road  Bryn Mawr  PWLLHELI  Gwynedd  LL53 2AR
Joan McKenzie  41 Dalkeith Road  EDINBURGH  EH16 5BU
The Global Manufacturing Co  FREEPOST  Clifden Buildings  CIRENCESTER  Glos  GL7 1CU
Youngs Motors Ltd  High Street  TAUNTON  Somerset  TA1 3SX
Dan Corrigan  2 Ennis Road  RATHKEALE  Co Limerick
Messrs J Cranleigh & Co  PO Box No 21  Surrey Road  NORWICH  Norfolk  NR1 3NG
Mr Yeoh Chee Yam  104 West Street  BRADFORD  West Yorkshire  BD1 1NL
```

7 Type envelopes or labels for exercises 1–5 in this unit.

Freepost

An organization wishing to receive a reply (or response to an advertisement) from customers, without them having to pay postage, may (by obtaining a licence from the Post Office) tell the customers to use the word FREEPOST on the envelope. The word is usually typed in capitals on a line by itself after the name of the organization.

Improve your spelling skill

Type each line of an exercise three times, then type the complete exercise once. Set the left margin at 15 or use pre-stored margins.

```
 1  view until merge awful chaos quiet forty really absorb centre
 2  lose occur gauge audio among video weird choice losing prefer

 3  paid guard media input recur queue depot canvas govern pursue
 4  quay basic alter diary truly lying reign height eighty ascend

 5  cheque usable cursor buffet unique wholly mislaid acknowledge
 6  debtor tariff fulfil coming friend humour leisure undoubtedly

 7  hungry murmur choose format argues misuse omitted immediately
 8  modern cancel except access genius serial console transferred

 9  mislaid relying dismiss useless forceful privilege stationery
10  editing college twelfth benefit February principal admissible

11  liaison minutes cursory woollen harassed Wednesday difference
12  usually grammar centred certain achieved dependent receivable

13  movable pastime synonym justify withhold perceived compliment
14  arguing marriage valuable omission function parallel envelope

15  develop exercise physical planning expenses guardian pleasant
16  believe courtesy received decision occasion familiar definite

17  pitiful forcible sentence transfer separate reducing feasible
18  proceed exercise physical hardware expenses guardian pleasant

19  knowledge agreeable competent underrate absorption colleagues
20  vaccinate committee benefited possesses accessible accidental

21  technical recognize inoculate recommend courageous wraparound
22  recipient erroneous transient emphasize especially repetition
23  courteous aggravate aggregate competent enthusiasm pagination
```

Language arts—apostrophe   See explanation on page 170

```
 1  My clerk's new word processor has many useful function keys.
 2  All our clerks' income tax records were in the Staff Office.
 3  The company's new laser printers were very swift and silent.
 4  The directors' cars were parked just in front of the office.

 5  Mr & Mrs Bob Cross's house was put up for sale on Wednesday.
 6  Kenneth Andrews' farm was put up for auction on 21 November.
 7  My children's playground was unusable because of the floods.
 8  The men's cricket bat will be found near the pavilion gates.

 9  We don't know at what time it's possible to visit her today.
10  James said, 'Do write and let me know your time of arrival.'
11  The desks measured 5' 11" x 2' 10" x 2' 6" and 6' x 3' x 3'.
12  I am certain that the word 'embarrass' has 2 r's and 2 s's.
```

Language arts—agreement of subject and verb   See explanation on page 170

```
 1  A daisywheel is a fast spinning disk that prints characters.
 2  Floppy disks are used for recording and storing information.
 3  You were our first customer when we opened our shop in town.
 4  He agrees with me, I agree with you, and they agree with us.
 5  Neither William nor Brian was at the meeting on Monday last.
 6  A new diary and a phone index are necessary for your office.
```

8   Type the following fully-blocked letter in open punctuation, from Leys Enterprises, on A4 letterhead paper.
(a) Suggested margins: 12 pitch 22–82, 10 pitch 12–74. (b) Type an envelope.

		Turn up
	Our ref NP/PQ346901M/WC	2 single spaces
	Your ref SPT/ZAM	2 single spaces
	3 April 1990	2 single spaces
Special mark	FOR THE ATTENTION OF SERGE P TRANTER	2 single spaces

Messrs Tranter, Gerrish & Partners
Beaumont House
Main Street
CONGLETON
Cheshire
CW12 3BT

Dear Sirs

POLICY NO PQ346901M

As a valued client of ours, it is important that you should
be kept aware of how your policy is progressing and also of
any new developments that may affect you or be of interest
to you.

To this end, I should be glad if you would let me know when
it would be suitable for me to call and see you.

In the meantime, I am obtaining details of the current value
of the units allocated to your policy.

I am enclosing some leaflets which give some idea of the
latest developments that may be of interest to you, and
also a stamped addressed envelope for your reply.

Yours faithfully
Name of   LEYS ENTERPRISES
organization

NIGEL PITTS
Investment Manager

Encs

NOTE: This exercise contains all the
parts of a business letter.
Keep your copy and refer to it
when necessary.

 Key in document 8 (filename POLICY) for 12–pitch printout. Embolden all words in block capitals and use the
word wraparound function. When you have completed this task, save under filename POLICY and print out one
copy. Recall the document and follow the instructions for text editing on page 171.

Exercise 12

Keys on page 170
Proofreading target: 7 minutes
Typing target: 4 minutes

The following exercise contains 15 errors. A correct version is not provided, so you will have to identify the errors by using your knowledge of typing layout, spelling, punctuation and correct grammatical expression. When you have noted all the errors, type a corrected version, proofreading your typed copy very carefully.

P R E S T E L

Prestal is a collection of specialist, educational and general databases which provide a wide range of information & services for a variety of users. It is part of british Telecom and was the worlds first viewdata service. At the end of 1987 there were about 300,000 pages of information and interactive services held on Prestel's own computors, from more than 1,000 organizations.

When you subscribe to Prestel you is given an identity number and password and a telephone number to dial to connect you to the Prestel network. The information is held on mainframe computers situated in different parts of the country and linked together to form a network. The services are made available to your microcomputer via the telephone and modem at local call telephone rates. The moden is a devise which allows a computer to be connected to a telephone line.

     The information includes news articles, storys, advertisments, reference information statistics, ect. A Prestel user can book holidays, send messages to other subscribers, order goods; etc.

The following exercise contains 14 errors. A correct version is not provided, so you will have to identify the errors by using your knowledge of typing layout, spelling, punctuation and correct grammatical expression. When you have noted all the errors, type a corrected version, proofreading your typed copy very carefully.

HEALTHY VDU SCREENS?

Is it safe to sit in front of a visual display unit allday? Or does it cause eye strain, backache, headaches frozen shoulders, or even misscarriages?

If there are any health worrys, it may be that stress come highest on the list caused by sitting with a fixed posture in front of a screen for more than four hours a day on work than is repetitive and requires a high degree of accuracy. It is wise to take plenty of brakes, get up and walk around a little, or do a different type of work for a short time, if poss. Make sure the lighting and ventilation in your office are adequate, and that your chair is adjustable so that you are sitting in a comfortable position; a detatchable keyboard is useful, as is a tilt and swivle screen; ajust the brightness of the print on the screen to suit your eyes. Remind yourself how lucky you are to have all the advantages of typing on a word processer! Or would you prefer to use an old manual type writer?

KEYBOARDING SKILLS

Before proceeding to the exercises below, you should type the following skill building exercises:

improve your spelling Nos 5 and 6, page 155.   **alphabetic sentence** No 3, page 156.
skill measurement No 16, page 158.   **record your progress** No 11, page 164.

PRODUCTION DEVELOPMENT

- *Correction of errors*—See **data store**, page 182.

- *Proofreading*—See **data store**, page 191.

1   In the exercise below, the sentences in COLUMN ONE have been repeated in COLUMN TWO. Those in column one are correct, but in each sentence in column two there is a typing error. Compare the sentences and see how quickly you can spot the errors. Then type the sentences correctly.

COLUMN ONE
1   Allan Jones is 10 years old.
2   It will take 18 months to complete.
3   The dog's collar was too tight.
4   Mary, Joan's sister, was ill.
5   The word processor cost £3,980.00.
6   Did Steven Browne start school today?
7   Order more ribbons for the printer.
8   You should be able to type at 30 wpm.
9   Take the disk from its box on the desk.
10 Make all your corrections neatly.

COLUMN TWO
1   Alan Jones is 10 years old.
2   It will take 18 months to compete.
3   The dogs collar was too tight.
4   Mary, Joan's sister was ill.
5   The word processer cost £3,980.00.
6   Did Steven Browne start school today.
7   Order more ribbons for the Printer.
8   You should be able to type about 30 wpm.
9   Take the disk form its box on the desk.
10 Make all you corrections neatly.

Further exercises on **proofreading** are on pages 148–154.

Typing from manuscript copy

You will have to type letters or documents from handwritten drafts. Take particular care to produce a correct copy. Before typing, read the manuscript through to see that you understand it. Check the completed document and correct any errors *before* removing the paper from the typewriter.

2   Type the following on A5 landscape paper. (a) Read the whole passage through before you start to type and locate and correct the three errors. (b) From the top edge of the paper turn up seven single spaces. (c) Suggested margins: 12 pitch 22–82, 10 pitch 12–72. (d) Single spacing. (e) Keep to the line-endings in the copy.

CONSUMER SAFETY

Consumers have a right to expect goods to be safe. But not all are. Look at the lables, follow the instructions and take particular care of those at greatest risk – the very young and the elderly. Remember to use you electric blanket carefully. Have it serviced regularly – most manufacturers say at least once every 3 years. Checks have shown that up to 70% are potentially dangerous.

See Typing Target Practice, R/E, page 14, for further exercises on Typing from manuscript

Exercise 10   **Keys on page 170**
                                                                                                                    Proofreading target: 5 minutes
                                                                                                                         Typing target: 3 minutes

The following exercise contains 12 errors. A correct version is not provided, so you will have to identify the errors by using your knowledge of typing layout, spelling, punctuation and correct grammatical expression. When you have noted all the errors, type a corrected version, proofreading your typed copy very carefully.

```
WALKING DOGS IN THE COUNTRYSIDE

It is just as important to keep your dog under control in the country-side as it
is when walking him in a towns. Your dog should be trained to be obediant.  There
are dog - training classes in most areas.  Take your dog - both you and he will
enjoy it, and it will give you confidence to now that you can control your dog.
He should stay when he is told come when called, sit and walk to heel on command.

Remember the following points when in the country -

1  Never allow your dog to chase anything - it is a bad habit which are hard
   to break.
2  The dogs lead should always be on when their are farm animals about, and do
   not allow him to run on to cultivated fields.
3  Make sure you know the country code yourself, & then you can train your dog
   in countryside awareness.
```

The following exercise contains 14 errors. A correct version is not provided, so you will have to identify the errors by using your knowledge of typing layout, spelling, punctuation and correct grammatical expression. When you have noted all the errors, type a corrected version, proofreading your typed copy very carefully.

```
     Staverton International Ltd., office furniture and equipment manufactures,
have reported losses for a number of years, but have now staged a strong recovery.
They were in good form last year, breaking the £1 million pre-tax profit barrier
for the first time.  There furniture is modern and functional and within the
price bracket of the smaller companys, eg, an executives desk in mahogany will
sell for approximatly £981.50p. the colours are bright and imaginative with
yellow's blues and greens being used for the upholstery.

Last years record braking results reflect a 27.7 % return on shareholders' funds.
This year has started strongly and there is a good order book.
```

Tabulation

Arrangement of items in columns

You may be required to arrange items in column form in such a way that they are horizontally centred on the page, with equal spaces between the columns and with equal margins. This can be done easily by means of the backspacing method you have already used in display work, or by using the arithmetical method.

Some *electronic keyboards* have an automatic function for setting out column work.

Tabulator key

All typewriters have three tabulator controls which you should locate on your machine as their positions vary on the different makes.

1 A tab set key to fix the tab stops.
2 A tab clear key to clear the tab stops.
3 A tab bar or key to move the carriage/carrier/cursor to wherever a tab stop is set.

Preliminary steps for arranging items in columns

1 Move margin stops to extreme left and right.
2 Clear all previous tab stops that may be already set. On most machines this can be done by pressing the clear key while returning the carriage, carrier or cursor. On other machines there are special devices for this purpose.
3 Insert paper seeing that the left edge is at 0.
4 Set the left margin and tab stops at the points given.
5 Test your tab stops by returning the carriage, carrier or cursor and then depressing the tab bar or key.

Typing the table

1 Type the main heading at the left margin.
2 Turn up two single (one double) spaces.
3 At left margin type first item in first column.

4 Tabulate to the second column and type first item; then tabulate to each of the remaining columns and type the first item.
5 Continue in the same way with the rest of the table.

NOTE: It is essential that you complete each horizontal line before starting the next line.

3 Carrying out the instructions given above, type the following table on A5 landscape paper. (a) Leave 51 mm (2 inches) at the top of the page, ie turn up 13 single-line spaces from the top edge of the paper. (b) Set the left margin at the point given; the figures in brackets are for 10 pitch. (c) Set the tab stops as shown. (d) Double spacing.

Left margin: 33(24)	FUNCTION KEYS ON A WORD PROCESSOR		1st tab: 45(36) 2nd tab: 57(48)
	Delete	Select	Menu
	Stop code	Justify	Merge
	Insert	Text tab	Line insert
	Erase	Tab clear	Line delete

Exercise 9

Keys on page 170
Proofreading target: 5 minutes
Typing target: 7 minutes

The details given in the handwritten exercise 9(b) are correct. There are a number of errors in the typewritten version in exercise 9(a). When you have noted the errors, type a corrected version, making sure that you proofread your own typed copy very thoroughly.

Exercise 9(a)

ADDRESSES OF PREMISES WHERE OUR EQUIPMENT IS INSTALLED

Name	Addresses	Date Instaled	Inspection due on
P M Coker & Sons Tel: (0373) 62445	Watermore House 21 Castle Street Frome Somerset BA11 3AS	September 1986	January 1990
Acoustic Treatment PLC Tel: (0603) 624091	Castle House Norwich NR2 1PJ	January 1987	September 1990
Batley Computor Services Ltd Tel: 0272 548967	2 Old Gloucester Road Hambrook Bristol BS16 1RP	March 1987	Nov 1990
Dandy Agency plc Tel: (0733) 653312	10a High Street Old Fleton Peterborough. PE2 9DY	April, 1987	December 1990

Exercise 9(b)

ADDRESSES OF PREMISES WHERE OUR EQUIPMENT IS INSTALLED

Name	Address	Date Installed	Inspection Due on
P M Coker & Sons Tel: (0373) 62445	Watermore House 21 Castle Street Frome [Somerset BA11 3AS	Sept 1986	Jan 1990
Acoustic Treatments PLC Tel: (0603) 623091 548964	Castle House Norwich NR2 1PJ	Jan '87	Sept '90
Batley Computer Services Ltd Tel: (0242) 548964	2 Old Gloucester Road Hambrook Bristol BS16 1RP	Mar '87	Nov '90
Dandy Agency plc Tel: (0733) 653312	10A High Street Old Felton Peterborough PE2 9JY	April 1987	Dec '90 (months in full, please)

(Do NOT type postcodes on a separate line)

4 Following the instructions given on the previous page, type this table on A5 landscape paper. (a) Leave 51 mm (2 inches) at the top of the page. (b) Set the margins and tab stops at the points given; the figures in brackets are for 10 pitch. (c) Double spacing.

```
          HOMOPHONES

          Same sound - different spelling and meaning
Left margin:                                                        1st tab: 41(32)
24(15)    dear - deer    road - rode    die - dye                   2nd tab: 59(50)

          light - lite   our - hour     whether - weather

          check - cheque weak - week     bare - bear

          write - right  guest - guessed mail - male
```

- *Horizontal centring (**steps to determine starting point for each column**)—backspacing method—See **data store**, page 187.*

Horizontal centring (steps to determine starting point for each column)—arithmetical method

1 Move margin stops to extreme left and right.
2 Clear all previous tab stops that may be already set.
3 Insert paper seeing that the left edge is at 0.
4 Calculate the number of characters and spaces in the longest item in each column and write these figures clearly in a rough diagram on a separate sheet of paper.
5 Allow three spaces between each column. Write these figures in the diagram.
6 Subtract the total calculated in point 5 from the total number of spaces across the page.

7 Divide the sum arrived at in point 6 by two, which will give you the point at which to set your left margin.
8 From the left margin, space along for each character and space required for the longest item in the first column, plus the three spaces allowed between the first and second columns. Set a tab stop and make a written note on your diagram of the point on the scale at which the tab stop is set.
9 Repeat for the remaining columns.
10 Type the table as described on the previous page.

5 Carrying out the instructions given above, type the following table on A5 landscape paper. (a) Leave 51 mm (2 inches) at the top of the page. (b) Leave three spaces between columns. (c) Double spacing.

Rough calculations for exercise 5.

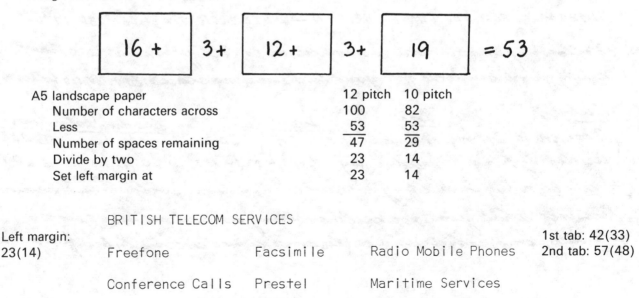

	12 pitch	10 pitch
A5 landscape paper		
Number of characters across	100	82
Less	53	53
Number of spaces remaining	47	29
Divide by two	23	14
Set left margin at	23	14

```
          BRITISH TELECOM SERVICES
Left margin:                                                           1st tab: 42(33)
23(14)    Freefone          Facsimile     Radio Mobile Phones          2nd tab: 57(48)

          Conference Calls  Prestel       Maritime Services

          Telemessages      Radio Paging  Directory Enquiries
```

Exercise 8

Keys on page 170
Proofreading target: 4 minutes
Typing target: 5 minutes

The details given in the handwritten exercise 8(b) are correct. There are a number of errors in the typewritten version in exercise 8(a). When you have noted the errors, type a corrected version, making sure that you proofread your own typed copy very thoroughly.

Exercise 8(a)

MEMORANDUM

FROM Paula Brooke-Little   DATE 11 September 1990

TO Giles Ladell   REF PB-L/TS/Eve

TIMETABLE FOR THE WINTER SESSION - SEPTEMBER 1990-DECEMBER 1990

Following enrolement, I am pleased to tell you that we have sufficient students for your two evening classes to run as folows:

Subject	Day	Time	Starting Date	Room No
Beginners' Typing	Monday	6.30-8.30 pm	18.9.90	B204
Audio Typing	Wednesday	6.15-8.15 pm	25.9.90	H207

I should be glad if you will confirm with your senior lecturer that you are still willing to take these extra classes, and that the times and dates are suitable for you.

Exercise 8(b)

MEMORANDUM

FROM *Paula Brooke-Little*   DATE *11 September 1990*

TO *Giles Ladell*   REF *BB-L/TSEV*
                                                  1990

TIMETABLE FOR THE WINTER SESSION— SEPTEMBER/TO DECEMBER 1990

Following enrolment, I am pleased to tell you that we have sufficient students for your two evening classes to run, as follows —

Subject	Day	Time	Starting Date	Room No
Beginners' Typing	*Monday*	*6.30 - 8.30 pm*	*25.9.90*	*B 204*
Audio Typing	*Wednesday*	*6.15 - 8.15 pm*	*20.9.90*	*B 207*

I shall be glad if you will confirm with your senior lecturer that you are still willing to take these extra classes, and that the dates and times are suitable for you.

Vertical centring

At this early stage in your training it is not necessary to centre the tables vertically with equal top and bottom margins. Follow the instructions given or leave a top margin of 25–51 mm (1–2 inches).

Typing column headings—blocked style

1 Remember that the column heading may be the longest item in the column, so you must take this into account when making your calculations for horizontal centring.
2 Column headings and column items start at the left margin and at the tab stops set for the longest item of each column.
3 Turn up two single (one double) after the main headings.
4 Turn up two single (one double) after the column headings, which may be typed in capital letters or small letters with initial capitals. The column headings are usually underlined if they are typed in small letters.

6 Type the following table on A5 landscape paper. (a) Leave 51 mm (2 inches) at the top of the page. (b) Centre the table horizontally. (c) Leave three spaces between columns. (d) Double spacing.

ENGLISH COUNTIES

A b b r e v i a t i o n s

Abbreviation	County in full	Abbreviation	County in full
Beds	Bedfordshire	Berks	Berkshire
Bucks	Buckinghamshire	Oxon	Oxfordshire
Worcs	Worcestershire	Northants	Northamptonshire
Wilts	Wiltshire	Hants	Hampshire

7 Type the following on A5 portrait paper. (a) Leave 51 mm (2 inches) at the top of the page. (b) Centre the table horizontally. (c) Leave three spaces between columns. (d) Double spacing. (e) Before you type this exercise, find the missing dialling codes from your telephone directory and enter them correctly in your finished copy.

INTERNATIONAL DIALLING CODES

Country	Code	Country	Code
Australia	010 61	France	010 33
Belgium	010 32	Hungary	010 36
Canada	010 1	Japan	010 81
Denmark		Malta	

8 Centre the following horizontally on A5 portrait paper in double spacing according to the instructions given for the previous exercises.

DISTANCES FROM LONDON

Town	Miles	Town	Miles
Liverpool	197	Stranraer	399
Birmingham	110	Aberdeen	492
Hull	259	Edinburgh	373

Keys on page 170
Proofreading target: 3 minutes
Typing target: 2 minutes

The information given in exercise 6(a) has been typed from exercise 6(b) given below. Exercise 6(b) is accurate, but there are 12 typing errors in exercise 6(a). When you have noted the errors, type the exercise. Proofread your own typed version very thoroughly and compare with exercise 6(b).

Exercise 6(a)

```
FIELD WALK

Sunday, 9 April                              Leader: Shan Porter

Meet at car park opposite the 'Barley Mow; turn off A4047 Wallingford–Reading
road at Black Root Farm.   (Map ref SU637856)  8.30–10.30 am.   A walk to see
marsh marigolds and here snipe drumming.   Wellies advised, binoculers useful.
No dogs.   Length of walk approximately 3½ miles. Suitable for all ages.
```

Exercise 6(b)

```
F I E L D   W A L K

Sunday, 10 April                             Leader: Shân Porter

Meet at car park opposite the 'Barley Mow'; turn off A4057 Wallingford–Reading
road at Black Route Farm.   (Map reference SU637856).   8.30–10.30 am.   A walk
to see marsh marigolds and hear snipe drumming.   Wellies advised, binoculars
useful.   No dogs.   Length of walk approximately 3¾ miles.   Suitable for all
ages.
```

The details given in exercise 7(b) are correct. There are 11 errors in exercise 7(a). When you have noted the errors, type a corrected version, in alphabetical order, making sure you proofread your own typed copy very thoroughly.

Exercise 7(a)

```
PAYE   – Pay As You Earn
GSCE   – General Certificate in Secondary
           Education
VDU    – Visual Display Unit;
R.S.A. – Royal Society of Arts
UNESCO – United Nations Educational,
           Scientific and Culture
           Organisation
BASIC  – Beginners All-Purpose
           Symbolic Instruction Code
FAX    – Facsimile telegraphy
EFTA   – European Free Trade Association
PTO    – Please Turn Over
E & OE – Errors & ommisions accepted
```

Exercise 7(b)

```
BASIC  – Beginners' All-Purpose Symbolic
           Instruction Code
E & OE – Errors and Omissions Excepted
EFTA   – European Free Trade Association
FAX    – Facsimile Telegraphy
GCSE   – General Certificate of Secondary
           Education
PAYE   – Pay As You Earn
PTO    – Please Turn Over
RSA    – Royal Society of Arts
UNESCO – United Nations Educational,
           Scientific and Cultural
           Organization
VDU    – Visual Display Unit
```

CONSOLIDATION PRACTICE

We have reserved this unit for consolidation so that you have an opportunity to apply the practices and procedures introduced in the previous units thus enabling you to revise where necessary, or practise keyboard techniques and drills in order to type more accurately or more quickly.

The examiner, and your employer, will be interested in how many documents you type in a given time; therefore, in addition to accuracy and acceptable layout, we have set a **production target time** for each exercise. It may be that at first you will only reach this target after concentrated practice.

If you make an error, stop and correct it. Of course, the more errors you make the more time you waste (!) in making corrections. When you have typed the complete exercise, check the whole document carefully and correct any errors you may find BEFORE removing the paper from the machine.

At the top of each page, type the date and the **production target**.

Production target—6 minutes

1   Type the following on A5 portrait paper. (a) Leave 25 mm (1 inch) clear at the top of the page. (b) Double spacing. (c) Suggested margins: 12 pitch 13–63, 10 pitch 6–56.

THE CONSUMER CREDIT ACT

Would you credit it?

The Consumer Credit Act was designed to ensure

'truth in lending'. Under the Act you must be

given certain information before you sign an

agreement. This includes the APR which is a true

and standard way of calculating interest. You

can, therefore, compare the cost of different

types of loans.

In simple terms, 30% APR will cost approximately

twice as much in interest as 15% APR.

Keys on page 170
Proofreading target: 4 minutes ⎞ for each
Typing target: 5 minutes ⎠ exercise

Read each passage carefully and compare with the correct copy typed below. Each line in the incorrect copy contains an error that may be spelling, spacing, hyphenation, omission of apostrophe, etc. When you have found and noted the errors, type the corrected passage using margins of 12 pitch 22–82, 10 pitch 12–72. Use blocked paragraphs. Do not type the figures down the left side.

Exercise 4

Exercise to be corrected

1 Visible indexing systems have the definate advantages of easy access

2 and clear labelling or indexing. The information can be seen at once

3 with very little or no handeling. Also cards can be inserted or removed

4 without disturbing others in the container. Visible card indexes may

5 be held flat in trays, in loose leaf binders, or they may hang from

6 walls, or they may be free-standing on table tops or desks.

Correct copy

1 Visible indexing systems have the definite advantages of easy access

2 and clear labelling or indexing. The information can be seen at once

3 with very little or no handling. Also cards can be inserted or removed

4 without disturbing others in the container. Visible index cards may

5 be held flat in trays, in loose-leaf binders, or they may hang from

6 walls, or be free-standing on table tops or desks.

Exercise 5

Exercise to be corrected

1 Prestel is a public database Retrieval service operated by British
2 Telecom. The data is stored on computers and accesed via telephone
3 lines. Various agencies subscribe to input information for annual
4 fee. The information is very varied: eg, household hints, sports
5 results. In order to retreive information a Prestel user can call
6 the computer centre on telephone lines, using a keypad. The informa-
7 tion will be shown on his television screen, which can be adopted for
8 Prestel use

Correct copy

1 Prestel is a public database retrieval service operated by British
2 Telecom. The data is stored on computers and accessed via telephone
3 lines. Various agencies subscribe to input information for an annual
4 fee. The information is very varied, eg, household hints, sports
5 results. In order to retrieve information a Prestel user can call
6 the computer centre on a telephone line, using a keypad. The informa-
7 tion will be shown on his television screen, which can be adapted for
8 Prestel use.

Production target—15 minutes

2   Type the following on A4 letterhead paper (Leys Enterprises). (a) Suggested margins: 12 pitch 22–82, 10 pitch 12–72. (b) Type an envelope to Miss Gwyneth Jones.

Ref MG/TY

(*Insert today's date*)

Miss Gwyneth Jones

(*Please type Miss Jones's address here. You will find it on page 42*)

Dear Miss Jones

HIGH YIELD CERTIFICATE 1468876

I enclose the above numbered certificate for your retention.

As requested, £600 has been re-invested into a new High Yield Certificate No 7905743, which is enclosed. The remaining money is enclosed in 2 cheques, one for £267.18 and the other for £280, both made payable to yourself.

I hope this meets with your requirements.

Yours sincerely

Martin Gosling
Branch Manager

Encs

Production target—15 minutes

3   Type the following on A5 landscape paper. (a) Leave a top margin of 51 mm (2 inches). (b) Centre the table horizontally. (c) Leave three spaces between columns. (d) Double spacing.

BROOKER & CO LTD

New Staff List

Name	Designation	Department	Extension
Elaine Cox	Secretary	Sales	2541
Jocelyn Lane	Administrator	Publicity	3043
Karim Mubarak	Translator	Export	1239
Colin Skelley			

(*Colin Skelley's designation, department and extension number are in the DATA FILES (filename STAFF) on page 174. Please insert them here.*)

Proofreading

Proofreading target for each exercise: 2 minutes
Typing target for each exercise: 3 minutes

In the exercises below, the sentences in COLUMN ONE have been repeated in COLUMN TWO. Those in column one are correct, but in each sentence in column two there is a typing error. Compare the sentences and see how quickly you can spot the errors. Then type the sentences correctly.

Exercise 1

Column one

1 A program for a computer is recorded on a disk.
2 The visual display unit looks like a TV screen.
3 A disk can hold 100 kilobytes or more.
4 A matrix printer is faster than a daisy-wheel printer.
5 Bar codes may be used in stock control.
6 Spreadsheet programs may be used for management accounting.

Column two

1 A programme for a computer is recorded on a disk.
2 The vizual display unit looks like a TV screen.
3 A disk can hold 101 kilobytes or more.
4 A matrix printer is faster than daisy-wheel printer.
5 Bar codes may be used in Stock control.
6 Spread sheet programs may be used for management accounting.

Exercise 2

Column one

1 Keep your shorthand notebook handy.
2 Date each page at top and bottom.
3 Do not interrupt the dictator.
4 Raise any queries at the end of dictation.
5 Rule a left margin for reminders.
6 Keep a pen or pencil by your notebook.

Column two

1 Keep you shorthand notebook handy.
2 Date each page at bottom and top.
3 Do not interupt the dictator.
4 Raise any queries at the end of dictation
5 Rule a left margin for the reminders.
6 Keep a pen or pencil, by your notebook.

Exercise 3

Column one

G A R D E N I N G - October

Tasks for the month

Plant fruit trees or soft fruit canes

Transplant cabbages, and lettuces

Plant hardy, spring-flowering plants

Mark out boundaries of new borders

SWEEP UP DEAD LEAVES

Column two

G A R D N I N G - October

Tasks for the Month

Plant fruit trees of soft fruit canes

Transplant cabbages, and lettuce

Plant hardy, spring flowering plants

 Mark out boundaries of new borders

SWEEP UP ANY DEAD LEAVES

Production target—8 minutes

4 Type the following on A5 landscape paper. (a) Read the passage through before starting to type. (b) Turn up 25 mm (1 inch) from the top of the page. (c) Suggested margins: 12 pitch 22–82, 10 pitch 12–72. (d) Double spacing. (e) Keep to the line-endings shown in the copy.

COMMUNICATIONS
Face the Fax
Important communications were often sent by hand, courier, post or the telex machine, until fairly recently.

The facsimile machine has seen a rise in popularity in the last few years as an often cheaper and speedier means of communication. There is a wide range of models to choose from, and it is often the job of the secretary to discover which model would be suitable for the organization by which she is employed.

Production target—8 minutes

5 Type the following on A5 portrait paper. (a) Read through the passage before starting to type. (b) Turn up 25 mm (1 inch) from the top of the page. (c) Suggested margins: 12 pitch 13–63, 10 pitch 6–56. (d) Single spacing. (e) Keep to the line-endings shown in the copy.

UNLEADED PETROL
What is it?
Unleaded petrol is fuel that has not had any lead added to it at the refinery to improve its octane rating. Instead, engine power and performance are maintained by using more octane components.

The environment
Lead is a poison. The more we reduce it in daily usage the more we reduce environmental pollution. Lead levels in leaded petrol have been cut by two-thirds since 1 January 1986, to 0.15 grams per litre.

6 (15 mins)

Would you please complete one of our Evaluation Forms for one of our clients, James Hodge. Unfortunately, I spilled coffee over his copy.

TOUR NO - 348

RESORT - Corfu

HOTEL - Santa Elena

DATE OF DEPARTURE - 26 Sept '90

COURIER'S NAME - Hazel Palmer

OUTWARD JOURNEY - Delayed 4 hrs at Gatwick

STANDARD OF HOTEL/s - Moderate

EXCURSIONS - Excellent

QUALITY OF PRE-TOUR INFORMATION -
   More information could have been given about the many excursions available & their prices

COURIER - Very helpful, polite & friendly

LOCAL GUIDES - Generally good

HOW DID THE TOUR RATE - Good

ADDITIONAL COMMENTS -
   I shall definitely visit Corfu again - one week wasn't long enough to see all the awe-inspiring sights.

KEYBOARDING SKILLS

Before proceeding to the exercises below, you should type the following skill building exercises:

proofreading No 3, page 148   **techniques and reviews** No 3, page 157.
skill measurement No 17, page 158.   **record your progress** No 12, page 164.

PRODUCTION DEVELOPMENT

Securing an acceptable right margin

Up to this stage in the book, you have always returned at the same point as the line-ends in the exercise from which you have been copying. This is not usually possible, of course, and in a great many exercises you will have to decide on your own line-endings and also see that you do not have an untidy right margin. If you are using a manual or electric typewriter, a bell will ring to warn you that you are nearing the right margin.

Before you can practise making your own line-endings, it is necessary for you to become accustomed to listening for an audible signal (margin bell, etc) that warns you that you are nearing the end of the typing line. On your own typewriter, find out how many spaces there are after you hear the margin bell or warning device before you reach the set right margin. If you are using an electronic keyboard, we suggest that you do not utilize the automatic return for the time being. Find out how the manual return works and what audible signal, if any, there is.

Most electronic keyboards have normal carrier return, justified right margin and automatic return. This automatic return is referred to as automatic word wraparound. Some have devices that indicate that you are approaching the right margin and some do not. Consult the handbook that accompanies your machine.

1   Type the following on A5 landscape paper and note the instructions in the text. (a) Use single spacing. (b) Suggested margins: 12 pitch 22–82, 10 pitch 12–72. (c) Listen for the audible signal, but follow the copy line for line.

> RIGHT MARGIN AUDIBLE-WARNING DEVICE
>
> Five to 10 spaces from the right margin a bell or other sig-
> nal on your machine will warn you that you are almost at the
> end of the writing line. It is necessary to train yourself
> to listen for this signal, and to react as follows:
>
> If the bell/device signals at the beginning of a new word of
> more than 5-10 letters, divide the word at the first avail-
> able point.
>
> If the bell/device signals at the end of a word, do not type
> a further word on that line unless it has less than 5-10
> characters (or 2 words such as 'for it' or 'I am', etc) or
> unless the new word can be divided at an appropriate point.

Margin-release key

If you cannot complete a word at the right margin, press the margin-release key (usually found at the top right or left of the keyboard). The word can then be completed. The margin-release key will release the left margin as well as the right one.

2   Type each of the following sentences exactly as it appears, using the margin-release key when necessary. (a) Use A5 landscape paper. (b) Double spacing. (c) Suggested margins: 12 pitch 22–82, 10 pitch 12–72.

> Text which is unjustified provides an uneven or ragged right margin.
> Reformatting text on a VDU will result in a change in line-endings.
> A system/program which is simple to use is known as 'user friendly'.

4   (20 mins)

Would you please type a letter to Ms A I Hewitt. Her address is on page 127.

Say that with reference to her holiday in Italy, departing on Mon 26 Nov 1990, we are writing to remind her that the balance is now due for payment. [Tell her that we look forward to receiving her remittance asap, & give her our best wishes for a very happy holiday.

Head the letter ITALIAN ALPS — Tour No H60
Don't forget the ref & date & type one carbon copy & an envelope. ✓Thank you.

5   (35 mins)

Please type the following on a card & enclose it with the letter to Ms Hewitt.

SUPERDEAL TRAVEL AGENCY
(Insert our address here)

Ref AC/(Yr initials)   Date

The ~~following~~ information given on the reverse of this card has just bn rec'd regarding ~~excursions~~ tours during yr proposed visit to Italy.

On the reverse of the card, please type the information that ~~which~~ I will give to you shortly. I have to check one of the figures.

● *Guide for dividing words at line-ends*—See **data store**, page 187.

3 Copy each of the following lines once for practice and then once for accuracy. (a) Use A5 landscape paper. (b) Suggested margins: 12 pitch 22–82, 10 pitch 12–72. (c) Single spacing. (d) Note that the hyphen indicates where the word would be divided at the end of a line. Observe where the word is divided and if no hyphen is given, where division is not possible.

```
tele-phones, trans-mitted, play-ing, atten-tion, ship-ments,
fisher-man, pre-eminent, self-confidence, prod-uct, kin-dred
satel-lites, excel-lent, pos-sible, bag-gage, magis-trates,
desig-nation, radi-ator, manu-script, per-fect, under-stand,
book, books, looked, shakes, paved, cleaned, ended, sailed,
entry, amazed, invent, sadly, £30.89, Coventry, Miss Reading
```

4 Type the following making your own right margin. If you feel it necessary, in order to avoid a ragged right margin, divide words at the end of the lines. (a) Suggested margins: 12 pitch 22–82, 10 pitch 12–72. (b) Double spacing.

```
T Y P E W R I T I N G

Homework Assignments
```

Once you have completed the keyboard, under the super-

vision of your tutor, it may be beneficial for you to

practise on your own typewriter, at home.

If you do not have a typewriter, you can still undertake

a certain amount of work. You can prepare exercises by

reading them through; there are points of theory that

you must know and be able to apply without hesitation;

exercises that you type in class can be checked and read

through at home.

If you spend some extra time working on your own, you will become a fast and accurate typist.

3 – (15 mins)

(One copy of the following memo, please, & then you can photocopy it later.)

URGENT   MEMORANDUM

To   All Staff   Ref (My initials, followed by an oblique & yr initials.)
      attending Travel & Tourism Course

From (My name & designation)   Date

         TRAVEL AND TOURISM COURSE }← (Centre)
           26 Nov to 14 Dec '90

Those staff who wl be attending the above course
which is to be held at the County Business College,
Sheep Street, are asked to note the following
change of times.

(Centre)→ {Mondays   9.00am to 3.00pm   (Change times to 24-hr clock.)
        {Thursdays   9.30am to 4.00pm

The total amt of hrs of study is unchanged.

DISTRIBUTION   Neville Walters
                 Kathleen Prior
                 Geoff Morgan
                 Marie Hunt

(Type a label to each of the above, please.)

KEYBOARDING SKILLS

Before proceeding to the exercises below, you should type the following skill building exercises:

improve your spelling Nos 7 and 8, page 155.　　**alphabetic sentence** No 4, page 156.
skill measurement No 18, page 158.　　　　　　　**record your progress** No 13, page 165.

PRODUCTION DEVELOPMENT

Typing measurements

When typing measurements note the following:

1　The letter 'x' (lower case) is used for the word 'by', eg 210 mm × 297 mm (space before and after the 'x').

2　ONE space is left after the numbers and before the unit of measurement, eg 210 (space) mm; 2 (space) ft 6 (space) in.

3　Groups of figures should not be separated at line ends.

4　Most abbreviations do not take an 's' in the plural, eg 6 in; 6 lb; 2 mm; 4 kg.

5　When using open punctuation there is no full stop after any abbreviation, unless at the end of a sentence.

1　Type each of the following lines three times on A5 landscape paper. (a) Suggested margins: 12 pitch 22–82, 10 pitch 12–72. (b) Pay particular attention to the spacing in the measurements.

```
One rug measures 82 cm x 76 cm; and the other, 65 cm x 44 cm.

The carpets were all 6 ft 6 in x 5 ft 7 in or 16 ft x 15 ft.

Send me 5 lb of potatoes, 2 oz of pepper, and 500 g of sugar.
```

Use of words and figures

1　Use words instead of figures for number one on its own and for numbers at the beginning of a sentence. But if number one is part of a list of figures, it should be typed as a figure, eg 'Follow instructions 1, 2 and 3'.

2　Use figures in all other cases.

2　Type the following exercise on A5 portrait paper. (a) Suggested margins: 12 pitch 13–63, 10 pitch 6–56. (b) Leave 25 mm (1 inch) clear at the top of the page. (c) Single spacing. (d) Read the passage through before starting to type. (e) Make your own line-endings. (f) Note the use of words and figures.

THE HISTORY OF THE STOCK EXCHANGE

Dealings in stocks and shares began with the merchant venturers in the 17th Century. In 1773 'New Jonathan's' Coffee House became the Stock Exchange, with some 500 subscribers and 100 clerks.

Although London was the largest exchange (until the 1914-18 war it was the world's largest) the growth of the Industrial Revolution prompted the establishment of local share markets in other parts of the country — more than 30 of them at the peak.

Seven exchanges in the British Isles amalgamated to form the Stock Exchange of Great Britain and Ireland in 1973.

② – (15 mins)

AC/2461/(Tr initials)

(Month & year only)

(Leave sufficient space for the name & address)

(Headed paper, please, and 2 carbon copies, one for Julian Fielding & the other for file.)

Dr

HOLIDAYS – 1991

You may feel that it's hardly the time to be writing to you with details of summer holidays, especially since it is just the start of winter. But, if you book now for ~~next~~ summer 1991, you wl be eligible for our incredible special offers.

If you book now, you can go on a holiday ~~almost~~ anywhere ⊙ summer in the world for a deposit of only £10 per person & nothing more to pay until 6 wks before you are due to leave. If you do settle earlier, you wl be entitled to a discount as well as our superb FREE gift. But hurry – this offer closes on 31 Dec '~~89~~ 90. [There are so many fabulous hols to choose from – a leisurely cruise, a 'once-in-a-lifetime' trip to the Sth Pacific, the wonders of the United States, & many more. If you take advantage of our offer, you could afford to go for longer.

For the ~~holiday you hv in mind best~~ advice on where to go – call in & ~~see us~~ soon. We shall be delighted to help you.

Yrs sinc

(My name & designation here, please)

PS Don't forget, our superb offer closes on 31.12.90 – so hurry.

- *Longhand abbreviations*—See **data store**, page 175.

3   After studying the list of abbreviations in the **data store** on page 175, read the following passage to see that you understand it; then type a copy on A5 landscape paper. (a) All abbreviations to be typed in full. (b) Suggested margins: 12 pitch 22–82, 10 pitch 12–72. (c) Single spacing. (d) Make your own line-endings.

INFORMATION TECHNOLOGY

LOCAL AREA NETWORKS

Personal computers hv. become an integral part of office life. Up to recent times individuals hv. bn. using them in isolation. Now more and more cos. are recognizing th., to be used to the full, they shd. be linked together in local area networks.

Well over 100 software packages are available to create these networks.

At its most basic level, a co. may hv. 5 personal computers spread abt. its depts., but only 2 printers wd. be nec. When they are linked, someone on the fourth floor can compose a letter on a desktop micro + hv. it printed out in the postroom.

4   Type the following on A5 portrait paper. (a) Suggested margins: 12 pitch 13–63, 10 pitch 6–56. (b) Single spacing. (c) Make your own line-endings.

PRESTEL

Prestel is part of British Telecom. It is not a single service, but a collection of specialist, educational + general databases wh. provide a wide range of info. + services for a variety of ~~uses~~ users.

There are, currently, approx. 300,000 pages of info. held on Prestel's own computers, from more than 1,000 cos. The info. is held on mainframe computers situated in different parts of the country, + linked together to form a network.

When you subscribe to Prestel, you are given the tel.no. to dial to connect you to the network, + yr. identity no. + password wh. allow you to log on to the system so th. info. can be recd.   (LOG)

① **40 mins**

Double spacing throughout except where indicated. Change 'abroad' to 'overseas' in each case.

SUPERDEAL TRAVEL AGENCY ← *Centre*

TRAVELLING ABROAD ← *Centre in sp caps*

YOUR HEALTH GUIDE ← *Centre in lc + u/scored*

There are various sensible precautions you should take if you are intending to travel abroad. *Many people forget that they may hv to pay thousands of pounds in medical costs if they got ill or hv an accident while abroad.*

1. <u>Check the requirements of your destination.</u> Find out about the health risks in the country you are visiting and the precautions you ~~can~~ *should* take.

2. <u>Consult your doctor.</u> See your doctor, at least 2 months before your holiday, and s/he will advise you and arrange vaccinations if required. Some of these can take time to become effective and cannot be given at the same time as other vacinations.

If you need to take prescribed medicines whilst you are abroad, you should check on their availability in the country/ies you are visiting.

3. <u>Have a dental check-up.</u> It may be <u>difficult</u> and <u>expensive</u> to get treat-ment while you are away. It is wise, therefore, to visit your dentist if you have any doubts about your teeth.

4. <u>Medical insurance.</u> Make certain you take out sufficient medical insurance. ~~if you~~ How much you need to pay for medical treatment abroad depends on the country ~~you are in~~ and the existence of any special arrangments for free or reduced cost medical treatment.

4.1 If you are visiting an EEC country, you may need form E111 . . .

Hanging paras + single spacing

4.2 If you are visiting any other country, medical insurance is <u>essential</u>. Check with your travel agent on the amount of insurnace you will need →and include enough cover to allow for the extra cost of travelling home in an emergency.

4.3 If you are visiting a country ~~which~~ *that* has a reciprical health care agree-ment with the UK, read pages 4-6 of the attached addendum.

5. <u>State Retirement Pension.</u> If you are recieving a Retirement State Pension, you must tell your local DSS office if you are going abroad for more than 3 months' at a time.

6. <u>Students.</u> If you are going to study in another EEC country, you may require a form other than E111. Write to OSS, Overseas Branch*, giving the dates your course begins and ends and your address abroad.

No matter where you are going - always check that your insurance cover is adequate. Your travel agent will be able to advise you.

---

*   *Newcastle upon Tyne, NE98 1YX*

You will find item No 3 in the Data Files (filename TRAV) page 174. Please enter here & renumber the remaining items accordingly.

KEYBOARDING SKILLS

Before proceeding to the exercises below, you should type the following skill building exercises:

proofreading No 4, page 149.　　　**techniques and reviews** No 4, page 157.
skill measurement No 19, page 159.　　**record your progress** No 14, page 165.

PRODUCTION DEVELOPMENT

Enumerated items

Paragraphs and items are sometimes numbered or lettered as follows. The numbers or letters may stand on their own or be enclosed in brackets. Always leave one clear linespace between enumerated items. Two character spaces follow the last figure, letter or bracket. There is always one clear linespace before and after enumerated items, eg

1^2 Address	$(1)^2$ Address	A^2 Address	$(a)^2$ Address
2　Telephone Number	(2)　Telephone Number	B　Telephone Number	(b)　Telephone Number

1　Type the following on A4 paper. (a) Use single spacing with double between each item. (b) Suggested margins: 12 pitch 22–82, 10 pitch 12–72. (c) Leave two character spaces after the item number. (d) Top margin: 51 mm (2 inches), ie turn up 13 single spaces from the top edge of the paper.

> ELECTRONIC MAIL
>
> Electronic mail is a new concept in communication. It has the advantages of privacy, speed, flexible timing (it may be sent or received during the day, night or weekend) as well as flexible storage - on system, disk or paper.
>
> The equipment required is as follows -
>
> 1　keyboard
>
> 2　computer terminal
>
> 3　screen and printer
>
> 4　modem or acoustic coupler
>
> 5　telephone or cable.

2　Type the following on A5 portrait paper. (a) Use single spacing with double between each item. (b) Suggested margins: 12 pitch 13–63, 10 pitch 6–56. (c) Leave two character spaces after the bracketed letters.

> WORD PROCESSING - Glossary of terms
>
> Students who use a word processor should be familiar with the terminology used if they wish to become fast and efficient operators.
>
> (a)　Ruler - a line that appears below the status line, showing the margins and tab settings.
>
> (b)　Tractor feeder - an attachment to a printer (usually dot matrix) that feeds continuous station-ery through using 2 circular belts with protruding studs that catch the sprocket holes in the paper.
>
> (c) Scrolling — moving text vertically or horizontally on the screen.
>
> (d) Selective printing — printing selected pages within a document, eg in a 20-page document to print only pages 8 & 14.
>
> (e) Pixels — is an abbreviation used for picture elements.

INTEGRATED PRODUCTION TYPING

SUPERDEAL TRAVEL AGENCY

OFFICE SERVICES – REQUEST FORM

Typist's log sheet

This sheet contains instructions that must be complied with when typing the documents. Read the information carefully before starting, and refer back to it frequently.

Originator ALVIN CARMICHAEL
Branch Manager   Department –   Date 5 Nov '90   Ext No / 30

Typists operating a word processor, or electronic typewriter with appropriate function keys, should apply the following automatic facilities: top margin; carrier return; line-end hyphenation; underline OR bold print (embolden); error correction; centring; any other relevant applications.

Remember to (a) complete the details required at the bottom of the form; (b) enter typing time per document in the appropriate column; and (c) before submitting this **log sheet** and your completed work, enter TOTAL TYPING TIME in the last column so that the typist's time may be charged to the originator.

Document No	Type of document and instructions	Copies – Original plus	Input form¶	Typing time per document	Total typing time ¥
1	Your Health Guide	1 original	AT		
2	Letter with 2 carbons & envelope	1 + 2	MS		
3*	An urgent memo	1 original	MS		
4	Letter to Ms Hewitt from brief notes	1 + 1	MS		
5	Enclosure for the above letter to be typed on a card	1 original	MS to print ⵢ		
6	Evaluation form to complete	1 original	MS		

(ⵢ I shall let you have this printed information shortly. I should like all this work returned to me in 2½ hrs, please as I shall not be in the office for the next 2 days).

				TOTAL	TYPING TIME

TYPIST – please complete:

Typist's name: Date received: Date completed:

                            Time received: Time completed:

If the typed documents cannot be returned within 24 hours, the office services supervisor should inform the originator. Any item that is urgent should be marked with an asterisk (*).

¶ T = Typescript   AT = Amended Typescript   MS = Manuscript   SD = Shorthand Dictation   AD = Audio Dictation
¥ To be charged to the originator's department.

Insetting matter from left margin

Matter may be inset from the left margin to give a certain part of the work greater emphasis. This matter may or may not consist of numbered items. You must follow any instructions given to you as to how many spaces to inset. There is always one clear linespace before and after inset matter.

When insetting matter you may either:

1 Set a tab stop at the point where each of the lines in the inset portion will commence; or

2 re-set the left margin.

When using this method, it is most important to remember to go back to the original margin when you have finished typing the inset portion. It is wise to make a reminder mark on the copy at the point where you need to revert to the original margin again.

Some electronic machines allow for a second temporary margin to be set while retaining the original margin.

3 Type the following on A4 paper. (a) Use single spacing, with double between the paragraphs and numbered items. (b) Suggested margins: 12 pitch 22–82, 10 pitch 12–72.

VALUE ADDED TAX

Value Added Tax (VAT) is not an overcomplicated tax, but inadequate methods of recording and accounting can make it so.

Ensure that the system used by your company is watertight. It should be

Inset
5 spaces

1 logical

2 well-regulated

3 easy to read so that your records will satisfy the most stringent inspection.

A well-regulated system for recording VAT is a positive step towards freeing your employees from unnecessary and frustrating paperwork whilst, quite possibly, increasing profits.

4 Type the following on A5 portrait paper. (a) Single spacing. (b) Suggested margins: 12 pitch 13–63, 10 pitch 6–56.

PERSONAL PENSION PLANS

There are abt. 10 million employees who hv. no co. pension scheme.

There are advantages in having a personal pension plan.

Inset 5 spaces

(a) You can retire at 50.

(b) Tax benefits are attractive. Until the age of 35 you can contribute up to 17.5% of yr. earnings to a personal pension.

Insurance cos., banks, unit trusts + bldg. socs. are now providing personal pension plans. The earlier you start a plan, the bigger yr. pension wl. be.

6   Centre and rule the following table.

Building Insurance ← (Caps)

Sum Insured	Annual Premium		
	Standard Cover	Premium Cover	Economy Cover
	£	£	£
£18,000	29.80	35.50	27.20
£20,000	33.00	39.00	30.50
£25,000	48.00	41.00	35.20
£40,000	66.00	78.00	58.30
£50,000*	82.50	89.50	73.50

* For each £1,000 thereafter add £2.00

(£30,000   48.25   56.50   42.00)

7   Centre and rule the following table.

ADVERTISEMENT RATES[1]

From January 1991

Paper[2]	Classified		Per line (minimum 3 lines)
	Cars	Situations Vacant	
	£	£	£
The Herald	3.95	4.50	1.16
The Tribune	4.10	4.85	1.16
Evening News	2.30	2.75	0.65
Advertiser	1.82	1.72	0.70

1 Per single column
2 Weekly

KEYBOARDING SKILLS

Before proceeding to the exercises below, you should type the following skill building exercises:

improve your spelling Nos 9 and 10, page 155.   **alphabetic sentence** No 5, page 156.
skill measurement No 20, page 159.   **record your progress** No 15, page 165.

PRODUCTION DEVELOPMENT

Variable linespacer

The variable linespacer is found on the left or right platen knob. By pressing this in, the platen roller can be moved to any position desired. Its purpose is to ensure that you have proper alignment of the details to be typed on dotted lines, ruled lines or when inserting details in a form letter or memo.

Memoranda (memorandums)

A message from one person to another in the same firm, or from the Head Office to a Branch Office, or to an agent, is often in the form of a memorandum—usually referred to as a 'memo'. Memoranda (the plural 'memorandums' is now widely accepted) may be typed on any of the usual sizes of paper. The layout of headings may vary from organization to organization.

Important points to remember when typing memos on headed forms

1   Margins: 12 pitch 13–90, 10 pitch 11–75. These margins may vary depending on the size of the form and the length of the message to be typed.
2   After the words in the printed headings leave two clear character spaces before typing the insertions and use the variable linespacer to ensure their alignment.
3   Date: correct order—day, month, year. The month is not usually typed in figures.
4   Some memos have a subject heading which gives the reader information about the contents of the memo. The heading is typed two single spaces below the last line of the printed headings, ie turn up two single spaces.
5   If there is no subject heading, start the body of the memo two single spaces after the last line of the printed headings.
6   The body of the memo is usually typed in single spacing, with double between paragraphs.
7   After the last line of the body, turn up two single spaces and type the reference. This is usually the dictator's and typist's initials which identify the department or person dictating the memo.
8   If an enclosure is mentioned in the body of the memo, this must be indicated by typing Enc (or Encs if more than one enclosure) at the left margin. After the reference turn up at least two single spaces before typing Enc or Encs.

NOTE: A memo with printed headings is given in the *Workguide and Resource Material* and may be copied.

1   Type the following memo on a printed A5 memo form. (a) Follow the instructions given above. (b) Suggested margins: 12 pitch 13–90, 10 pitch 11–75.

MEMORANDUM

From   Jeram Jhaj, Sales Director

To   Bernard Adler, Assistant Sales Director

Date   3 April 1990

Turn up 2 single spaces

ANNUAL REVIEW

Turn up 2 single spaces

I enclose the forms to be completed for the sales staff in respect of the Annual Review. You will note that the forms this year are slightly different and 4 questions have been added.

Would you please return the completed forms by Friday, 20 April.

Turn up 2 single spaces

JJ/FG

Turn up 2 single spaces

Encs

- *Centred style tabulation*—See **data store**, pages 193 and 195.

4 Centre and rule the following table.

Alphabetical order of method, please

METHODS OF REPROGRAPHY

Method	Approximate number of copies
Offset-litho	1,000 plus
Facsimile	One at a time
Carbon	1 to 10
Spirit	150 plus
Ink (stencil)	1,000 plus
Word Processing	Unlimited

5 Centre and rule the following table.

International Paper Sizes ← *Emphasize*

Please type in size order

Paper	Sizes in millimetres
A2	420 x 594
A4	210 x 297
A3	297 x 420
A5 (landscape)	210 x 148
A5 (portrait)	148 x 210
A7	74 x 105
A6	105 x 148

2 Type the following on a printed A5 memo form. (a) Suggested margins: 12 pitch 13–90, 10 pitch 11–75.
(b) Mark the memo URGENT as indicated.

<u>URGENT</u>   MEMORANDUM

From Miriam Fox, Public Relations Director   Ref MF/14/29/WY

To All Heads of Department   Date 5 April 1990

PUBLIC RELATIONS

Will Heads of all Departments please notify relevant staff that all enquiries
from the press or other media about the company, should be referred to the
Public Relations Department. No conversations about any matter relating to
the company should be entered into with the media.

3 Type the following on a printed A5 memo form. Suggested margins: 12 pitch 13–90, 10 pitch 11–75.

                          MEMORANDUM

From Jeremy Nott, Secretary, Staff Committee   Ref JN/TL

To All Staff   Date 9 April 1990

ANNUAL OUTING

Following the recent meeting of the Staff Committee it has been decided that
the date for this year's annual outing will be changed from June to September.
The venue is unchanged – a day trip to Boulogne.

I will let you have the exact date and further details in due course.

4 Type the following on a printed A5 memo form. Suggested margins: 12 pitch 13–90, 10 pitch 11–75.

FROM Serge Winterton, Director
TO   Toni Hampton, Head of A9 Section   (Insert today's date)

CAR PARKING
I hv noticed th several staff from yr section are parking in
'A' car park wh is reserved for senior management.
I shd be glad if you wd inform yr staff of co policy on
this matter. I am enclosing the registration nos of
the cars concerned.

(TYPIST – Please type the reference here – Mr Winterton's
initials followed by your own.)

---

3 Type the following table and rule on completion.
  NB   K equals thousand. Retain the abbreviation.

Please use a capital K throughout

THE COMPUTER INDUSTRY

E x p e n d i t u r e - 1988/89

User Section	Expenditures			
	Hardware		Software	
	1988	1989	1988	1989
Engineering	£460k	£368k	£121k	£125k	/Trs
Retail and Distribution	£711k	£437k	£107k	£99k
Public Utilities ..	£941k	£724k	£262k	£242k
Financial ,, ..	£877k	£978k	£360k	£212k
Education ,, ,,	£355k	£343k	£104k	£48k
Public Administration ,,	£578k	£520k	£90k	£109k
Process Industry ,,	£467k	£505k	£186k	£128k
~~Other Industry~~ ,,	£433k	£477k	£128k	£99k
Research ,, ,,	£324k	£299k	£102k	£84k

Can you check these figures in the Data Files (filename FINAN) page 173, please.

Key in document 3 (filename FINAN) for 10-pitch printout. Embolden the main headings, use the save function for the first horizontal line and copy this where necessary. Also use the vertical line key. When you have completed this task, save under filename FINAN and print one copy. Recall the document and follow the instructions for text editing on page 172.

Before proceeding to the exercises below, you should type the following skill building exercises:

proofreading No 5, page 149.
skill measurement No 21, page 159.
techniques and reviews No 5, page 157.
record your progress No 16, page 165.

PRODUCTION DEVELOPMENT

Forms

Information that is to be typed opposite headings should be on the same line as the base of the printed heading and, therefore, it is important to know how close your typewriter prints to its alignment scale. Type a sentence and study exactly the space between the typing and the scale so that, when you insert a form and wish to align your typing with the bottom of the printed words, you will know how much to adjust the paper with the variable linespacer.

When typing over ruled or dotted lines, no character should touch the ruled or dotted line. Therefore, with the variable linespacer adjust the typing line so that, when typed, the descending characters y, p, g, etc, are very slightly above the dotted or ruled line. Business organizations have a great variety of forms that have been printed, or duplicated, with guide headings, boxes, columns, etc, and the typist has to type in additional information.

When the insertion is typed on the same line as the printed heading, there are two clear spaces before the start of the insertion. Where the insertion comes below a printed heading, it is typed on the next line. However, if the column is deep and the information to be inserted is short, it will look better with a clear space between the printed heading and the inserted matter.

1 There is a skeleton of the form below in the *Workguide and Resource Material* and copies may be duplicated. Insert the form into your typewriter and then type in the handwritten words, following the layout given.

DIRECT DEBITING INSTRUCTION

Please complete, then return the form to Broadlands Trust, Park Avenue, GRANTHAM, Lincs, NG31 5LL

Membership No TV 2496 ....

The Manager .... Somerton .... Bank

Full address of your bank branch 2 White Street ....

Great Dunmow Essex .... Postcode CM6 2BR ....

Name of account holder Cliff T Ware ....

Account No | 8 | 4 | 6 | 0 | 1 | 5 | 3 | 9 |

I instruct you to pay Direct Debits from my account at the request of Broadlands Trust.

Signature .... Date 14 May 1990 ....

---

2 Complete another form, dated today, in respect of Joan MacKenzie. Her membership number is PY07298 and she banks with Lowshire Bank, 26 Queen Street, Edinburgh, EH2 3ER (Account number 65096511).

TYPIST — I am not sure whether Ms Mackenzie's name is spelt correctly. Would you check it please? You will find it on p.42.

PRODUCTION DEVELOPMENT.

● *Blocked style tabulation—subdivided headings*—See **data store**, page 196.

1   Type the following table and rule on completion.

S A V I N G S   P L A N

Investment of £20 per month

over 11 years

Age at outset		Cash Sum Paid	Yield
Female	Male		
		£	%
18-35	18-31	5,492	12.68
44	40	5,461	12.59
54	50	5,357	12.26
64	60	5,222	11.83

2   Type the following table and rule on completion.

lc/   Price-List
             Uniform medal ribbons* } *Emphasise*

Length of ribbon	Price per metre			
	16 mm	25 mm	32 mm	35 mm
	£	£	£	£
50 metres	1.15	1.30	1.50	1.55
100 "	0.70	0.85	0.95	1.05
200 "	0.52	0.56	0.71	0.82
500 "	0.44	0.50	0.62	0.68
1,000 "	0.40	0.45	0.59	0.62

Retain ditto marks

Double spacing

* Corded finish

3 Using a copy of the printed form from the *Workguide and Resource Material*, complete the details for Sir Joseph Bliss. You will find his address on page 42. Date the form for tomorrow.

LEYS ENTERPRISES

TYPIST – Please type in the handwritten details

6-9 Druce Road, Cox Bank, CREWE, Cheshire, CW3 2AF
Telephone: 0270 701387   Fax: 0270 709822

Item *5 boxes Facsimile rolls – Code No 3184*

I enclose crossed cheque/PO for the total amount £ _____ payable
to LEYS ENTERPRISES, or I wish to pay £ *43.43* _____ by

TYPIST – Insert tick in ink

(Please tick appropriate box)

☐ Access   ☑ Visa   ☐ Diners   ☐ American Express

Your card expiry date *August 1991*

Card No *4929 601 424 828*

Signature _____   Date _____

Name and address for delivery (BLOCK CAPITALS):

TITLE |S|I|R|_|_|_| INITIALS |J|_|_|_|_|_|_|

SURNAME |B|L|I|S|S|_|_|_|_|_|_|_|_|_|_|_|_|_|_|_|_|_|_|_|_|_|_|

NUMBER AND ROAD |_|_|_|_|_|_|_|_|_|_|_|_|_|_|_|_|_|_|_|_|_|_|_|_|_|_|_|

DISTRICT |_|_|_|_|_|_|_|_|_|_|_|_|_|_|_|_|_|_|_|_|_|_|_|_|_|_|_|_|

TOWN |_|_|_|_|_|_|_|_|_|_|_|_|_|_|_|_|_|_|_|_|_|_|_|_|_|_|_|_|_|

COUNTY |_|_|_|_|_|_|_|_|_|_|_|_|_|_|_|_|_|_|_|_|_|_|_|_|_|_|_|_|

POSTCODE |_|_|_|_|_|_|_|_| TELEPHONE NO |0|2|1|_|3|5|4|_|5|3|8|3|

Deletions

It is sometimes necessary to delete letters or words in a form, form letter or a circular letter. For instance, in the exercise below the Revd N P Carter-Bond wishes to pay Leys Enterprises by cheque. You will therefore need to delete the oblique sign and PO. To delete printed characters, use an x aligned with the characters already printed.

4 Complete another form, dated today, for the Rev N P Carter-Bond of 12 High View, Chorlton, Crewe, Cheshire, CW4 3PF. The remaining details are in the Data Files (filename LEYS) on page 173.

5 Complete a Hospital Record Form (a skeleton can be found in the WORKGUIDE AND RESOURCE MATERIAL) for Miss Joanna Hazell of 3 Forest Hill, Headington, Oxford, OX3 0BB (tel 0865 818312). She was born on 1.1.70 in Oxford & has been employed as a shorthand-typist for the last 18 months. Her National Health Service No is JP/216/4 — Dr Olive Downing is her GP & her address is – Mount House, 12 Kings Drive, Headington, Oxford, OX3 2PL (tel 0865 864273).

---

4 Would you please retype the memo on the previous page from Josh Kerby but omit the final paragraph & the Distribution List. It is to be sent to Allan F. Chapman, Managing Director. Date it today, & in place of the last paragraph type —

Please let me know if you wish to hv any further information, & I wl make arrangements to come to yr office to discuss the position with you.

• *Alternative placement of name and address of addressee*—See **data store**, page 178.

Centring the home address on the page

Your home address may be centred on plain paper when typing a semi-blocked or blocked personal letter.

5 Type the following semi-blocked personal letter on plain A5 paper, using open punctuation.

23 West Street WAREHAM Dorset BH20 5LH

15 January 1991

Dear Sir SERVICING OF CENTRAL HEATING BOILER← (Centreheading)

You informed me, two weeks ago, that a representative of your company would be coming to service my central heating boiler yesterday, Monday 14 January.

I waited in all day but to my annoyance no one called. I telephoned your office and was told that your engineer had been delayed and that I was to make another appointment.

The only convenient date for me is Thursday, 24 January at 10.30 am, and I shall expect your engineer without fail.

Yours faithfully

Wayne Chastleton

The Managing Director
P J Hollis & Co Ltd
WAREHAM
Dorset
BH18 2PF

PRODUCTION DEVELOPMENT

Typing sums of money in columns

Refer to the instructions given on page 36 with regard to the typing of decimals. Then note the following:
The £ sign is typed over the first figure in the £'s column.
Units, tens, hundreds, etc, fall under one another

	Example	£
		461.76
		34.99
		1.21
		956.00

1   Type the following on A5 portrait paper, taking care to type the decimal points, units, tens and hundreds figures under one another. (a) Leave three spaces between the columns. (b) Double spacing.

£	£	£
384.89	217.80	789.45
108.00	209.12	387.45
90.07	40.87	30.76
2.00	9.77	3.66

Interliner lever

The interliner lever may be found on the right or left side of the typewriter. Locate this on your machine. The interliner lever frees the cylinder from the ratchet control, so that the cylinder may be turned freely forward or backward as required. When the lever is returned to its normal position, your machine will automatically return to the original spacing.

Double underscoring of totals

If you have to type double lines underneath the totals, use the interliner. When typing totals, proceed as follows:

1   Type the underscore for the first lines above the totals. (Do not turn up before typing the first lines). These lines extend from the first to the last figure of the longest item in each column, including the total.

2   Turn up twice and type the totals.
3   Turn up once and then type the lines below the totals.
4   Turn the cylinder up slightly by using the interliner lever and type the second lines. Then return the interliner lever to its normal position.

2   Display the following on A5 landscape paper. (a) Single spacing for the main part. (b) Leave three spaces between columns. (c) Follow the instructions for the total figures. (d) Decimal points must fall under one another.

£	£	£	£	
228.90	12.34	212.34	109.87	
404.75	566.78	33.44	654.57	
323.25	90.12	105.62	1,010.85	
1,234.56	35.45	1,212.05	354.25	
789.00	1,237.95	343.18	1,213.65	
654.32	220.16	331.26	434.12	← Do not turn up
				← Turn up 2 single spaces
3,634.78	2,162.80	2,237.89	3,777.31	
				← Turn up 1 single space
				← Use interliner

Memoranda—semi-blocked

Revise the points given on page 57 about the typing of memos. The layout of the printed forms used for memos varies considerably, but the same rules for typing them apply. It is preferable to leave two clear character spaces after the words in the printed headings before typing the insertions, and to use the variable linespacer to ensure their alignment. Never type a full stop after the last word of an insertion, unless it is abbreviated and full punctuation is being used. A memo form with printed heading is given in the *Workguide and Resource Material*, and copies may be duplicated.

3 Type the following semi-blocked memo on a printed A4 memo form, using full punctuation.

PERSONAL   M E M O R A N D U M

From   Josh Kerby, Finance Director   Ref. JK/pp/(Yr initials)

To   All Staff   Date (Tomorrow's)

                    INSURANCE - CONTRACTED-OUT SCHEME

        Please read the following information carefully. It affects _all_ employees.

YOUR CHOICE

        Since 1 July 1988 every employee can now choose whether or not to be a member of SERPS (the Government's State Earnings Related Pension Scheme). If you are not in our pension scheme, it is a very important choice. Even if you are in our scheme or about to join, you have the choice of being in or out of SERPS. If you opt out, your National Insurance Contributions (is) effectively reduced with the balance going to an insurance company or other financial institution to provide a pension from State Pension Age to replace your SERPS benefit. The difference between being in or out of SERPS could be substantial. So how do you make up your mind?

HOW TO CHOOSE

        What's best for a friend or colleague may not be the right choice for you, so (its) important to check. However, the chart attached can go a long way in helping you find the right answer. Because of the terms offered by the (Goverment), the younger you are the greater the potential advantage of in opting out of SERPS. If you have not been in a pension scheme before and possibly even if you have, the Government will pay a valuable bonus into a pension arrangement which opts out of SERPS. For someone on average earnings of just over £200 per week, this could amount to over one thousand pounds. (figs) £

WHAT NEXT?

        If you are not in our pension scheme, then a personal pension with an Ins Co will ensure that you can take advantage of the money offered by the Govt. Even if yr age suggests you are better off remaining in SERPS, a personal pension can help to provide the income you need at retirement. Come & discuss it with me, or my assistant, Derek Smith. Ring extension 214 for an appt.

DISTRIBUTION -   Accounts Department   (Please centre ditto marks
                  Despatch   "   under the word Department)
                  Sales   "

Att. (1)

Form letters

Many documents that businesses use will contain similar information and wording and, in order to save time, form or skeleton letters, containing the constant (unchanging) information, are prepared and are duplicated or printed, and only the variable items (name and address, etc) are inserted by the typist in the blank spaces that have been purposely left to accommodate them.

The electronic keyboard and the VDU have made production of repetitive text very much easier and time saving. The skeleton letter, containing the constant information, is keyed in and stored on a disk. When required, it can be retrieved by pressing a function key, and any insertion can be made quickly and easily (there is no difficulty with alignment when you have a VDU) and the complete letter printed out, so that it looks like an original— as distinct from a duplicated or printed document with the variables added.

Filling in form letters

The following steps should be taken when you fill in a form letter:

1 Insert the form letter into the machine so that the first line of the body of the letter is just above the alignment scale.
2 By means of the paper release adjust the paper so that the base of an entire line is in alignment with the top of the alignment scale (this position may vary with different makes of machines) and so that an 'i' or 'I' lines up exactly with one of the guides on the alignment scale.

3 Set margin stops. The margins should be set to correspond to the margins already used in the duplicated letter.
4 Insert the details in the appropriate spaces. Remember to leave one clear space after the last printed character before starting to type the 'fill in'. The date, the name and address of the addressee and the salutation should be typed against the left margin.
5 Complete the insertion details.

3 Following the instructions given above and using a copy of the printed letter from the *Workguide and Resource Material*, type in the handwritten details.

THE CENTRAL HOSPITAL
Park Hall, OXFORD, OX2 1AL   Telephone 0865 432968

Our ref OG/261/42/5pr

23 May 1990

Mrs Olive Patterson
3 Partridge Lane
Boar's Hill
OXFORD
OX3 2BC

Dear Mrs Patterson

An appointment has been made for you to attend Mr Maynard's
clinic on Monday, 11 June   at 2.00 pm
for a consultation.

If you are unable to keep this appointment, please notify the hospital
immediately.

Yours sincerely

O GRANTHAM
Medical Records Officer

Charges

The fee required to obtain the USSR and Polish visas (are) £25 per person for UK passport holders.

USSR

(i)   Please sign the enclosed application form.

(ii)   Please forward three recent, identical, passport-sized photographs approx. 4 cm x 4 cm (1½" x 1½"). _(Please check the size in the Data Files (filename USSR), page 174)_

(iii)   Please forward a valid 10-year passport.

Check-list

Please tick against each item to make sure that ~~they are~~ *it is* enclosed with your reply and post immediately.

(Inset 51 mm (2"))

1.   Full 10-year British Passport   *lc*

2.   Photographs (five)

3.   All completed visa forms

4.   (Check) ma~~k~~*d*e payable to Happihols Ltd.
         (£25 per person)

Poland

(i)   Completed application form in triplicate, & signed.

(ii)   Please forward 2 identical, passport-sized photographs, as above.

(iii)   Please forward a valid 10-yr passport. (The Polish Embassy requires that the validation of yr passport exceeds that of the req'd visa by a min of 6 mths.)

Yrs sinc

CLAIRE T. FLEMING
Manager

b.c.c.   Paul St. John Palmerston, Reservations Clerk
         File

Key in document 2 (filename HOLS) for 15-pitch printout. Embolden the subject heading and the shoulder headings. Use the word wraparound function. When you have completed this task, save under filename HOLS and print one original and two copies. Retrieve the document and follow the instructions for text editing on page 172.

---

4   On another copy of the form letter from The Central Hospital complete the following details.

The reference is OG/264/42/fpr and the date is 29.5.90. The letter is to be sent to MR GARY ARNOLD, 18 ELAND LANE, JERICHO, OXFORD, OX2 6PR, & he must attend the Skin clinic on Thurs, 14 June at 1045 hrs for an x-ray.

Invoices

An invoice is the document sent by the seller to the purchaser and shows full details of the goods sold. The layout of invoices varies from organization to organization according to the data to be recorded. Invoices are printed with the seller's name, address and other useful information. A trader registered for VAT who supplies taxable goods to another taxable person, must issue a VAT invoice giving the VAT registration number, tax point, type of supply, etc.

5   Type the following invoice on a copy of the form that can be found in the *Workguide and Resource Material*. Set the left margin and tab stops for each column at the starting point for the headings in each column and then type the information exactly as it appears.

INVOICE   1234

JAMES CORRIGAN & SONS LIMITED
Dublin Road
Thurles
Co Tipperary

NOTE: After the second horizontal line turn up two single spaces and type the £ sign in the appropriate columns at the tab stops. Then turn up another two spaces before starting the items.

Telephone (062) 56986

Figures—

Units must always be typed under units, tens under tens, etc. Follow the text layout carefully when typing the total column.

12 June 1990

Mr & Mrs J O'Rourke
39 Cranston Drive
Thurles   Co Tipperary

Where possible, leave two clear spaces after the vertical lines before typing the items—with the exception of the money columns where decimal points must fall underneath one another.

Quantity	Description	Price	Total
		£	£
2	Waterford Crystal Vases	75.00	150.00
1	Waterford Crystal Fruit Bowl	86.00	86.00
3	Waterford Crystal Sherry Glasses	25.00	75.00
1	Waterford Crystal Decanter	120.00	120.00
			431.00
	Delivery charge		8.50
			439.50
	Prices include VAT E & OE		

- *Blind carbon copies*—See **data store**, page 179.

Semi-blocked letters—continuation sheets

See page 110 for general information about the use of continuation sheets. When using the semi-blocked style of letter, the name of the addressee is typed at the left margin, the page number is centred in the typing line and the date ends at the right margin (backspace one for one from right margin).

Mr L W R Hanlan   2   27 March 1990

2 Type the following semi-blocked letter with two carbon copies. On the carbon copies only, mark one copy for Paul St. John Palmerston, Reservations Clerk, and the other one for the file. Use full punctuation. Type a label to Col. and Mrs. Dunn.

Please type all figures as figures; shoulder headings in closed caps - not underlined

Our ref. CTF/4948/(Yr initials)   *Today's date*

Col. & Mrs. W. Dunn,
2 Malthouse Close,
WELSHPOOL,
Powys,
Wales.
SY21 8SR   *Subject heading centred in closed caps*

Dear Col. & Mrs. Dunn,   TOUR NO. 4948

     The following information concerns Visa Application for the USSR and Poland. The embassies concerned will not accept visa applications from individuals who apply (separetely.) Therefore, visas must be obtained in accordance with the following instructions.

When to apply

     Passports and completed USSR and Polish visa application forms must be sent no earlier than <u>six weeks</u> before departure to:

                    The Manager,
                    Happihols (Visa Section),   *Centre this line &*
                    20 South Street,   *start all the others*
                    CARDIFF,   *at the same point*
                    South Glamorgan,
                    Wales.   CF4 9DF

Complete documentation

It is essential that you submit the correct documentation to our office as given above, as to rectify any omissions may take so long as to make it impossible for us to apply for your visas.

Passport

     You will require a full ten-year British passport (a yearly (visitors) passport is not acceptable).

Late bookings

     In respect of bookings made within 4 - 6 weeks before depar-ture, we will forward the application forms to you immediately for completion. These forms must be returned to us within seven days to allow them to be dealt with.

6   Type the details that follow on to another invoice form.

Invoice No: 8390   Supplier: As ex 5, page 63   Date: 19 June 1990
Purchaser: McCluskey Bros   10 Castle St   Thurles   Co Tipperary

   6   Cut glass wine goblets   £35.00   £210.00
   2   Cut glass candlesticks   £30.00   £60.00
   1   Cut glass bowl   £75.50   £75.50

The delivery charge is £6.50. Please calculate and insert the total figures.

7   Type the details from the invoice below on to a suitable form which can be found in the *Workguide and Resource Material*.

INVOICE   NO 8301

MAGNET OFFICE EQUIPMENT PLC
33 Magnet Buildings
ENNISKILLEN   Co Fermanagh   BT74 6DX

Telephone (0365) 23480
VAT registration No 008 3765 87   Fax (0365) 25879

                                        Date 5 June 1990

T MacMannus & Co Ltd
2 Dowell Lane
ENNISKILLEN   Tax point 05.06.90
Co Fermanagh   BT74 7AA   Type of supply Sale

Your order No PUR 7/90   Account No P/3209   Advice note No 23456

Quantity	Description	Unit cost	Total cost
		£	£
3	Open plan acoustic screens	128.63	385.89
1	Roller blind cupboard	178.99	178.99
1	Double pedestal desk	359.95	359.95

VAT SUMMARY
Code   %   Goods   Tax
1   15 £924.83 £138.74

Total goods	924.83
Discount	0.00
Total VAT	138.74
TOTAL	£1,063.57

Subject to our conditions of
sale. Copy on request.

E & OE

KEYBOARDING SKILLS

Before proceeding to the exercises below, you should type the following skill building exercises:

use of apostrophe Nos 9–12, page 155.   **alphabetic sentence** No 13, page 156.
skill measurement Nos 38 and 39, page 162.   **record your progress** Nos 31 and 32, pages 168–69.

PRODUCTION DEVELOPMENT

Semi-blocked letters

The following points should be noted when typing semi-blocked letters.

1 **Date:** This ends flush with the right margin. To find the starting point, backspace from the right margin once for each character and space in the date.
2 **Reference:** Type at the left margin on the same line as the date.
3 **Special marks:** PERSONAL, PRIVATE, URGENT, etc, are typed in the same style and position as in fully-blocked letters.
4 **Subject heading:** Centre the heading in the typing line.
5 **Body of letter:** The first word of each paragraph is indented, usually five spaces, from the left margin. Tap in and set a tab stop for paragraph indent.

6 **Complimentary close:** Start this approximately at the centre of the typing line.
7 **Signature:** As in fully-blocked letters, turn up a minimum of five single spaces to leave room for the signature. Type the name of the person signing, starting at the same scale point as the complimentary close.
8 **Designation:** Begin to type the official designation (if any) at the same scale point as the complimentary close, ie immediately below the name of the person signing.
9 **Enclosure:** Typed in the same style and position as in fully-blocked letters.
10 **Punctuation:** Semi-blocked letters and fully-blocked letters may be typed with open or full punctuation.

1 Type the following semi-blocked letter from Leys Enterprises on headed A4 paper, with two carbon copies on bank paper, one for Jocelyn P. Barton and the other one for the file. Use full punctuation. Type an envelope to Ms. Kennerton.

Our ref. PIF/PI 386204F/GP   29th November 1990

URGENT

Ms. F. S. Kennerton,
241 Bridge Road,
OXFORD.
OX2 8RW

Dear Madam,

ORDER NO. PI 386204F

Thank you for your recent order which is being despatched to you tomorrow. Please allow a further 2-3 days for the P.O. to effect delivery.

We are very sorry that we have been forced to extend our normal 28-day despatch period, but we are extremely busy at the moment. We do hope this has not inconvenienced you in any way.

[We are enclosing a copy of our latest catalogue.]

Yours faithfully,
LEYS ENTERPRISES

PAULA I. FIELD
Sales Department

c.c. Jocelyn P. Barton
        File

Credit notes

1 Used to cancel an incorrect invoice.
2 Used for crediting goods or packing cases returned.
3 A supplier who credits a customer for goods/services relating to taxable supplies, must issue a VAT credit note, which should give: VAT registration number, amount credited for each item, rate and amount of VAT credited, etc.
4 See also information about **window envelopes** on page 197.

8 Type the details from the credit note below on to a suitable form which can be found in the *Workguide and Resource Material*.

CREDIT NOTE   NO 2487

MAGNET OFFICE EQUIPMENT PLC
33 Magnet Buildings
ENNISKILLEN   Co Fermanagh   BT74 6DX

Telephone (0365) 23480
VAT registration No 008 3765 87

Fax (0365) 25879

Date 13 June 1990

```
T MacMannus & Co Ltd
2 Dowell Lane
ENNISKILLEN
Co Fermanagh        BT74 7AA
```

Original tax invoice No 8301
Date of invoice 05.06.90

Reason for credit	Quantity	Description	Total	
			£	
Damaged in transit	1	Roller blind cupboard	178	99
		Total credit	178	99
		Plus VAT	26	85
		TOTAL	£205	84

E & OE

VAT SUMMARY
Code	%	Goods	Tax
1	15	£178.99	£26.85

Enumerated items—roman numerals blocked to the right

See page 79 for information about enumerated items. As well as being blocked to the left, roman numerals may be blocked to the right with or without full stops. Full stops are never used with brackets. There should be two spaces after the full stop, bracket or after the numeral without a full stop. With open punctuation it is not usual to type a full stop after the enumeration. As indented paragraphs are used in the exercise below, the roman numeral with the most characters, ie iii, starts at the indent, which means that it will be necessary to indent an extra two spaces for i, and one extra space for ii and iv, eg

```
                                    i
                                   ii
                                  iii
                                   iv
```

4   Type the following in double spacing, using indented paragraphs.

Insurance← (Centre in sp caps)

The Hurricane of 1987← (Centre in closed caps)

The hurricane of 1987 was the worst storm to hit the South East of Britain since records began.

Nineteen people lost (there) lives, 3,000 miles of telephone lines (was) brought down and thousands of homes were without electricity for days – the worst power failure since the Second World War.

(/) If you ever have to make a claim ~~under~~ against your insurance policy, it is worth remembering –

(Indent 7 spaces)
→ i.   if your house is made uninhabitable, most insurance (companys) will pay for the costs of additional (accomodation) whilst your own home is restored to a habitable condition;

(Indent 6 spaces)
→ ii.   full rebuiding means the full cost of rebuilding in the same size, form, style, and conditions as previously;

(Indent 5 spaces)
→ iii.   any electric, gas or water supply pipes which may be damaged will usually be repaired at no extra cost to you;

(Indent 6 spaces)
→ iv.   most ins cos wl pay architects', surveyors' + legal fees, if nec.

There is little we can do to prevent a similar storm striking us again, but we can at least make sure that we are fully covered by insurance.

PRODUCTION DEVELOPMENT

- *Special signs, symbols and marks*—See **data store**, page 192.

- *Constructing special signs, symbols and marks*—See **data store**, page 192.

1   Type each of the following lines three times. Use double spacing.

$\underline{/7}56 \div 12 = 63\underline{7}$ $\underline{/1}2 \times 5 = 60\underline{7}$ $\underline{/2}00 \div 2 = 100\underline{7}$ $\underline{/1}0 + 15 = 25\underline{7}$

$\underline{/2}0 + 6 \div 2 = 13\underline{7}$ $\underline{/2}00 \times 2 \div 4 + 30 = 130\underline{7}$ $\underline{/4}0 + 6 \div 2 = 23\underline{7}$

Superscripts (*superior or raised characters*)

A superscript is a character that is typed half a space above the line of typing. To type a superscript, turn the paper down half a space and type the character(s) to be raised; then return to the original typing line. If your machine does not have half spacing, use the interliner. In the exercise below, notice the degree sign. On its own it is typed immediately after the figure, but when followed by C (Centigrade/ Celsius) or F (Fahrenheit), there is a space between the figures and the degree sign but no space between the degree sign and the letter C or F. Use lower case o for the degree sign, unless your keyboard has a degree sign on it, eg 10 °C. Superscripts are used for typing degrees and mathematical formulae, eg $a^2 - b^2$.

Subscripts (*inferior or lowered characters*)

A subscript is a character that is typed half a space below the line of typing. To type a subscript, turn the paper up half a space and type the character(s) to be lowered; then return to the original typing line. If your machine does not have half spacing, use the interliner, eg H_2O, $C_{12}H_{22}O_{11}$. Subscripts are used for typing chemical formulae.

2   Type the following lines three times each. (a) A5 landscape paper. (b) Double spacing.

Subscripts are used in typing H_2SO_4, $CaCO_3$, N_2O and CO_2.

Superscripts are used for typing the degree sign 4 °C.

A right angle equals 90°; 1° equals 60', and 1' equals 60".

At 10 am the temperature was 4 °C; at 2 pm it was 20 °C.

$ax + b^2 = a^2 - bx.$ $a^2 (a - x) + abx = b^2 (a - b).$ $x^2 - a^2.$

3   Turn to page 192 and practise typing the special signs, symbols and marks.

UNIT 36   See Typing Target Practice, R/E, page 27, for further exercises on
Special signs, symbols and marks, Superscripts, Subscripts   66

Indented paragraph headings

See page 31 for paragraph headings. The paragraphs may be indented and the headings typed in either of the forms given on page 31. A full stop may be typed after the paragraph heading, two spaces being left after the full stop.

2   Type the following in single spacing with indented paragraphs.

<u>Changes in the world's climate</u> ← ⟨CAPS & CENTRE⟩

<u>The Greenhouse Effect</u> ← ⟨Centre⟩

    Our weather appears to grow more and more erratic. It is known that it is necessary to research the oceans if we are to understand and appreciate any future climatic changes.

    <u>Green plankton.</u> Plankton drift between the poles and the equator. They form a greater mass of living things than even the Amazon Forest. ~~It is controlled~~ In cold water they can absorb carbon dioxide; in the tropics they release it. Carbon dioxide is crucial to the greenhouse effect; the balance of it is controlled almost entirely by those plankton, but we don't yet know how.

    CO₂. All we know is that the amount of CO₂ has doubled in recent yrs. If the plankton cannot absorb this extra CO₂, the planet will heat, the ice caps will melt, & that will cause great difficulties for the world.

    <u>Ocean research</u> Britain leads the world in ocean research, but a good deal more information needs to be gathered.

Shoulder headings

See page 32 for shoulder headings. The paragraphs that follow the shoulder headings may be indented, but the shoulder headings are displayed in the same form as they are when followed by blocked paragraphs.

3   Type the following in double spacing with indented paragraphs.

⟨Shoulder headings in alphabetical order⟩

CARING FOR HOUSEPLANTS ← ⟨Centre⟩

LIGHT

    Most plants require a bright, but not direct light. It is preferable to keep them a maximum of 1.5 metres from a window.

Feeding ← ⟨CAPS⟩

    A plant should be fed only when it is growing. Over feeding ~~will~~ ✓ burn the roots and could kill the plant.

TEMPERATURE

    Warm temperatures of at least 50 to 60°F (10 to 15°C) are req'd as most indoor plants originate from the tropics.

REPOTTING

    Repot yr houseplants each yr in the spring. Use a 1cm larger pot & a good quality potting compost.

WATERING

    The exact watering requirements will depend partly on the position of the plants. In winter, when plant growth almost stops, less water is needed.

Accents

When a typewriter is used for a great deal of foreign correspondence, the keys are usually fitted with the necessary accents. However, when accents are used only occasionally, the following are put in by hand in the same coloured ink as the ribbon.

Usually typed as special characters are:
diaeresis and umlaut = quotation marks typed over letter, eg Düsseldorf
cedilla—letter c, backspace and comma, eg Alençon

   /   \\   ^   ~
acute grave circumflex tilde

4   Type the following on A5 landscape paper. Use double spacing.

```
Heinz Schmüde, 18 Münchnerstrasse, Düsseldorf, West Germany.

Mme P Sené, 10 Boulevard Dalez, Alençon, France.

Señor Pedro Quijote, Carret del Legs, Bejar, Salamanca, Spain.
```

> Some word processors and word processing software have special symbols, such as accent marks, that can be inserted during typing.

5   Type each of the following lines three times on A5 landscape paper. Double spacing.

```
From afar there came to our ears the call "Cuckoo!  Cuckoo!"
They had spent $300 on presents and came home with only 90¢.
The asterisk (*) is used for a reference mark in a footnote.
250 ÷ 5 + 50 ÷ 4 = 25; 25 x 5 - 15 ÷ 2 = 55; $125 ÷ 5 = $25.
```

Ornamental borders—see also data store, page 176.

Information displayed in the form of a notice, menu, etc, may be given more emphasis, and made more eye-catching, by the use of an ornamental border—as in exercise 6 below.

Brace

The brace is used by printers for joining up two or more lines. To represent the brace in typing, use continuous brackets as shown in exercises 6 and 7.

6   Type the following on A5 portrait paper. (a) Double spacing except for the bracketed items which should be in single spacing. (b) Type an ornamental border as shown.

```
O o O o O o O                         O o O o O o O
o                                               o
O    COACH TIMETABLE                            O
o                                               o
O    London to Oxford      Oxford to London     O

     0715) Not Sundays     1745
     0815)
     0845)                 1755) Saturdays only
                           1815)
     0915                  1835)

     0935                  1855
O                                               O
o    0955) Saturdays only  1915) Not Sundays    o
O    1015)                 1935)                 O
o                                               o
O o O o O o O                         O o O o O o O
```

KEYBOARDING SKILLS

Before proceeding to the exercises below, you should type the following skill building exercises:

proofreading Nos 12 and 13, page 154.   **techniques and reviews** No 12, page 157.
skill measurement Nos 36 and 37, page 162.   **record your progress** No 30, page 168.

PRODUCTION DEVELOPMENT

Paragraphing

There are three different forms of paragraphing, viz, indented, hanging and blocked.

Blocked paragraphs

As you have already learnt, all lines in blocked paragraphs start at the left margin. When typing in single spacing, it is usual to turn up two single spaces between paragraphs. However, if double spacing is used, an extra space or spaces should be left between paragraphs, ie turn up three single or two double spaces.

Indented paragraphs

When using indented paragraphs, the first line of each paragraph is indented from the left margin, usually five spaces. This indentation is made by setting a tab stop five spaces to the right of the point fixed for the left margin. When using indented paragraphs, two single or one double space is turned up between paragraphs when typing in single or double spacing.

Hanging paragraphs

When using hanging paragraphs, the second and subsequent lines of each paragraph are usually inset two spaces to the right of the first line. This type of paragraph may be used to draw particular attention to certain points. (See page 132; enumerated items i, ii, iii and iv in exercise 4.)

Headings centred in the typing line

Main and subheadings may be centred in the typing line when using any of the above paragraphs, although it is more usual to block headings when using blocked paragraphs and centre headings when using indented paragraphs. To centre headings in the typing line, find the centre point by adding the two margins together and dividing by two. Then backspace from this point, one space for every two characters and spaces in the heading.
Examples: Margins set at
   12 pitch 22–82 $22 + 82 = 104 \div 2 = 52$ (centre point)
   10 pitch 12–72 $12 + 72 = 84 \div 2 - 42$ (centre point)
   12 pitch 13–63 $13 + 63 = 76 \div 2 = 38$ (centre point)

1   Type the following in double spacing with indented paragraphs. Centre the main heading and subheading in the typing line. Suggested margins: 12 pitch 22–82, 10 pitch 12–72.

                              38(29)
                    THE TELECOMMUNICATIONS MARKET
                              45(36)
                           Feature Phones
            27(17)
Indent   Feature phones can be useful and profitable for small
5 spaces

       businesses such as solicitors, accountants or insurance

       agents. Most have memories and there can be extras such as

       a microphone, a timer, a digital memory and/or a print out.

       In order to use a feature phone, it must, by law, be maintained

       by a BSI engineer, and you must have one of the master sockets.

Indent   There are phones with fully-digitalized key systems with
5 spaces

       a microprocessor built into the handset.

                    , Callers can be put 'on hold,'

Handwritten or printer's bracket

This has to be replaced by the round brackets, used in exercise 6, on the previous page. Where lines of unequal length are bracketed together, the brackets are typed immediately after the last characters in the longest line. All brackets in any one group are typed at the same scale point.

7 Type the following on A5 landscape paper. (a) Use the same linespacing as in the exercise. (b) Leave five spaces between the columns. (c) Replace the handwritten brackets with round brackets.

```
SPACING BEFORE AND AFTER PUNCTUATION

    Full stop              Two spaces at end of sentence.

    Comma        )                                              NOTE: It is permissible
    Semicolon    }         No space before, one space after.    to type the single-line
    Colon        )                                              text against any of the
                                                                lines to which it
                                                                refers.

    Dash                   One space before and one space after.

    Hyphen                 No space before and no space after.

    Exclamation sign )     No space before, 2 spaces after at end
    Question mark    }     of sentence.
```

- *Proofreaders' marks*—See **data store**, page 190.

8 Type a copy of the following on A4 paper. (a) Make all the necessary corrections. (b) Suggested margins: 12 pitch 22–82, 10 pitch 12–72. (c) Double spacing.

```
Acid Rain ← ( Sp caps )

Acid rain is made up from different various components which
interact with mist or rain and are converted into acids.// It
comes mainly from car exhausts and power stations, but it can
also come from industry.

  It is disastrously affecting the lakes, rivers and trees through-        ( In full )
  out Europe and North America.  In Germany approximately 50% of
  trees are seriously affected.  The average UK rainfall is 10 times
  more acid than normal rain - even old buildings are being corroded.
                                              ancient
```

// The Gov. needs to act asap. by introducing legislation wh.
wd. state that all vehicles cars shd. run on unleaded petrol.
This wd. def. reduce exhaust pollution. Industry can
be persuaded to run on low sulphur fuels - so that,
by the mid-1990s, acid rain wd. be a thing of the
past.

UNIT 36   See Typing Target Practice, R/E, pages 27–28, for further exercises on *Handwritten or printer's bracket, Proofreaders' marks*   **68**

8 Type this exercise in single spacing, following the display given as an example at the foot of the page. Type the items in alphabetical order.

DATA BANK*

Tailpiece

This is an illustration or ornamental motif at the end of a page, unit or chapter and is made up by combining characters, such as hyphen, colon, etc.

```
            :-:-:-:-:-:
            -:-:-:-:-
             :-:-:-:
              -:-:-
               :-:
                -
```

Time

1 Twenty-four hour clock

As international travel has become more popular, we are all more aware of the 24-hour clock. It always consists of four figures with no full stops; for example:

0001 hours (one minute after midnight) 0700 hours (7.00 am) 1200 hours (noon) 1300 hours (1.00 pm) 1800 hours (6.00 pm) 2359 hours (11.59 pm). Midnight is always represented by the word 'midnight'.

2 am/pm and o'clock

Words or figures may be used with o'clock: one o'clock, 9 o'clock. Use *am* and *pm* with figures with no space between the two letters; see examples above. There is a full stop after each letter when using full punctuation, eg 4.00 p.m.

Proportional spacing

With proportional spacing, the characters do not all take up the same amount of space. As in printing, each character is given its natural width. For example, an n is wider than an i, an m is wider than an n and a capital M is wider than a lower-case m. The characters are not measured in spaces but in terms of units. One of the outstanding features of proportional spacing is that the typed copy appears to be printed rather than typed.

Bibliography

A bibliography is a list of books, magazines, or newspaper articles, included in footnotes at the end of a chapter or book to show the source from which the information has been taken, or as a reading list for people who want to go further into the subject. The items are listed alphabetically according to the author's last name which is typed in upper and lower case. The author's name is typed first followed by the forename(s) or initials. With full punctuation, use the comma and full stops as follows:

Drummond, A. M. and Coles-Mogford, A., *Typing First Course*, McGraw-Hill, Maidenhead, 1988.

With blocked style, it is usual to block all lines although the second and subsequent lines for any one item may be inset five to ten spaces. The titles of the books are typed in upper and lower case and underlined, or in sloping type, because the printer will set them in italic.

Hyphen

This is used to replace the word 'to' in certain instances. Examples:

The firm's address was 19–23 North Street. He lived from 1901–1976. This date could also be typed 1901–76, but you must be careful if the dates spread over two centuries, eg 1707–1806 (NOT 1707–06). The dash is also used to replace 'to'.

House style

An organization may decide that letters, memos, reports, etc should be displayed according to certain conventions or style. This would mean that all letters sent to customers and clients would have the same layout. If the organization you work for has a particular house style which differs from your training or preference, you **must** conform to it without deviation.

* Taken from *Applied Typing, Fifth Edition*, Archie Drummond and Anne Coles-Mogford, published by McGraw-Hill Book Company (UK) Ltd.

EXAMPLE:

```
D A T A   B A N K*

BIBLIOGRAPHY

A bibliography is a list of books, magazines, or newspaper articles, included
in footnotes at the end of a chapter or book to show the source from which the
```

● *Footnotes*—See **data store**, page 186.

Standard margins

In the following and subsequent exercises fewer instructions will be given about margins and layout of documents. If you are not given any instructions, you should decide what you consider to be the most suitable margins for the length of document and type of display. One point to remember is that, as far as possible, the document should be balanced horizontally on the page, ie approximately equal margins on either side, unless you are given special instructions to the contrary. If you are given specific measurements (millimetres/inches) for margins—say 25 mm (1 inch) on the left and 13 mm ($\frac{1}{2}$ inch) on the right—it is wise to measure and mark the paper, in pencil, before inserting it into the machine.

● See **data store**, page 188, for further information about **margins**.

9 Type the following on A4 paper. (a) Double spacing, except for the footnotes which must be typed in single spacing with double between each one. (b) Suggested margins: left 38 mm (1$\frac{1}{2}$ inches), right 25 mm (1 inch).

Cordless Telephones ← *(CAPS + underline)*   *(Correct the circled words)*

A common standard

A new generation of cordless telephones capable of making calls abroad is *(bieng)* developed. A common standard for cordless telephones across Europe would revolutionize business communications in the 1990s, as the models available now have limited use in range and capacity. // At the moment[1], it is not possible to have *(to)* many in one area as ~~users~~ pick up other conversations.

The next generation of cordless telephones will have as many as 40 channels with a higher capacity, so they will be more secure for use by business.

It is envisaged that tiny transmitter *(recievers)* would be mounted on top of telegraph poles and other vantage points[2] to pick up and relay calls over hundreds of miles.

---

1 1989

2 You would drive close to one of these points and dial in the usual way.

10 PORTABLE COMPUTERS

(A4 paper + double spacing. Margins as in exercise 8)

Portable computers* are now light-weight but powerful working tools for the mobile high flyer. They can function as neat, desk-top personal computers, then fold away + be carried home or on a bus trip, complete with info stored on disk. [These portable computers can (a) analyse spreadsheets + a/cs complete with charts + graphs, (b) incorporate word processing software. [They weigh approx 9 lb to 20 lb + hv liquid crystal or supertwist *(SUPERTWIST)* screens built into the lid.

If the laptop has a modem** fitted, the sec can also keep in contact with the office + base computer by plugging into the telephone + dialling the co, even from a cellular car phone.

MODEM

** Converts data from digital signals to analog signals wh can be sent via telephone lines.

* Prices range from approx £400 to £2,500.

Typing from print

Today, most firms keep on hand a wide variety of type sizes and styles for use in typing documents of all kinds and especially for preparing camera-ready copy (CRC). The increasing use of electronic keyboards and other sophisticated machines now available for desktop publishing, means that many organizations print their own circulars, leaflets and catalogues. If you are using an ordinary typewriter and are copying from previously printed matter, make good use of the following in order to make your work more eye-catching.

1 Where a word(s) is in italic print, underline the word(s) when typing, or print in italic if it is available to you.
2 Where a word(s) needs to be emphasized, use bold type, underline (but not if you are already using the underscore for italic print), spaced capitals or spaced small letters, or closed capitals.

Horizontal centring—all lines centred

Follow the points given for horizontal centring on page 34, but do not set a left margin and centre EACH line, not just the longest one.

- **Vertical centring**—See **data store**, page 183 (Display).

6 Type the following on A5 landscape paper. Set a tab stop at the horizontal centre point of the page, eg 12 pitch 50, 10 pitch 41. Centre each line horizontally and the whole notice vertically. Type an ornamental border.

```
X-X-X-X-X-X-X-X-X-X-X-X-X-X-X-X-X-X-X-X-X-X-X-X-X-X-X-X-X-X-X
-                                                           -
X               M I C R O   J A R G O N                     X
-                                                           -
X                 Banner - the main headline                X
-          Bullet - solid blobs before text for emphasis    -
X                 DTP - desktop publishing                  X
-    Automatic pagination - automatic numbering of pages    -
X                 CPI - characters per inch                 X
-                                                           -
X                                                           X
-         For   speed   and   expertise                     -
X                                                           X
-                                                           -
X          BE FAMILIAR WITH COMPUTER TERMINOLOGY            X
-                                                           -
X-X-X-X-X-X-X-X-X-X-X-X-X-X-X-X-X-X-X-X-X-X-X-X-X-X-X-X-X-X-X
```

7 Type the following two job advertisements on one sheet of A5 portrait paper, centring each line horizontally and the whole notice vertically. Use any form of emphasis available to you to highlight individual words/lines.

Sales Manager
(Director Designate)
Database management
systems
Thames Valley
c.£30,000 + car + benefits

-------ooOoo-------

European
Personnel Manager
Human resourcing on a
European scale
Berkshire-based
c.£18,000 + car

KEYBOARDING SKILLS

Before proceeding to the exercises below, you should type the following skill building exercises:

improve your spelling Nos 13 and 14, page 155.   **alphabetic sentence** No 7, page 156.
skill measurement No 24, page 159.   **record your progress** No 19, page 166.

PRODUCTION DEVELOPMENT

- *Carbon copies*—See **data store**, page 179 (4.14).

- *Photocopying*—See **data store**, page 179 (4.14.5).

Simple display in fully-blocked letters

Emphasis may be given to important facts in a letter by displaying these so that they catch the eye of the reader. In fully-blocked style, this display may start at the left margin, with one clear space being left above and below, as in the specimen letter that follows.

1 Type the following letter from Leys Enterprises on A4 letterhead paper. Use 25 mm (1 inch) margins on either side. Take one carbon copy and type an envelope of suitable size.

NOTE: The date has been typed on the same line as the reference and ends level with the right margin. To do this, backspace once for every character and space in the date, from the right margin. A number of organizations prefer to have the date typed in this position. Follow house style or layout of input from which you are copying.

Our ref   MH/OP/4357   3 July 1990

M Dubois Esq   NOTE: If the postcode is typed on the same
100 Druids Cross Road   line as the last item in the address,
Calderstones   leave two to six character spaces after
LIVERPOOL   L17 7YB   the last word before typing the code.

Dear Mr Dubois

SPECIAL OFFERS

It gives me great pleasure to invite you to become an investor in a
major launch of 3 new unit trusts. If you invest within the launch
period, you will receive the following offers:

SPECIAL OFFER NO 1 - 50p fixed price
SPECIAL OFFER NO 2 - Early bird discount

The valuable offers listed above could mean additional pounds to you.
So please make certain to get your investment in by ←

*TYPIST - Please check the date in the Data Files (filename OFFER)
page 174, + type it here.*

For more information about the funds, please refer to the brochure
enclosed.

Yours sincerely

MARJORIE HOLLINGTON
Investment Manager

Forms of address with full punctuation—addressing envelopes

The guide to the addressing of envelopes, given on page 42, applies with the exception of inserting punctuation after abbreviations and at line-ends. It should be noted that Miss is not an abbreviation and, therefore, does not require a full stop.

Examples:

Mr. M. James   Dr. O. Coleman   Messrs. W. O. Horne & Sons   Ms. N. Gray

```
Mrs. W. Fallon,              E. P. Freeman, Esq., M.A., B.Sc.,
24 St. John's Street,        T. R. Beach & Co. Ltd.,
BOSTON,                      2 Herne Bay Road,
Lincs.                       BANBURY,
PE21 6AA                     Oxon.        OX16 8LB
```

Points to note:
1 Full stop after an initial, followed by one clear space.
2 Comma at the end of each line except for the last line before the postcode, which is followed by a full stop.
3 NO punctuation in postcode.
4 Comma after surname, followed by one space before Esq.
5 Full stop and NO space between the letters of a degree, but a comma and space between each group of letters.
6 Notice recognized abbreviation for Oxfordshire.

3 Type each of the following lines twice in single spacing. Use margins of 12 pitch 20–80, 10 pitch 11–71. Notice that there is NO full stop in the 24-hour clock.

```
Ms. W. K. Fleming will see you at 9 a.m. or 2 p.m. tomorrow.
Address the letter to P. W. St. John-Lloyd, Esq., M.D., B.A.
Miss U. B. Wallace will meet Mrs. L. V. Stait at 1400 hours.
```

4 Address C6 size envelopes to the following. Use blocked style and full punctuation. Mark the envelope to Ms. Hewitt 'CONFIDENTIAL', and the envelope to K. C. Brennan P.L.C. 'FOR THE ATTENTION OF MR. G. MADDEN. Do not copy the single quotation marks.

```
Ms. A. I. Hewitt, O.B.E., 17 Park Road, SWINDON.  SN2 2NR
K. C. Brennan P.L.C., 3 High Street, SEASCALE, Cumbria.  CA20 1PQ
Mr. T. Morgan, NAGROM, Bond Street, CRAWLEY, W. Sussex.  RH10 0ND
Mrs. L. M. Mulligan, 8 New Street, OMAGH, Co. Tyrone.  BT78 1AA
K. S. Mulcahy & Sons, 10 Carlow Street, WEXFORD, Irish Republic.
Mr. W. Chisholm, 5 High Street, LOSSIEMOUTH, Morayshire.  IV31 6AA
F. J. Jones p.l.c., Llangawsai, ABERYSTWYTH, Dyfed.  SY23 1AA
```

Half-space corrections

You can squeeze in an extra letter, eg type four letters where there were originally three, or spread a word with a letter less than the incorrect word, eg type a four-letter word where there were five letters before. Inserting a word with an extra letter:

1 Erase incorrect word.
2 Move carriage to second letter of the erased word.
3 Depress backspace key, hold it down and type first letter of new word, release backspace key and tap space bar once; hold down backspace key, type second letter, and repeat process.

Inserting a word with a letter less:

1 Erase incorrect word.
2 Move carriage to third letter of the erased word.
3 As in 3 opposite.

Alternatively: By means of the paper release lever, move the paper so that the printing point is half a space to the left of the erased word, or place printing point half a space to the right so that $1\frac{1}{2}$ spaces precede and follow the word.

Electric/electronic keyboards: Some of these keyboards have a half-space key and some manual machines have a half-space mechanism on the space bar.

---

5 Type lines 1, 2, 3 and 4 exactly as shown; then squeeze the word **them** in each of the two blank spaces in line two and spread the word **her** in each of the two blank spaces in line four. Use margins of 12 pitch 22–82, 10 pitch 12–72.

```
1  I told her that I will call.  I told her that I will call.
2  I told     that I will call.  I told     that I will call.
3  I told them that I will call.  I told them that I will call.
4  I told     that I will call.  I told     that I will call.
```

Column display in fully-blocked letters

When the matter is to be displayed in columns, three spaces should be left between the longest line of one column and the start of the next. The first column may start at the left margin and tab stops are set for each of the other columns, as explained on page 45.

2 Type the following letter from Leys Enterprises on A4 letterhead paper. Take a carbon copy and type an envelope. Mark the letter and envelope PRIVATE.

Ref TRF/IN   16 April 1990

Ms Jacqui Zahajkewch
Flat 12
Cedarhurst Drive
Waterdale
DONCASTER   DN1 3HR

Dear Ms Zahajkewch   ~~EXPENSES A/c 1990~~

In accordance with the provisions of your lease, I give below a comparison of your proportion of the expenses for the year ended 31 March 1990 and the previous year.

	1989	**1990**
Provision for major repairs	£180.00	£220.00
Grounds maintenence	21.00	24.00
Insurance, cleaning and electricity	44.50	48.25
Management expenses	18.75	21.90
	£264.25	£314.51

The amount outstanding on your account is £49.90, and I ~~shall~~ *shd* be glad if you would forward this sum, *at yr earliest convenience.*

Yrs sinc

THOMAS R FEARN
Management Accountant

Key in document 2 (filename LEASE) for 12-pitch printout. Use the decimal tab key when typing the sums of money. Embolden the word PRIVATE and the subject heading. When you have completed this task, save under filename LEASE and print out an original and one copy. Recall the document and follow the instructions for text editing on page 171.

3 Please type a similar letter to MRS MURIEL TYLER who lives at flat 36. All her expenses are reduced by £10 each year, as her flat is smaller. Will you, therefore, reduce all the figures, with the exception of the amount outstanding, by £10, please, when you type the letter.

(the totals by £40)

PRODUCTION DEVELOPMENT

Open punctuation

Up to this point in the book all the exercises have been displayed with open punctuation. This means that full stops have not been inserted after abbreviations, and business and personal letters have been typed with the omission of commas after each line of the address, and after the salutation and complimentary close. The modern trend is to omit punctuation in those cases as it simplifies and speeds up the work of the typist. However, punctuation is always inserted in sentences, so that the grammatical sense is clear.

Full punctuation

It is also acceptable to insert punctuation after abbreviations and after each line of an address as well as after the salutation and complimentary close. Grammatical punctuation is always inserted. Open and full punctuation must NEVER be mixed: a document must be typed in either open or full punctuation.

● *Abbreviations*—See **data store**, page 175.

1   Type the following sentences, using open punctuation. Note the use of abbreviations.

Mr & Mrs P R Fielding were told to see Dr M Grant-Phillips at St Paul's
Hospital at 4.30 pm and not 10.30 am.

The lorries, motor cycles, coaches, etc, were all parked in a small area which
measured only 800 sq ft.

Tyler & Royston plc is a large company, but A C Grosvenor & Co Ltd is more well
known, although employing fewer staff.

Leave a top margin of 25 mm (1 in), a left margin of 38 mm (1½ in) and a right
margin of 13 mm (½ in), when typing the report for Ms D Carpenter BSc.

2   Type the following sentences, using full punctuation. Compare the sentences with those in exercise 1,
     noting the differences in the use of the full stop after abbreviations.

NOTE: One space after a full stop at the end of an abbreviation, unless it occurs at the end of a sentence when
you leave two spaces. No space after a medial full stop within an abbreviation.

Mr. & Mrs. P. R. Fielding were told to see Dr. M. Grant-Phillips at St. Paul's
Hospital at 4.30 p.m. and not 10.30 a.m.

The lorries, motor cycles, coaches, etc., were all parked in a small area which
measured only 800 sq. ft.

Tyler & Royston p.l.c. is a large company, but A. C. Grosvenor & Co. Ltd. is more
well known, although employing fewer staff.

Leave a top margin of 25 mm (1 in.), a left margin of 38 mm (1½ in.) and a right
margin of 13 mm (½ in.), when typing the report for Ms. D. Carpenter, B.Sc.

Postscripts

Sometimes a postscript has to be typed at the foot of a letter, either because the writer has omitted something he wished to say in the body of the letter, or because he wishes to draw special attention to a certain point. The postscript should be started two single-line spaces below the last line of the complete letter (but before the enclosure notation, if there is one) and should be in single spacing. Leave two character spaces after the abbreviation PS, which has no punctuation with open punctuation, but a full stop after the S with full punctuation.

4 Type the following letter on A4 letterhead paper. Take a carbon copy and type an envelope. Use suitable margins.

ML/TP   *Insert today's date*

URGENT

Cassels (Trading Co) Ltd
Kingston Road Trading Estate
LEATHERHEAD
Surrey   KT22 7LY

Dear Sirs   CENTRAL HEATING APPLIANCES

Thank you for your letter enquiring about the installation of a central heating system in your offices. *property* *recently acquired*

Like all modern systems, solid fuel central heating is simple to regulate.

Inset 5 spaces

1 Manual control. This straightforward control simply regulates the air supply to your system.

3 Time switch. This allows you to choose at what time you want the heating to come on and go off.

2 Room thermostat. You choose the temperature you would like and when that temperature is reached the appliance switches itself off.

We are SFAS approved instalers of new systems or extensions to your existing system,

I am enclosing our brochure which give you all the information you may require when making your choice about which system of heating to install.

Yours faithfully   *& we sh be delighted to help you in any way we can.*

MAVIS LUCKETT
Sales Department

PS   It is worth considering having double glazing fitted in your new offices as this will greatly increase the efficiency of the heating system when it is installed.

For this information see Data Files (filename HEAT) on page 173.

Key in document 4 (filename HEAT) for 10-pitch printout. Embolden the word URGENT and the subject heading. When you have completed this task, save under filename HEAT and print out an original and one copy. Recall the document and follow the instructions for text editing on page 171.

5 Type the travel itinerary, following the display indicated in the exercise. Retain ditto marks.

TYPIST – Please leave one space clear at the points marked X and 2 spaces clear at the points marked XX

```
Itinerary
X
Jon Bromley's visit to Bristol
X
20th, 21st and 22nd November 1990
XX
Tuesday 20 November
X
1325 hours    Taxi from office to New Street Station, Birmingham.
1405 "        Depart from Platform 7.
1620 "        Arrive Bristol (Temple Meads).
```

← Highlight these lines.

Accom booked for 1 night at the Grand Hotel, Broad St – telephone 0272 216453.
Dinner at Grand Hotel with Ben Goldsmith.

XX
~~Tuesday~~ **Wed** 21 November ← *Highlight as above.*

X

1000 hours Town Clerk's office, Council House – tel 0272 217154.
Discussion abt new factory. Correspondence in file No 1.

1130 " Appt with Frederick Manson, Manager, Secure Building Society, 7 Temple Gate.
(Please check address in Data files (filename ITIN) page 173.)
– tel 0272 217091. Correspondence in file No 2.

1700 " Depart Grand Hotel. Ben Goldsmith will collect yr luggage + drive you to Weston-Super-Mare.

1745 " Arrive at Weston-Super-Mare. (Atlantic)
Accom booked at Grand Hotel, Beach Rd – telephone 0934 654321.
Dinner @ Grand Atlantic Hotel with Peter + Joan Salmon + Ben Goldsmith.

XX
Thur ~~Wed~~ 22 Nov ← *Highlight as above.*

X
0930 hours Depart Weston-Super-Mare.
Dining car on train.

1222 " Arrive New St, Birmingham.

Key in document 5 (filename ITIN) for 15-pitch printout. Embolden any words that need to be highlighted. When you have completed this task, save under filename ITIN and print one original. Recall the document and follow the instructions for text editing on page 172.

INTEGRATED PRODUCTION TYPING

These simulated office tasks are preceded by a **typist's log sheet** (copy in the *Workguide and Resource Material*). Refer to the **log sheet** for instructions and relevant details before and during the typing of the documents.

Timing

Today, because of the number of automatic functions on certain electronic keyboards (as compared with, say, a manual typewriter), it is impossible to set an average timing for any one document. In some typewriting examinations you should complete all questions; therefore, we suggest that your objective is to type the **integrated production typing projects** in the 2 or 2½ hours allowed, and, to help you judge just how much **time you can afford to spend on each task**, we have allocated the maximum number of minutes you should devote to any one task in order to finish the paper within the stipulated time. This time includes proofreading the typed page before removing it from the machine and making corrections where necessary.

Reading the manuscript or typescript through to see that you understand the contents (which is of paramount importance), deciding on linespacing and margins, reading and following instructions, are all essential typing techniques that require immediate decisions and must be carried out speedily and accurately. Therefore, within the timing of 2 or 2½ hours, we have left 15 minutes unused so that you can spend the first 10 minutes reading through the complete script, marking the special points to watch for and corrections to be made, deciding on what paper to use, what margins to set, where carbon copies are required, etc, and another five minutes for a final check to see that each task has been attempted and each instruction followed. Of course, it may be that you will take less time than that stated, and this is good as you will then have time in reserve.

Any writer, when preparing a draft or editing a script, may unwittingly make a mistake—it may be a word spelt incorrectly; an apostrophe in the wrong place or no apostrophe at all when there should be one; it may be that the verb does not agree with the subject. You have to correct these mistakes when you are typing. In practice exercises we draw your attention to the words by circling them; in all but the first **integrated production typing project** we do not circle them: you have to watch for the errors and correct them, just as you would do in business.

Folders

Keep the typed documents in a folder marked FOR SIGNATURE, and the folder (with the tasks in document number order, together with the **log sheet**) should be handed to your teacher when you are sure that all the documents (in any one group) are MAILABLE and ready for approval and signature where appropriate. Also, keep a separate folder for the documents that have been approved/signed—file the documents under the **log sheet** number and in document number order.

Mailable documents

The contents must make sense; no omissions (you could have a serious omission and the document may still make sense); no uncorrected errors (misspellings, incorrect punctuation, typing errors, etc); no careless corrections (if part of the wrong letter(s) is showing, the correction is not acceptable); no smudges; no creases. Consistency in spelling, in format, in typing sums of money, etc, is vital. Occasionally, your teacher may return a document marked C & M (correct and mail). This means that there is an error that will not be difficult to correct, and after a neat correction the document may be mailed.

Typist's log sheet

The information in the **typist's log sheet** will follow a pattern: name of employer will be at the top; the name of the originator and the department (where appropriate) will be handwritten; the date may or may not be given, but letters and memos must have a date unless there are instructions to the contrary. If you have access to a word processor, a text-editing electronic typewriter or a correction only electronic typewriter, follow the general instructions given on the **log sheet** against the symbol 💻 and enter your name, date and starting time near the bottom of the sheet. When all the documents have been completed and are ready for approval/signature, calculate and enter the TOTAL TYPING TIME at the bottom of the last column, and also record the date and time of completion.

Urgent

Note that any input marked with an asterisk (*) is urgent and should be dealt with first. Type the word URGENT at the top of the document, and see that it is ready for approval/signature within 40 minutes of your starting time.

Stationery requisition

Before starting the **integrated production typing**, you should read it through and decide on the quantity and kind of stationery you will require for all the tasks, and then fill in a **stationery requisition form** which you should hand to your teacher for approval. You will need headed paper for business letters and memoranda; bond white paper for top copies of other documents; bank paper for carbon copies; carbon paper, envelopes, cards, labels, etc. You may allow yourself a few sheets more than you require, but you should in no circumstances give yourself unlimited supplies. Most employers keep a strict control over the use of stationery. In an examination, your supply of typing paper will be limited. Of course, you will have readily available some means for correction of errors, ruler, pen, pencil, dictionary, etc.

Justified right margin

The right margin in typewriting cannot be completely regular as in printing, but for purposes of display, it may be made regular by adopting the printer's method. This is known as 'justifying', ie the space between words is increased (where necessary) so that the last character in each line is typed at the same scale point.

For this purpose a draft must be typed, making certain that no line extends beyond the point at which the right margin is set. Read through the draft copy and indicate where additional spaces should be left so that when the passage is retyped, and the additional spaces inserted, all lines will end at the same scale point.

NB   It would be wrong to try and justify 'short' lines.

Most word processing machines have a function key that will automatically justify the right margin.

3   Set margins at 12 pitch 22–82, 10 pitch 12–72, and type the following exercise. Take the paper out of the machine and, on the typescript, mark where an extra space(s) should be inserted to justify the right margin. Insert another sheet of paper and type the same passage with a justified right margin.

WINSTON CHURCHILL MEMORIAL TRUST
The Trust finances Travelling Fellowships to 100 British citizens annually from all walks of life, to undertake worthwhile projects overseas. Since 1965 approx 2,300 Churchill Fellowships hv bn awarded. Successful applicants contribute to every field of endeavour & their impact is considerable - both to the individual & to the country. // It is a living memorial to a great British statesman.

- *Ditto marks*—See **data store**, page 183.

Itinerary

If your employer has appointments outside the office, an itinerary may have to be prepared for him which will enable him to know exactly where he should be at any given time. If short, the schedule may be typed on a card, or paper of any convenient size. The display used varies, but it is useful to use side headings for the times of the appointments as in the example below.

4   Display the following itinerary on a card.

Angela Thornley-Grant's

I T I N E R A R Y

(Please retain the ditto marks.)

for Wednesday, 14 November 1990

1030 hours	Company car outside office building
1115 "	Arrive at Hartwell & Hunt's
1130 "	Meeting with Sales Director - Alan Goode
1245 "	Lunch at Saxony's with Alan Goode and
	Marilyn Lee, Sales Director, Anderson Bros
1415 "	Company car to meet you at Saxony's
1730 "	Interviews for Sales Rep for western region /uc
5	in your office

UNIT 49   See Typing Target Practice, R/E, page 62, for further exercises on
Justified right margin, Appointments itinerary, Ditto marks

124

Distractions

As an office worker, it is a necessity of life that you should be able to cope with interruptions and distractions which are a normal part of the office scene. Your boss may ask you to make alterations to a script (already in your possession) while you are engrossed in typing an urgent or complicated document; you may be interrupted by the telephone; a client may call to see your boss, etc. You should be sufficiently accomplished to be able to return to your typing unaffected by these distractions. To simulate office conditions, your tutor may interrupt you while you are working on the **integrated production typing** tasks and give you alterations to an exercise, or hand you an additional task. The distractions/interruptions are printed in the *Workguide and Resource Material* and may be photocopied so that you can complete the projects in their entirety. Examining bodies may incorporate this form of distraction during a typing examination.

Dates

A business document is of very little use unless it is dated and has a reference as to its origin. Documents, other than letters and memos, are usually dated at the bottom of the last page with the reference either before or after the date. When you are at business, follow the house style. Typewriting examiners for certain boards will penalize you if you date any document (unless there are instructions to do so) apart from letters and memos.

Superfluous wording

If you add a word(s) not in the script, eg a reference in a letter when it is not given, then you may be penalized by the examiner. Similarly, if you insert a line before a footnote and there is no line in the script, then you may be penalized.

Check very carefully to ascertain what the examiner does and does not accept.

Resource material

The *Workguide and Resource Material* is loose-leaf, and record sheets, printed letterheads, forms, form letters, etc, may be copied and these will make your typing much more realistic.

2 Type the following income and expenditure account.

J C PRITCHARD (1971) CO LTD

Income and Expenditure Account for the Year ended 31 December 1990

	1989	1990
	£	£

EXPENDITURE

		1989	1990
Fees		867	1,010
Stationery		7,391	9,137
Meetings		1,300	1,187
Delegations		682	940
Hire of halls		4,634	4,650
Groups		4,300	4,134
Printing and publications		1,153	880
Events		2,037	3,103
Films and equipment		140	71
Donations		19	140

Please check the total figures for each year. 22,623   25,252

Income ← _CAPS_

Insert leader lines

Grant	10,500
Interest	4
Halls	11,357
Groups	751
Publications	3
Events	193
Films	118
Excess expenditure over income	2,326

Insert total figure

You will find the '89 figures in the Data Files (filename EXPEN) page 173. Please insert them here.

🖥 Key in document 2 (filename EXPEN) for 12-pitch printout. Embolden the main heading and use the automatic underline feature and the decimal tab key. When you have completed this task, save under filename EXPEN and print out original. Recall the document and follow the instructions for text editing on page 172.

UNIT 49 See Typing Target Practice, R/E, pages 60–61, for further exercises on
**Financial statements—income and expenditure account**

123

INTEGRATED PRODUCTION TYPING

SCOTNEY and Sons Limited
OFFICE SERVICES – REQUEST FORM

This sheet contains instructions that must be complied with when typing the documents. Read the information carefully before starting, and refer back to it frequently.

Typist's log sheet

Originator GRAHAM SCOTNEY Managing Director   Department —   Date Today's   Ext No 424

Typists operating a word processor, or electronic typewriter with appropriate function keys, should apply the following automatic facilities: top margin; carrier return; line-end hyphenation; underline OR bold print (embolden); error correction; centring; any other relevant applications.

Remember to (a) complete the details required at the bottom of the form; (b) enter typing time per document in the appropriate column; and (c) before submitting this **log sheet** and your completed work, enter TOTAL TYPING TIME in the last column so that the typist's time may be charged to the originator.

Document No	Type of document and instructions	Copies – Original plus	Input form¶	Typing time per document	Total typing time Ұ
1	Memo to all the staff	1 + 1	MS		
2	Table giving special price reductions	1 top	AT		
3	Letter, envelope to Mrs Stewart	1 + 1	MS		
4	Credit note (I will let you have	1 top Re form	Printed shortly)		
*5	Notice about Re use of computers	1 top	AT		
6	Personal letter to Sir Richard Gardner (+ an envelope)	1 + 1	MS		
				TOTAL ·TYPING TIME	

TYPIST – please complete:

Typist's name: Date received: Date completed:

Time received: Time completed:

If the typed documents cannot be returned within 24 hours, the office services supervisor should inform the originator. Any item that is urgent should be marked with an asterisk (*).

¶ T = Typescript   AT = Amended Typescript   MS = Manuscript   SD = Shorthand Dictation   AD = Audio Dictation
Ұ To be charged to the originator's department.

KEYBOARDING SKILLS

Before proceeding to the exercises below, you should type the following skill building exercises;

proofreading No 11, page 153.   **techniques and reviews** No 11, page 157.

skill measurement No 33, page 161.   **record your progress** No 28, page 168.

PRODUCTION DEVELOPMENT

- *Financial statements*—See **data store**, page 185.

1   Type the following balance sheet.

PRITCHARD & PREECE

B a l a n c e   S h e e t   -   31 December 1990

Liabilities and Reserves		Assets	
	£'000		£'000
Shares	4,951,718	Mortgages	4,901,332
Deposits and loans	760,792	Investments and cash	1,096,113
Taxation and other liabilities	89,885	Fixed assets ..	75,104
General reserve ..	238,7977	Other assets ..	2,022
Deferred tax	6,299		
	6,047,571		6,047,674

Please check the totals — they should be the same.

Key in document 1 (filename SHEET) for 10-pitch printout. Embolden the main heading and use the automatic underline feature, the vertical line key and the decimal tab. When you have completed this task, save under filename SHEET and print out original. Recall the document and follow the instructions for text editing on page 172.

① (10 mins) One top copy on headed memo paper + one carbon copy. please.

FROM (Insert my name + designation here. please.)

To All Staff

(Today's date)

ANNUAL HOLIDAYS

stet/ You wl all be delighted to ~~know~~ learn. that it has bn

the h decided to increase / holiday entitlement of all members

of staff by 3 days, to take effect from (insert date here -

NP/ 2 weeks from today). [You wl all be receiving a notification

within the next ten days, setting out how this affects

yr particular holiday entitlement.

(Type the reference here — my initials followed by the oblique + yr initials.)

② (10 mins)

SPECIAL PRICE REDUCTIONS*

Code No	Catalogue Price	New Price
	£	£
MD241	39.95	36.95
TP402	21.95	15.95**	/ Trs
FW157	42.95	36.95
JK534	34.95	26.95	/ Trs
BL387	26.95	15.95

* Available for one month only

** Small size only

6 - 20 mins

Display the following as a folded leaflet.

INSIDE RIGHT

To be held at

THE CORN EXCHANGE

High Street

AMERSHAM

Viewing: Thurs 15.11.90

from 10.30 am to 8.0 pm

INSIDE LEFT

A U C T I O N

Friday 16.11.90

Commencing at 9.30 am

ANTIQUE AND OTHER FURNITURE

TOYS, DOLLS, MODELS

and effects

FRONT COVER

THE LESTER KELLY PARTNERSHIP

E S T A T E   A G E N T S

108 South Street

Amersham

Bucks

HP6 5AP

Telephone: (0203) 33232

---

(3) (20 mins)

GS/10/8/ (Yr initials)   (I top + I carbon, please. And don't forget the envelope.)

(Date)

Mrs A Stewart

(You wl find her address in the Data Files) (filename PRICE) on page 174.

Dr Mrs S ————————

SPECIAL PRICE REDUCTIONS

We are very pleased to be able to offer you, for one month

J7   only, ~~the chance to order from our cat.~~ special price
reductions on certain of the goods shown in our cat.
For example —

Code No	Catalogue Price	New Price
MD 241	(Insert prices from the table on the	
BL 387	previous page.	)

NP   [We aim to despatch goods within seven days, but please
allow a little time for delivery. You wl find, enclosed
with yr order, details on how to return goods if
J7   you ~~are not satisfied~~ find it nec to do so for any
reason.
We recom you call our freefone no, with credit card info
handy, + our friendly staff wl be happy to take yr order.
Yrs sinc

GRAHAM SCOTNEY
Managing Director
PS Our new cat, with all the latest styles wl be
despatched to you next month.

_____

(4) (15 mins)

Please send a credit note to Mrs Baker. All the details
are in the Data Files (filename NOTE) on page 174.

_____

④ — (10 mins)

(Display the following attractively on a card.)

F R E E

V A L U A T I O N   S E R V I C E

Lester Kelly's remain independent Estate Agents
who have specialized in residential property for
many years.
For advice on marketing & valuation, call on our
expertise now.

THE LESTER KELLY PARTNERSHIP
(Insert address & telephone no here, please.)

_____

5 — (20 mins)

(Send a letter to Mme Chantal Deveraux enclosing
details of the cottage at 4 Mill Street. Her address
is on page 107. The ref is — my initials, an oblique
& yr initials. Don't forget the date — & also type
an envelope, please.)

4 MILL STREET
I am enclosing details of the cottage at 4 Mill Street,
Amersham.
[This desirable property has been the subject of considerable
(Complete this paragraph from the details of the property
on page 115, up to . . . of woodwork renewed.)
[If you wish to view this property when you are in this
country, the keys may be obtained from our office in
South Street, Amersham.
Yrs sinc
(My name & designation here)

(5) 15 mins   A4 paper

<u>N o t i c e</u>

USE OF PERSONAL COMPUTERS

<u>Guide to good practices</u>   (CAPS)

The following is intended as a guide to all users of (computors).

1 <u>Keyboards</u>

Trs/ Don't eat, smoke (or) drink while using a computer. Any type of
'foreign matter' can seriously damage the keyboard.

2 VISUAL DISPLAY UNITS ← (Small letters, underlined as in No 3)

The tops of monitors and screens should not be covered while the
computer is switched on. The surfaces of the screens are very
(sensative) to scratching. ~~Scratched screens have been known to
implode.~~

3 <u>Disks and Disk Drives</u>   (storage)

Disks should be stored in a/box with invidual disks placed in
(seperate) envelopes. ←

The above guide lines should allow more hours of trouble-free
use and lower repair charges.
(Keep the disk drive door closed at all times, to prevent
dust & other particles entering.)

(6) 20 mins

(Send a letter to SIR RICHARD GARDNER. He is Chairman
of Gearing Components plc, Witton Place, Main Road,
FOLKESTONE, Kent, CT20 1 A2.)

I am very sorry but it wl be nec for me to postpone
our business lunch arranged for this coming Monday
(insert date, please), as I hv. to attend a Board Mtg. A
week on Mon. (insert date) wd. be suitable to me if that
suits you — same time, same place.
Sincerest apologies & warmest regards.

(Type our ref. GS/Yr initials, today's date & Sir Richard's
name & address, but leave about 8 single spaces after that
so I can write in the salutation. Also do NOT type
my name & designation at the end.)

3 — (25 mins)

(Please rearrange the table so that the 'size' column comes before 'accommodation'.)

'Riverside' ←
Luxury Flats ← (Use any method to emphasize these 2 lines.)

'Riverside' is a unique development, with landscaping to a high standard & offering a wide range of accom. The flats, from a studio type to a large, 2-bedroomed penthouse, each hv their own allocated parking space, whilst those above the ground floor also hv balconies.

Flat No	Accommodation	Size
Flat No 1, 3* & 5 (Studio)	Living room	17' 0" x 12' 3"
	Kitchen	7' 8" x 7' 7"
Flat No 2, 4 & 6* (One-bedroomed)	Living room	12' 8" x 12' 4"
	Kitchen	(I will check the size of the kitchen & give it to you shortly.)
	Bedroom	14' 0" x 10' 7"
Flat No 7*, 9 & 11 (Two-bedroomed)	Living room	14' 5" x 13' 2"
	Kitchen	8' 11" x 8' 1"
	Dining area	8' 11" x 6' 3"
	Bedroom 1	12' 10" x 8' 10"
	Bedroom 2	12' 10" x 8' 11"

* Already sold.

(Do not rule.)

KEYBOARDING SKILLS

Before proceeding to the exercises below, you should type the following skill building exercises:

proofreading No 7, page 150.   **techniques and reviews** No 7, page 157.
skill measurement No 25, page 159.   **record your progress** No 20, page 166.

PRODUCTION DEVELOPMENT

- *Roman numerals*—See **data store**, page 191.

1   Type the following on A5 paper. Use double spacing.

```
Refer to Section IX, Chapter II, Page 340, Paragraph 2(iii).
Read parts XVI, XVII, and XVIII, subsections ii, vi, and ix.
The boys in Forms VI and IX will take Stages I, II, and III.
Charles II, Henry VIII, George IV, James VI, and Edward III.
```

Enumerations using roman numerals

When roman numerals are used for enumerations, they may
be blocked at the left, eg
(i)⁴   Title of book   Leave four spaces after right bracket.
(ii)³ Name of author   Leave three spaces after right bracket.
(iii)² Publisher   Always leave two spaces after right bracket in *longest* number.

2   Type the following in single spacing on A4 paper. The coloured arabic figures indicate the number of spaces
to be left after the roman numeral and are not to be typed.

```
SECRETARIAL VACANCIES

FOR COLLEGE LEAVERS ← ⟨lower case + u/score⟩ with initial caps

If you are interested in applying for one of the following ⟨vacancys,⟩
please send your CV and letter of application to the address on the
enclosed circular.                                    ⟨given⟩

I⁴    SECRETARY TO THE PRINCIPAL                         Code: Sec.2641

College leaver required; 80 wpm shorthand; 50 wpm typing; word pro-
cessing training. £8,500 pa, plus ⟨lunchon⟩ vouchers and pension
scheme.
                                                         5017
II³   PROPERTY COMPANY IN MAYFAIR                        Code: Sec.50⟨⟩

Audio typing; general secretarial duties; no shorthand.  £7,500 pa,
plus profit-sharing scheme.

III²  FRENCH INVESTMENT BANK                             Code: Sec.6386

90/100 wpm shorthand; 50 wpm typing; word processing cert.  A bright,
outgoing personality required.  £9,000 pa, plus perks.
```

⟨See Data Files (filename JOBS) page 173,
for new IV.⟩

(Inset) { structural defect. It should be stressed that the likelihood of any serious problem arising is very remote, but you hv peace of mind knowing you are protected. ←

The exterior masonry surfaces of yr property hv been specially coated with a protective application wh wl guard against dampness, corrosion & the need for constant redecorating // I should be glad if you would complete the attached slip & forward it to the builders so that they hv yr details on file.

Yrs sinc

Our houses are sound and, as our many customers will readily confirm, reliable & trouble free.

Betti Goddard
SALES DIRECTOR

- -

Please forward to:
Devlin Developments

Insert address here. You will find it on page 107

NAME .. . .
ADDRESS . . . .
. . . .

Postcode . . . . Telephone number . . . .

Type an envelope to Mr & Mrs Greene & a label to Gavin Matthews, please.

• **Draft copies**—See **data store**, page 184.

3

DRAFT

Television of the future ← (CAPS)   ⟨*A4 paper*⟩

Choice and quality ← ⟨*Spaced lower case*⟩

⟨*Retain abbreviation*⟩

Viewers will have the choice of 20 or more TV channels by the year 1993, including 'pay as you view' TV.

There wl be

l.e. | I | A new Channel 5 by 1993 with various companies providing services at different times of the day. It will be available across 70% of the country.

~~II   Two satellite channels are to be launched in 1990.~~

⟨*Renumber accordingly*⟩

H | III | By the mid 1990s there will be ~~available across~~ up to 30 local TV stations using revolutionary microwave technology.*

IV *British Satellite Broadcasting is due to go on the air in Sept '90 wh means th viewers wl hv the option of five gov-backed channels.*

Eventually, the licence fee will be replaced. The BBC wl begin to raise funds thro' subscription services & sponsorship.

* *Local operators wl use microwave transmitters, sending out waves rather like those used in domestic ovens.*

⟨*Channel 6 is likely to follow soon afterwards.*⟩

Key in document 3 (filename TV) for 10-pitch printout. Use the word wraparound function and type the main heading in bold. When you have completed this task, save under filename TV and print one copy. Retrieve the document and follow the instructions for text editing on page 171.

2 — (30 mins)

(Two carbon copies, please — one for the file & one for Gavin
Matthews at Devlin Development. Mark the letter PRIVATE.)

Our ref BG/Sales/4061P/(Yr initials)

Mr & Mrs W Greene
6 Daroby Court
Camomile Green
Amersham
Bucks HP6 5AP

(Change 'house/s' to 'home/s'
throughout.)

Dr Mr & Mrs G———

GUARANTEED STANDARDS — TEN-YEAR WARRANTY

You wl be pleased to know that yr house has bn thoroughly
checked during construction & that it complies with guaranteed
standards. This means that the builders hv ensured that
it wl be as trouble free as poss.

(The ten-yr warranty wl protect you in the unlikely event
of any major defect arising.

The ten-yr warranty ← (CAPS, no u/score)

(a) The first two yrs
     The builders hv undertaken to put right almost any
     problems that may arise during the first two yrs of
     the life of yr house. This does not include
     'shrinkage cracks' wh often occur appear in new
     houses, or for electrical fittings.

(b) The remaining yrs
     Please contact yr builder if you hv any major

(Inset 13 mm (½") both sides)

Modification and rearrangement of material

In an office, your employer may give you specific or general instructions about altering the layout of a document, and these instructions should be followed very carefully.

If in an examination you are directed to modify or alter the layout of an exercise, these instructions MUST be followed, otherwise marks will be lost. Before starting to type, carefully read through the task and mark the script clearly in ink where any alterations have to be made. For example, if items have to be rearranged in date order, write 1, 2, 3, 4, etc, against the items in the order in which they should be typed. Time spent in preparation, will lead to greater accuracy and speed in typing.

4   Type the following on A4 paper in double spacing.

```
RELIGIOUS FESTIVALS IN 1989

------oOo------

Sikh

Birthday of Guru Nanak Dev Ji        13th November
Birthday of Guru Gobind Singh Ji     14th January
Martyrdom of Guru Arjan Dev Ji        7th June
Baisakhi                             13th April

------oOo------

Hindu

Janmashtami                          24th August
Maha Shiv Ratri                       6th March
Diwali                               29th November

------oOo------
```

Type in date order, please

Date order

5   Type the following on A5 portrait paper in double spacing.

Names of authors to be in alphabetical order

FAMOUS BRITISH AUTHORS

Name	Born	Died
DICKENS, Charles	1812	1870
SHAKESPEARE, William	1564	1616
HARDY, Thomas	1840	1768
✓ STERNE, ~~Laurence~~	1713	1928
KIPLING, Rudyard	1865	1936
GOLDSMITH, Oliver	1730	1774

UNIT 39   See Typing Target Practice, R/E, page 35, for further exercises on
Modification and rearrangement of material

81

BEDROOM 1 — 13' x 8' 6" with double radiator, window overlooking the front.

BEDROOM 2 — 14' x 9' with radiator, window overlooking the front.

BEDROOM 3 — 15' 2" x 6' 6" with radiator, 2 windows overlooking the rear, fitted cupboard.

BATHROOM — with coloured suite of panelled bath, pedestal wash-basin, low-level WC, radiator.

(leave 3 single lines clear)

Outside ← (Spaced)

(Double Spacing here)

There is no garden at the front of the property, but at the side there is parking space with a delightfully landscaped little garden with a small area of lawn surrounded by flower & shrub borders, wood panel fencing ensuring privacy & a concrete path. . . .

(leave 3 single lines clear)

RATEABLE VALUE — ←

SERVICES — All main services connected.

PRICE — ←

(These figures are in the Data Files (filename PROP) on page 174. Please insert them.)

(Insert the month & year here, please.)

Side headings

These headings are typed to the left of the set left margin. Side headings are usually typed in closed capitals with or without the underscore, but lower case may also be used. The following steps should be taken:

1 First decide on left and right margins.
2 Set right margin.
3 Set a tab stop at the point where you intended to set the left margin.
4 From the tab stop set in point 3, tap in once for each character and space in the longest line of the side headings, plus three extra spaces.
5 Set the left margin at this point.
6 To type the side headings, use the margin release and bring typing point to tab stop set in point 3.

If you are using an electronic keyboard, you may have the facility for setting a second left margin (often referred to as an **indent margin**) instead of using the tabular mechanism.

---

6   Type the following on A4 paper in single spacing. Set a tab stop at 12 pitch 18, 10 pitch 15, for the side heading. Margins: 12 pitch 32–88; 10 pitch 29–72.

THE SINGLE MARKET

By the end of 1992 the trade barriers which prevent Europe from being a single market will have come down. ~~This will open up substantial new opportunities for British business.~~

MARKETING   A third larger than the American market and more than double the Japanese, the wider European market will offer new opportunities for British business.

Production   Exploiting new markets and responding to competition will mean radical changes.

FINANCE   Effective financial management - especially cost control - is vital in the larger European market.

INFORMATION   IT systems ~~must be up to date~~ could make the differ-
TECHNOLOGY   ence between competitive success or failure.
                 An efficient up-to-date

7   Type the following on A4 paper in the order indicated, but do NOT type the figures. Retain the side headings.

KEEPING FIT

Keeping yourself in good shape physically means you can get more fun out of life.

(2) JOGGING   *The idea is to jog along at a pace th makes you no more than moderately breathless.*

(4) STAYING   *The average person swallows abt*
    SLIM   *half a ton of food a year! Exercise can help you stay slim by burning up calories, but make sure you don't overeat;*

(1) CYCLING   *Cycling is free, fun & faster than walking & an excellent way to build up stamina of heart & lungs.*

(3) SWIMMING   *This is just abt the best all-round form of exercise there is. Because yr body is supported by the water, yr spine & joints can move more freely.*

    e.c.   *Strike the right balance.*

UNIT 39   See Typing Target Practice, R/E, page 36, for further exercises on **Side headings**   **82**

① 380 mins

Headed paper for the first sheet, plain bond for the second. Keep to the linespacing shown.

Ref: 1218

Draw a rectangle here

51 mm x 38 mm

(2" x 1½")

A B S O L U T E L Y   I M M A C U L A T E

TOWN CENTRE COTTAGE

4 Mill Street

Amersham Bucks

Leave 3 single lines clear

This desirable property has been the subject of considerable expenditure

in recent years, and offer a beautifully presented, 3-bedroomed home.

The cottage is constructed of brick and stone sermounted by a slate roof,

and has recently been rewired, replumbed and had a considerable amount

of woodwork renewed. // The decor is in pristine condition and the fittings

in both the kitchen and bathroom are lovely modern units. Outside there

is parking space and also a small, but beautifully landscaped garden

which provides an ideal sitting-out area.

Leave 3 single lines clear

A c c o m m o d a t i o n

① COVERED PORCH - with steps to entrance door.

④ DINING ROOM   - 14' x 8' 8" with window overlooking the front, telephone
point, double radiator.

③ SITTING ROOM   - 13' 4" x 13' with window overlooking the front, TV point,
window to side, double radiator, built-in cupboards.

② KITCHEN   - 14' 8" x 6' fitted with an excellent range of modern
units comprising electric cooker point, plumbing for
automatic washing machine, flourescent striplight,
double raditor, half-glazed hardwood door to side.

⑤ LANDING   - with hatch to roof space.

TYPIST - Type the above items in numerical order, but do not type the figures.

UNIT 48   *Integrated production typing project—No 3*   115

KEYBOARDING SKILLS

Before proceeding to the exercises below, you should type the following skill building exercises:

improve your spelling Nos 15 and 16, page 155.   **alphabetic sentence** No 8, page 156.
skill measurement No 26, page 160.   **record your progress** No 21, page 166.

PRODUCTION DEVELOPMENT

- *Circular letters*—See **data store**, page 181.

1   Type the following on A4 letterhead paper (Leys Enterprises). As the name and address of the addressee is
    not being typed, turn up two single spaces after typing 'Date as postmark' and type the salutation.

TE/nlp   Date as postmark

Dear Reader

The positive new image of Business Information ← *CAPS - not underlined*

I have pleasure in attaching your copy of the first issue of
the 'new look' Business Information.

However, the trademarks of Business Information remain the
same - we shall continue to report on the latest news and
developements that have always made the magazine one of the
most reliable in the business world.

This exciting ~~new~~ image heralds a new era for the magazine and
it's readers which will ensure Business Information best meets
your needs. This significant investment has produced a journal
that carries even greater pace and impact, and delivers a
greater reader interest than ever before.

We hope you like what you see.

Also, the appts section wl continue to provide you with yr best source of job adverts when looking for career development.

Yours *sincereley*

TONI ELLIOT

Publishing Editor

Att (1)

INTEGRATED PRODUCTION TYPING

THE LESTER KELLY PARTNERSHIP

OFFICE SERVICES – REQUEST FORM

Typist's log sheet

This sheet contains instructions that must be complied with when typing the documents. Read the information carefully before starting, and refer back to it frequently.

Originator BETTI GODDARD Department Sales
Sales Director

Date 18.10.90

Ext No 29

Typists operating a word processor, or electronic typewriter with appropriate function keys, should apply the following automatic facilities: top margin; carrier return; line-end hyphenation; underline OR bold print (embolden); error correction; centring; any other relevant applications.

Remember to (a) complete the details required at the bottom of the form; (b) enter typing time per document in the appropriate column; and (c) before submitting this **log sheet** and your completed work, enter TOTAL TYPING TIME in the last column so that the typist's time may be charged to the originator.

Docu-ment No	Type of document and instructions	Copies – Original plus	Input form¶	Typing time per document	Total typing time ¥
1	Details of cottage (2-page)	1 + 1	AT		
2	Letter with tear-off to Mr & Mrs Greene (plus envelope & label)	1 + 2	MS		
3	Table of accommodation at 'Riverside'	1 top	MS		
4	Display, on a card	1 top	MS		
5	Letter from brief notes (plus envelope)	1 top	MS		
* 6	Folded leaflet	1 top	MS		
	(I would like the leaflet before I go out, please. I should be back in approx 2½ hrs – leave the other typing in my basket for me, please.)				
				TOTAL TYPING TIME	

TYPIST – please complete:
Typist's name: Date received: Date completed:
                        Time received: Time completed:

If the typed documents cannot be returned within 24 hours, the office services supervisor should inform the originator. Any item that is urgent should be marked with an asterisk (*).

¶ T = Typescript   AT = Amended Typescript   MS = Manuscript   SD = Shorthand Dictation   AD = Audio Dictation
¥ To be charged to the originator's department.

2 Type the following on A4 letterhead paper (Leys Enterprises), with a carbon copy. Turn up 10 single spaces after typing the reference, so that the date and the name and address of the addressee may be inserted before the letter is sent out.

RS/48/92/pr

Dear Sir/Madam (MORTGAGE & PENSION SERVICES)

The attached newsletter highlights two of our services which we hope you will use as an existing client.

As an (independant) co *(IN FULL)* we are able to offer totally impartial (advise) and our aim is to provide you with a fast and efficient personal service.

INSET 5 SPACES

(a) <u>Mortgage Service</u>. This service is useful, not only when you move house, but also to ensure that your existing arrangements are correctly structured in (todays) competitive market.

(b) <u>Pension Service</u>. Like most of our clients you have no doubt been bombarded with literature on the pension changes. Our service is designed to provide specific advice on your own particular needs.

Yours faithfully
LEYS ENTERPRISES

Please do not hesitate to contact us if you wd like to discuss either of these services in more detail

Russ Simonds
Finance Department

Att (1)

3 *Send the top copy of the above letter to Mrs Margot Lawden. You will find her address on page 42. Insert today's date, & type an envelope, please. Don't forget to delete the oblique & the word Sir in the salutation.*

2

Date

Stewart McDowell, Office Manager

As you no doubt know this simply means sending messages down telephone wires from one microcomputer terminal to another via a mainframe computer. The mainframe apparently acts as a kind of mail-box & sorting office. Each person has access to the mailbox thro' a password or code. (via an acoustic coupler - a device that allows computer data to be sent down the phone)

Messages to be sent down the wires are stored in the appropriate segment of the mailbox. When the recipient taps in her/his codeword on her/his terminal, any messages waiting to come thro' will flash up on her/his screen.

And it does save money - as well as time.

Please look into this & come & see me in my office on Wed of next week (insert date) at 1400 hrs

Can you check, please, in the Data Files (filename ELEC) page 173, to see if I have another appointment at this time.

PB/IR

Distribute to - Alec Milton, Sales Director
                 File

I understand that once subscribers are linked up, they can dial up a whole host of other services thro' what are known as electronic gateways.

Key in document 2 (filename ELEC) for 10-pitch printout. Embolden the subject heading and use the wraparound function. When you have completed this task, save under filename ELEC and print out an original and take two carbon copies. Retrieve the document and follow the instructions for text editing on page 172.

Circular letters with tear-off portion

Sometimes a letter will have a tear-off portion at the foot, so that a customer can fill in certain details and return the tear-off portion to the sender.

After typing the complimentary close leave a minimum of four clear spaces, ie turn up five single spaces and then type, from edge to edge of the paper, continuous hyphens or continuous dots; then turn up two single spaces and type the information on the tear-off portion.

When blank spaces are left on the tear-off portion for details to be filled in, use continuous dots or the underscore and double spacing. Remember to leave one clear space after the last character typed before starting the dots or underscore and one clear space at the end of the dots or the underscore before the next typed character if there is one, eg

```
        (space)          (space)          (space)
Surname .............. Christian names ...........
```

4 Type the following personal business letter on A4 paper. It is not necessary to leave space for the name and address of the addressee.

Backspace this line from the right margin & start all lines at this point.

14 The Hollow
Pateley Bridge
North Yorkshire   HG3 5NJ

July 1990

Dear

Some time ago you kindly volunteered to help serve coffee to our members before the talks and lectures we have on Thursday and Friday evenings.

Irs/ This would involve *arriving at the Hall at 7.00pm* making and serving the tea, coffee and biscuits (all the necessary equipment will be provided) and clearing it away before the lecture starts at 8.00pm. // If you are able to help,

NP the committee would be grateful if you could return the attached form *asap* so that a rota can be organized.

Sincerely

ANNABEL SHERGOLD
Membership Secretary

- -

NAME ....

ADDRESS ....

.... Telephone No ....

I shall be available on the following evenings. (*P* please tick those evenings when you will be able to help, and return the form to me.)

Inset 3 spaces

Thursday, 20 September	......	Friday, 7 December	......
Friday, 19 October	......	Thursday, 12 January	......
~~Thursday,~~ *Friday* 9 November	......	Friday, 17 February	......

Quotation marks

When two or more paragraphs are quoted, the quotation marks are placed at the beginning of each paragraph and at the end of the last paragraph only.

With ellipsis, there is a space after the initial quotation mark and before the first dot, and a space after the third dot and before the final quotation mark.

2   Type the following two-page memo with two carbon copies, one for Alec Milton, Sales Director, and the other one for the file. Type two labels, one for Mr Milton and the other for Mr McDowell.

PRIVATE

TO   Stewart McDowell, Office Manager   *change personal computers to PCs throughout*

FROM   Parveen Bashire, General Manager

DATE   *Insert tomorrow's date, please*

The electronic office –
The ability to compete in 1992 and beyond   *Please give each line of the heading a different emphasis.*

As the single market becomes a reality, I think it is time we looked at updating our office systems in the light of the new technology. The fast flow of information is vital ~~to our success~~. //Although our Accounts Branch is computerized, our typists have become word *processer* operators and our managers have their own personal *computors*, I feel that, to create a truly electronic office, our computers should be incorporated into 1 system.

Then our managers would be able to call up information whether on the main company computer, on their own PC or on a database halfway across the world. Our systems must be able to intercommunicate.

I read an article recently, an extract of which I give below.

Inset 6 spaces from left margin.   " . . . local area networks allow different types of personal computers to exchange information and share expensive *recourses*, ie, printers.

"Software to link microcomputers to main frames allows the managers to extract information ... to hunt for stored information by using a few key words."

I understand there are certain difficulties – the data may be in a different form from that we are used to wh cld mean we hv to learn a new set of skills to manipulate the data.

"EMAIL"

I feel we must also look at electronic mailing systems.

5

At̶ l̶e̶t̶t̶e̶r̶h̶e̶a̶d̶ papes, please, + one carbon copy on plain bank paper. (A4)

7390652/G61

Leave sufficient space here for date + name + address

Dear Sir/Madam

Holiday of a lifetime ← CAPS

At Getaway Travel we pride ourselves on finding the very best holidays anywhere in the world. And we know that you, as a previous traveller with us, really enjoy getting away somewhere special. // So why not see if we can make your most exotic holiday dream come true?

check this fig in the Data Files (filename HOLS) page 173.

When you have booked your holiday, you will be entitled to a free Travel Guide worth up to £10.99. It's illustrated in colour, and contains a wealth of facts about the places you'll visit. Just complete the voucher below and post it to us with details of your holiday and the Guide will be sent to you free of charge. // *come in + see us + that holiday of a lifetime wl soon become a reality.*

yrs sinc

JIM O'LEARY
Branch Manager

Pop in to yr local Get-T-, you'll find a wide range of brochures to take you almost any place you choose,

- -

Please send me my FREE travel guide for   U.C.

Double Spacing

DESTINATION ....
TOUR OPERATOR ....
DATE OF DEPARTURE .... RECEIPT NO ....
NAME ....
ADDRESS ....
.... Postcode ....

7390652/G61

⌨ Key in document 5 (filename HOLS) for 12-pitch printout. Use the word wraparound function and embolden all words in capitals. When you have completed this task, save under filename HOLS and print one top and one carbon copy. Retrieve the document and follow the instructions for text editing on page 171.

6 *Now complete the carbon copy. Date it June 1990 + address it to yourself. Don't forget to amend the salutation. Imagine then that you have just received this letter + complete the tear-off slip by typing in a destination of your choice. You booked with MIRABELLE TRAVEL TOURS (rec no HS 4026/41) + will be leaving on 22 August — so fill in your name + address + have a good holiday!*

2

14 September 1990

Akmal Ramzan & Son

catalogue and you will see that it is full of bargains of top quality items you use every day in your office.

(Inset 38mm (1½") both sides) For instance, you <u>can save</u> as much as 75% on certain (stationary) items.

We also have a very special offer on some of our computer-based equipment. Video typing is here, and here to stay, but the range and variety of equipment can be bewildering. Many businesses who are contemplating a new purchase or an upgrade of present equipment find it impossible to decide exactly what (there) requirements are. // Can you answer the following questions?

(Inset 25mm (1") from left margin; double spacing)

(1) Is the system right for my size of business?
(2) Will it be right in two (years) time?
5 (3) How wl 1 finance it?
(4) wl 1 need to employ a consultant?
3 (5) Is the application software readily available?

We can give you the answers to these & any other questions you may hv. Whatever the size of or co, we wl advise you which equipment wld be suitable for you & give you info on all the latest developments. No other co gives such a comprehensive service.

<u>ORDERING IS EASY</u>

If you know what you want after looking thro' our cat, simply tel us FREE OF CHARGE & tell one of our friendly, helpful staff what you need. We wl process or order asap & deliver it to you within 2 or 3 days from the vast stock in our computerized warehouse. //We look forward to hearing from you.

Yrs ffy

DEREK COPE-FENTON Sales Director

PS You wl find all the ordering details in the centre of the catalogue on page 10 (check this in the Data Files (filename DRCT) page 173. Call us now or, if you prefer, you can FAX or order or send it FREEPOST.

cc Despatch Department
File

Key in document 1 (filename DRCT) for 12-pitch printout. Embolden the subject heading and use the wraparound function. When you have completed this task, save under filename DRCT and print out an original and take two carbon copies. Retrieve the document and follow the instructions for text editing on page 172.

PRODUCTION DEVELOPMENT

- *Blocked tabulation with single-line column headings*—Refer to unit 28, page 45, for the method to be used when arranging items in columns.

- *Footnotes*—See **data store**, page 196.

NOTE: It is not usual to type a line above the footnote when it occurs after a table.

1   Use A5 paper. Follow the linespacing used in the exercise.

E R R A T A   (TYPE IN PAGE ORDER, PLEASE)

Please mark these (few) corrections in your catalogue now to avoid
any delay in the despatch of your goods.

Page	Catalogue No	Description	Correction
747	NP 2469	Jeans	33" inside leg
315	BL 1032	Navy skirt	
314	FT 3249	Grey suit	Large sizes only
318	TW 4955	Black check dress	
752	VP 1431	Trouser suit	Synthetic material
202	OR 5432	Waist slips*	100% nylon

* Short, long and medium

- *Leader dots*—See **data store**, page 195.

2   Display the following on A5 paper. Insert leader dots.

SOME UNITED KINGDOM AIRPORTS

Name	Telephone Number
London - Heathrow Airport	01-759 4321
Lydd Airport	0679 2041
London - Gatwick Airport	0293 28822
Aberdeen Airport	0224 722331
Exeter Airport	0392 67433
Leeds and Bradford Airport	0532 509696

Alphabetical order of airports, please.

PRODUCTION DEVELOPMENT

Continuation sheets for letters and memos

When a letter or memo extends to extra pages, these continuation sheets are typed on plain paper, which must be the same size, colour and quality (ie bond paper) as the first sheet. It is usual to type the following details at the top of the second and subsequent pages, starting on the fourth single-line space from the top of the paper.

No of page   It is preferable to type this information in double spacing. Turn
Date   up a minimum of three single spaces and continue with the remainder of
Name of addressee   the letter.

When a continuation sheet is needed, the letter must be so arranged that at least three or four lines are carried over to the continuation page. On no account must the continuation page contain only the complimentary close and the name of the writer. Do NOT divide a word from one page to the next. Leave approximately 25 mm (1 inch) clear at the bottom of the page before continuing on to the extra sheet. It is a good idea to mark the sheet lightly in pencil at 38 mm ($1\frac{1}{2}$ inches) up from the bottom to remind you, or, if a backing sheet is used and no carbon copy, you may wish to draw a heavy line on the backing sheet, so that it will show through as an indication to you that you are nearing the bottom of the paper. The word CONTINUED or PTO or a CATCHWORD may be used. (The first word or two that appear on the continuation page are typed in the bottom margin on the previous sheet and are known as catchwords.)

Additional carbon copies

It is quite often necessary to type more than one carbon copy, any extra ones being for the information of others concerned. If this is the case, the name(s) of these people is (are) typed either:

1   in the top right or left corner, or
2   at the foot of the letter or memo.

The names are usually typed one under the other and preceded by the words 'Copy for...', 'Distribute to...' or 'cc...'. When the completed letter is removed from the typewriter, the individual names are ticked or underlined. A carbon copy should also be taken for the file. See page 183 for further information about distribution lists.

eg

1st carbon	2nd carbon	3rd carbon
cc J Atkinson ✓	cc J Atkinson	cc J Atkinson
Mrs A Farmer	Mrs A Farmer ✓	Mrs A Farmer
File	File	File ✓

1   Type the following two-page letter on A4 paper. Mark the letter FOR THE ATTENTION OF MR J RAMZAN. Take one carbon copy for the file and one for the Despatch Department. Type an envelope.

Our ref   DC-P/Sales/4021F/pr   14 September 1990

Akmal Ramzan & Son
Insert address here from page 107

Dear Sirs
← (OFFICE EQUIPMENT)
Here is a unique opportunity to make big savings in all your office supplies - buy <u>direct</u> from us - (Britains) leading office supplies company. //We are enclosing our new, comprehensive

3

(A4 paper)

F O R   S A L E

Apartments – HOLLYBUSH COURT[1]

GROUND FLOOR ← (Initial caps)

Type	Facilities	Price
		£
Rose	Garden door; double aspect lounge; faces ~~north~~ west	72,625
Jonquil	Faces ~~west~~ north; patio	71,841

1st Floor[2]

Daisy	Double aspect lounge; faces east	68,875
Rose	Separate kitchen/dining room	74,326

[1] All 2-bedroomed

[2] Lifts to all floors

TYPIST – There are 2 apartments available on the 2nd floor. The details are in the Data Files (filename SALE) on page 174. Type them here, please

---

4

CLEANING ← (Sp caps)

Half-price offer ← (Closed caps)

(Leave a 51 mm (2") top margin.)

We are in yr. area for 2 wks. offering our Special Cleaning Scheme.

	Normal Rate £	Special Cleaning Scheme* £
CARPETS**		
Lounge	18.00	9.00
Complete 3-bedroomed house	67.00	33.50
Dining room	9.00	4.50
UPHOLSTERY		
3-piece suites	38.00	19.00
CURTAINS		
Full length	24.00	12.00
Half length	18.00	9.00

* All prices exclusive of VAT.

** We move the furniture.

Key in document 4 (filename CLEAN) for 10-pitch printout. Embolden all words in capitals. When you have completed this task, save under filename CLEAN and print one copy. Retrieve the document and follow the instructions for text editing on page 171.

Top margin — 38mm (1½")

25 mm (1") margins on either side. Leave 2 clear lines at points marked *

GENERAL INFORMATION

*

Walks last 1-2 hours, are conducted at a leisurely pace and are informal. They all start and finish at the same place. Please be there 15 minutes before starting time.

*

Please come prepared with stout footwear and waterproof clothing.

*

Dogs are permitted, provided they are kept under control.

*

Don't forget your binoculars!

*

All events are free. ← Highlight this line.

Top & side margins as page 2

Align dates with right margin & highlight them in the same way.

Sunday, 29 July 1990

Naming Wild Flowers
(Valley Country Park - 2.0 pm)

Saturday, 11 August 1990

Summer Stroll
(Spindleberry Leys - 10.30 am)

Wednesday, 2 September 1990

Beginners' Bird Watching
(Valley Country Park - 4.30 pm)

Sunday, 21 October 1990

Guided Walk
(Lockington Common - 2.0 pm)

Sunday, 3 February 1991

You will find the title of this walk in the Data Files (filename WALK) on page 174.
(Valley Country Park - 10.30 am)

------oOo------

Key in document 3 (filename WALK) for 10-pitch printout. Use the 'flush right' facility for page 3 and embolden all words that require emphasis. When you have completed this task, save under filename WALK and print one copy. Retrieve the document and follow the instructions for text editing on page 172.

Blocked tabulation—horizontal ruling

A neat and pleasing appearance may be given to column work by ruling in ink or by the use of the underscore key. An 'open' table has no ruled lines. A 'ruled' table has the column headings separated from the column items by horizontal lines above and below the headings, and below the last line in the table. When typing a ruled table, proceed as follows:

1 Decide on a suitable top margin.
2 Set the left margin in the usual way.
3 It will be necessary to set a right margin at the point where the typed horizontal lines will end. To do this, from the last tab stop, tap space bar once for each character and space in the longest line of the last column and set the right margin at the point reached.

4 Type main heading and subheading (if there is one) at the left margin. Turn up TWO single spaces and type the underscore from margin to margin.
5 Turn up TWO single spaces and type the column headings and then ONE single space and type the underscore again from margin to margin.
NB Remember to turn up ONCE before and TWICE after each horizontal line (in single spacing).

5 Type the following on A5 landscape paper.

Turn up

2 spaces ——▶ MID-WEEK BREAKS

2 spaces ——▶ _____

2 spaces ——▶ Town   Hotel   Address
1 space ——▶
2 spaces ——▶ _____

Leamington Spa   White Hart   Forest Hill
Stratford-on-Avon   Red Lion   Shakespeare Drive
Abingdon   The Lamb Inn   St Giles' Road
1 space ——▶ _____

NOTE: Column headings are not usually underlined when the table is ruled.

Blocked tabulation with columns of figures

When columns in a table contain figures, care must be taken to see that units come under units, tens under tens, etc. Where there are four or more figures, these are grouped in threes starting from the unit figure, a space being left, or a comma inserted, between each group. When typing blocked tabulation, the £ symbol is placed above the first figure in the longest line.
NOTE: When typing continuous matter, it is preferable to insert a comma between the groups, rather than leave a clear space.

6 Type the following on A5 landscape paper in double spacing.

Turn up

2 spaces ——▶ DEPARTMENTAL TURNOVER

2 spaces ——▶ _____

2 spaces ——▶ DEPARTMENT   1988   1990   1989
1 space ——▶
2 spaces ——▶ _____

DEPARTMENT	1988	1990	1989
	£	£	£
Hardware	1,985,240	995,985	1,172,248
Soft furnishing	2,864,000	3,869,435	4,084,908
Perfumes and cosmetics	853,467	890,569	1,029,000
Stationery	908,980	1,011,108	899,978

1 space ——▶ _____

Folded leaflets

The contents and display of folded leaflets varies enormously; it is therefore important to follow the layout given and any instructions very carefully. Brief details are usually typed on the front cover and further information on the inside pages 2 and 3. Occasionally, some brief details may be typed on the back cover. The paper may be folded and then fed into the machine, but unless great care is taken, it may crease. If possible, insert the paper lengthwise but, before doing so, mark the page numbers clearly in pencil as a guide. The following diagram will help:

FRONT SIDE OF PAPER (UNFOLDED)

fold

back page	front page

REVERSE SIDE OF PAPER (UNFOLDED)

fold

page 2	page 3

3   Type the following folded leaflet, displaying the information according to the instructions given and the display shown.

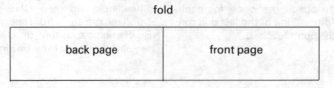

FRONT PAGE

Use A4 paper + turn up at least 38 mm (1½") from the top edge.

COUNTRYSIDE

← Leave 3 single lines clear

EVENTS IN

Shropshire

← Leave 2 single lines clear

1990/1991

Leave 25 mm (1") clear

Issued by the Recreation Services

Blocked tabulation—horizontal and vertical ruling

In addition to the horizontal lines, a boxed table has vertical lines and the left and right sides may or may not be closed in by vertical lines. The vertical lines between the columns must be ruled exactly in the middle of each blank space. It is therefore advisable to leave an odd number of spaces between the columns—one for the vertical ruling and an equal number on either side of the ruling. If the outside verticals are to be ruled, the horizontal lines must extend (usually two spaces) to the left and right of the typed matter. To rule the vertical lines, take the following steps:

1 First set left margin and tab stops.
2 From the last tab stop, tap space bar once for each character and space in the longest line of the last column plus two spaces (if you are allowing three spaces between the columns) and set right margin at point reached.
3 After typing main heading and subheading (if there is one), turn up two single spaces and return to left margin.
4 Press margin release key and backspace two (if you are allowing three spaces between the columns). This gives you the starting point for the horizontal lines which will extend to the right margin.

5 Move to first tab stop and backspace two (if you are allowing three spaces between the columns); at this point make a pencil mark for the first vertical line.
6 Move to the next tab stop and backspace two; at this point make a pencil mark for the second vertical line.
7 Continue in the same way for any additional columns.
8 When you have typed the last horizontal line, mark the bottom of each of the vertical lines.
9 Horizontal lines may be ruled by underscore and the vertical lines in matching colour ink; all lines may be ruled by using the underscore, or all lines may be ruled in ink.
10 Do not allow the vertical lines to extend above or below the horizontal lines. They must meet precisely.

If you are using an electronic keyboard, you may have the facility for setting out the columns and inserting the vertical lines. Refer to the manufacturer's handbook.

NOTE: When marking the top of the vertical lines, make a note of the scale points at which they have to be drawn so that when you have typed the bottom horizontal line, you will know exactly where to make the pencil marks.

7 Type the following table on A4 paper. Rule the lines carefully.

HOLLYBUSH COURT

Estimated costs per month

	Rose	Jonquil	Daisy
	£	£	£
Service charge	15.50	14.50	12.95
Ground rent	6.00	5.00	4.00
Water rate	4.87	4.87	4.87
Management services	10.45	9.45	8.45
Warden's salary ...	6.75	6.75	6.75
TOTAL			

Please calculate and type in the total figures.

UNIT 41   See Typing Target Practice, R/E, page 41, for further exercises on
Blocked tabulation—Horizontal and vertical ruling

90

KEYBOARDING SKILLS

Before proceeding to the exercises below, you should type the following skill building exercises:

proofreading No 10, page 153. **techniques and reviews** No 10, page 157.
skill measurement No 31, page 161. **record your progress** No 26, page 167.

PRODUCTION DEVELOPMENT

- *Aligned right margin*—See **data store**, page 176.

1 Type the following telephone index in double spacing. Put names in alphabetical order according to surname (if a personal name) or the first word of name (if an impersonal name). Margins: 13 mm (½ inch) on either side. Align (block) right margin.

Example in open punctuation

BROWN, A J, 46 Thomas Street, Leeds, LS2 9JT 0532 21376
FISHER, L, & Co Ltd, 20 Clifton Road, Northampton, NN1 5BQ 0604 6868

Akmal Ramzan & Son, 6 Crown Drive, Bedworth, Warwicks, CV12 8QR 0203 316890
Liam Kennedy Car Sales Ltd, 12 New Street, Dublin 8 .... 01 48440
McBridge (Sports) Ltd, 6 Park Street, Rosyth, Fife, KY11 2JL 0383 215585
Jones Bros, 13 Carmarthen Road, Swansea, West Glamorgan, SA5 7BL 0792 687141
Devlin Developments, PO Box 26, Cambridge, CB1 2JT 0223 66510
P F Simcox & Co Ltd, 2 Mill Street, Nottingham, NG1 6BW 0602 414014
Inge Schneider, Kapellenstrasse 8, Geissberg, Wiesbaden 6200, Hesse,
   West Germany 06121 341201
Chantal Deveraux, 25 rue de Paris, 03000 Moulins, Bourbonnaise,
   France .... (70) 44 00 58

Brief notes

You may be asked, in the office or in an examination, to type a letter or memo from brief notes. The following procedure should be adopted:

1 It is often wise to type a rough draft, making sure you get the points in the correct order, usually in the order they are given in the brief notes.
2 Avoid short, disconnected sentences and decide where to paragraph.
3 There is no need to correct typing errors if you make a rough draft as it will waste time, but verify dates, people's names, etc, and type them accurately.
4 Remove the paper with the rough draft from the machine and read carefully what you have typed, making any further amendments that may be necessary.
5 Insert a fresh sheet of paper, with appropriate carbon copies, if needed, and type a final copy ready for despatch.

2 Please send a letter, dated today, to Frank Harmer, Sales Director of Jones Bros, & say that I look forward to seeing him at the meeting to be held at the Queens Hotel, Birmingham, on Tuesday, 17 July. Ask him if he would let me know whether ~~or not~~ he could have dinner with me that evening at the hotel so that we could discuss marketing strategies overseas.
Mr Harmer's address is in exercise 1 above. Include our ref —
HB/46/21/ Yr initials .

HARRY BARTRAM
Managing Director

- *Multiple-line headings*—See **data store**, page 194.

NOTE: If an item in the descriptive column takes up more than one line, type the figures against the last line of the item, as shown in exercise 8, below.

8

ALL RISKS INSURANCE

The Cost

The table below gives the annual premium, according to area*, per £100 of sum insured.

ITEM	COST IN AREA 1	COST IN AREA 2	COST IN AREA 3
	£	£	£
1 Unspecified personal possessions** (minimum sum insured £1,000)	3.00	2.00	1.50
2 Personal Money and Credit Cards (limit £300)	3.00	3.00	3.00
3 Specified personal possessions including valuables	2.00	3.00	1.50
4 Pedal ~~cycles~~ bikes (limit £200 per cycle)	3.00	3.00	3.00

lc (against item 2)
stet (against item 4)

* See attached list for areas.
** Does not cover contact lenses.

Possessions owned by yr. family, permanently living with you, can be included.

Key in document 8 (filename INS) for 12-pitch printout. Embolden the column headings. When you have completed this task, save under filename INS and print one copy. Retrieve the document and follow the instructions for text editing on page 171.

3 Type the following information on a postcard.

GLYN JAMES MANUFACTURING COMPANY
Gwynfa Street   SWANSEA   SA5 2RG

Ref BE/Sh.T/20   24 August 1990

I wish to acknowledge your letter, dated
20 August, applying for the post of shorthand-
typist in the Sales Department.

Your application is receiving attention and I
will contact you again after the closing date
for applications, *wh is 29 Aug.*

*Address the
reverse side to –
Freda Sellwood-Davis
(see previous page)*

4   WILLIAM J MARSHALL BDS & Associates   Dental Surgeons
26 Charlotte Buildings   Park Lane   Rubery   Rednal   B45 2JR
Tel: 021-453 552[1]

---

*I wish to remind you th yr six-monthly
check wl be due by the end of this month.*
*Wld you, therefore, please call in or tel
the surgery to make an appointment.*
*As you know, it is nec th you hv this
regular inspection.*
Insert today's date here

5   *LEYS ENTERPRISES*
Please insert address. You wl find it on p 39

Ref AF/pb/8312   *2 Oct '90*
Thank you for yr order No 8312 for *Insert the
item after ' for '. You wl find it in the Data
Files (filename ORDER) page 174.*

*Unfortunately, we are out of stock of this par-
ticular item. However, we wl forward yr order
to you asap – hopefully by the end of Oct.*

INTEGRATED PRODUCTION TYPING

THE NEWTOWN BUILDING SOCIETY

OFFICE SERVICES – REQUEST FORM

Typist's log sheet

Originator *Ben Badby* Department *Admin* Date *Today's* Ext No *21*
Chief Executive

> Typists operating a word processor, or electronic typewriter with appropriate function keys, should apply the following automatic facilities: top margin; carrier return; line-end hyphenation; underline OR bold print (embolden); error correction; centring; any other relevant applications.

Remember to (a) complete the details required at the bottom of the form; (b) enter typing time per document in the appropriate column; and (c) before submitting this **log sheet** and your completed work, enter TOTAL TYPING TIME in the last column so that the typist's time may be charged to the originator.

Document No	Type of document and instructions	Copies – Original plus	Input form'	Typing time per document	Total typing time ¥
1	'Buying a new house'	1 Original	AT		
2	Memo	1 + 1	MS		
3	Repayment mortgage table	1 Original	MS		
4	Letter, with label, to Mr & Mrs Simons	1 + 1	Printed		
5	Letter to MS Anders, + an envelope	1 + 1	MS		
6	'Notice of Unit Allocation' form to complete (I will let you have the blank form shortly.) The details are in the Data files (filename UNIT page 174)	1 Original	Printed		
			TOTAL TYPING TIME		

TYPIST – please complete:

Typist's name:

Date received: Date completed:
Time received: Time completed:

> If the typed documents cannot be returned within 24 hours, the office services supervisor should inform the originator. Any item that is urgent should be marked with an asterisk (*).

¶ T = Typescript   AT = Amended Typescript   MS = Manuscript   SD = Shorthand Dictation   AD = Audio Dictation
¥ To be charged to the originator's department.

2 Type the following letter of application from Freda Sellwood-Davis, on plain bond paper with a carbon copy on bank paper.

26 Park Road
Craig Cefn Parc
Swansea   SA6 5JT

Your Ref   BE/Sh.T/20

20 August 1990

Mr Brian Evans
Personnel Officer
~~Please take address for CV~~

Dear Sir

I wish to apply for the post *that* ~~which~~ was advertised in (todays) Evening Mail, for a shorthand-typist in the Sales Dept. I NP have just left Swansea Comprehensive School having taken a secretarial course there in my final year. *I am very interested in the post you hv available as, during my last yr at school, I carried out work experience so yrs co, & found it most enjoyable & interesting.*

I was told, at th time, th if a suitable vacancy arose, my application wd be given careful ~~serious~~ consideration.

I am enclosing my CV, & sh be available for interview at any time.

Yrs ffy

FREDA ~~SMALLWOOD~~-DAVIS
SELLWOOD

Postcards

Many firms send postcards [A6—148 mm × 105 mm (5$\frac{7}{8}$ inches × 4$\frac{1}{8}$ inches)] in acknowledgement of letters and orders. These formal acknowledgements are typed like memos without a salutation or complimentary close. Note the following:

1 The firm's name may be printed, typed at the left margin or centred, usually about four single spaces from the top of the card.
2 Margins: 13 mm ($\frac{1}{2}$ inch) on either side is preferable.
3 Use single spacing with double between paragraphs which may be blocked or indented.
4 After typing the firm's name and address, it is usual to turn up two single spaces and type the reference at the left margin with the date backspaced from the right margin on the same line.
5 Turn up two single spaces and type the main body of the postcard.
6 The name and address of the addressee is typed on the reverse side, parallel to the longest edge.

See Typing Target Practice, R/E, page 52, for a further exercise on Postcards

BUYING A NEW HOUSE

Change the word 'house' to 'home' throughout

The process of buying a new house can be difficult and slow.

But if you put yourself in our hands at the Newtown Building

✓ Society, we can offer facility *ties that will* ~~which could~~ help things to run

smoothly.

1 <u>A choice of mortgages.</u> We offer a choice of repayment

mortgages, endowment mortgages or a combination of both,

up to £300 thousand.

2 <u>Choice of properties.</u> We are happy to grant mortgages on

virtually any type of house, from a 3-bedroomed semi to a

converted windmill.

3 <u>Method of repayment on your house.</u> ~~Your method~~ *This* will depend

on the type of mortgage you choose. Below is a typical

example of mortgage costs on a repayment mortgage. ~~with~~

~~interest calculated at 12.25% but, of course, this may vary~~

~~from time to time.~~

Insert the table here from overleaf, but do not include the main heading or the ruling.

② *10 Mins*

Send a memo, please —
To: Diana Bellamy, Management Assistant
From: Ben Badby, Chief Executive BEN
(Insert date)
It has bn. some yrs. since we revised our Direct Loan Application Form. // I am enclosing a copy so that you can read it + let me hv. yr. suggestions for up-dating + improvements. I am asking Alison Hopper to give me her ideas also - you may wish to hv. a word with her.
BC/ (yr. initials)
Please type a subject heading - DIRECT LOAN APPLICATION FORM

KEYBOARDING SKILLS

Before proceeding to the exercises below, you should type the following skill building exercises:

improve your spelling Nos 19 and 20, page 155.   **alphabetic sentence** No 10, page 156.
skill measurement No 30, page 160.   **record your progress** No 25, page 167.

PRODUCTION DEVELOPMENT

- *Curriculum vitae (cv)* — See **data store**, page 182.

1   Type the following exercise on A4 paper. Suggested left and right margins 25 mm (1 inch).

```
        C U R R I C U L U M   V I T A E

        NAME              Freda Sellwood-Davis (Miss)

        ADDRESS           26 Park Road, Craig Cefn Parc,
                          Swansea, SA6 5JT

        TELEPHONE         0792 62068

        DATE OF BIRTH     22 Feb '73

        NATIONALITY       British  Typing stage III (Awaiting results)

        EDUCATION         Swansea Comprehensive School
                          (1984-1990)

        QUALIFICATIONS    GCSE: History (Grade B)          List subjects
                                French (Grade D)           in alpha
                                English Language (Grade C)  order
                                Cookery (Grade A)

        SECRETARIAL       Pitman Certificates: Shorthand - 80 wpm
        QUALIFICATIONS                         Typing - Stage II

                          Course Work: Word Processing - Grade A
                                       Office Procedures - Grade B

        WORK EXPERIENCE   Three week's work experience at -
                          Glyn James Manufacturing Company, Swansea.
                          I carried out general typing, dealing
                          with the post in the mailing department,
                          and some word prosessing.

        INTERESTS         Music, swimming, cycling
    CAPS
        Referees          Miss Rogers
                          Headmistress
                          Swansea Comprehensive School
                          High Street
                          Swansea  SA2 4TO    Telephone: 0792 37521
```

*Insert the name & address of the second
referee here, please. You wl find it in
the Data Files (filename CV) on page 173.*

③ 20 mins

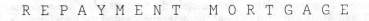

R E P A Y M E N T   M O R T G A G E

lc/

Amount	Term	Total Payable[1]	Percentage per annum	Repayments per month[2]
	Years	£	%	£
£20,000	15	43,635.14	12.9	241.77
	20	53,419.53	12.9	222.10
	25	63,909.41	12.9	212.64
£50.000	15	108,948.82	12.9	604.43
	20	133,412.90	12.8	555.25
	25	159,634.78	12.8	531.60

1 Includes an estimate of expenses.
2 There may be a small variation in the final payment.

④ 15 mins

Can you find a copy of a letter we sent to Mrs W Davies. It is in the Data Files on page 173, under filename MORTGAGE, I think. Please send the same letter, dated today of course, to - Mr & Mrs R P Simons, N2 Close End, Bishop's Castle, Shropshire, SY9 7DG, but insert a subject heading ANNUAL MORTGAGE STATEMENT. Don't forget to take a carbon copy & type a label. Oh, & alter the reference - it shd be the same as in the memo you hv just typed to Diana Bellamy.

END

SY

Decimalized enumeration

In addition to the methods of enumeration already introduced, it is modern practice to use the decimal point, followed by a figure, for the subdivisions. For example, 4(a) and 4(b) would become 4.1 and 4.2, and 4(a)i and 4(a)ii would become 4.1.1 and 4.1.2. This method of enumeration is often used when numbering minutes. When using open punctuation, the decimal point must be inserted. Leave two clear character spaces after the final figure, not a full stop.

4   Type the following exercise on A4 paper. Suggested left and right margins: 25 mm (1 inch).

LEYS ENTERPRISES

(Insert address here. You will find it on page 39)

Minutes of a meeting of Sales representatives for the South-west region held in the main building in Druce Road, on Tuesday, 4 September 1990 at 2.0 pm.

PRESENT: Alan Cox *(Chairman)*   *(Change to 24-hour clock, please)*

Jo Steinberg, Bob Anderson, Glyn Watts, Brenda Abbotts, Bill Julyan, René Grant, Ivan Parojcic

22.1   APOLOGIES FOR ABSENCE

(Inset 6 spaces) 22.1.1   An apology was *(recieved)* from Geoffrey Raynor who was in Germany on business for the company.

22.1.2   An apology was also received from Patricia Fowler who was in hospital recovering from a major operation. Best wishes were sent for her speedy return to good health.

22.2   MINUTES OF LAST MEETING

The minutes of the meeting held on 3 July '90 had already bn circulated & were taken as read. They were approved, & signed by the Chairman:

22.3 MATTERS ARISING

There were no matters arising from the minutes

22.4 REPORTS

(Inset ~~Inset~~ 6 spaces) 22.4.1 Glyn Watts, Brenda A— & Bob A— gave full & comprehensive reports for their particular areas.

22.4.2 Bob Anderson was commended for his excellent efforts in his first 4 mths with the Co.

22.5 CELLULAR TELEPHONES

The chairman reported that cellular telephones are to be fitted in all cars used by senior management & sales staff as from the end of Oct.

22.6 AOB *(in full)*

The chairman said that he had rec'd a report from Geoffrey R— who was in Düsseldorf, & his visit was proving most successful.

22.7 DATE OF NEXT MTG

Wed 10 Oct '90 @ 1430 hrs

CHAIRMAN...................................... DATE............................

⑤ 25 mins

MARLEY

Type the following letter to Ms Chloe Anders, Five Acres, Marley Lane, WINDERMERE, Cumbria, LA23 2EW. with a carbon & an envelope. Mark the letter & envelope PERSONAL.

Our Ref BC/10/8/(Yr initials)

Dr Ms A———

High Yield A/c ← (CAPS, no u/score)

I am enclosing yr annual statement wh shows how much interest yr a/c has earned this yr. [I am also delighted to announce our higher/new, interest rates from Dec this yr.

Inset 10 spaces {

Interest Rate %	Minimum Investment of
9.25	£10,000
9.50	£25,000

As one of our major investors, you already know the benefits of investing in our High Yield A/c.

We are continually seeking new ways to provide you with the best return on yr capital. Our H— Y— A— is (only) one of the ways we can help you make the most of yr savings.

We hv branches nation wide, where our staff are only too willing to help you. Please contact yr local branch if you need guidance or financial advice.

Yrs sinc

BENJAMIN CADBY ← Chief Executive

PS Yr nearest local branch is in the high St. Windermere. uc

⑥ 10 mins

Please complete a UNIT ALLOCATION FORM. The details are in Data Files (filename UNITS) page 174.

Minutes of meetings

Details of any decisions, resolutions or business discussed at a meeting, are recorded and preserved. These are known as minutes. Each minute is usually numbered as this facilitates indexing. The order in which the minutes are typed always follows the order in which the items appeared on the agenda. As well as being numbered, each minute will have a heading which may be typed as a side heading or as a shoulder heading. A description of the meeting, including the date, time and place appears first together with a list of those present with the chairman's name first followed by the names of the officers/members. After the minutes have been approved, the chairman will sign them; a space may be left for signature when the minutes are being prepared together with a space for the date on which the minutes are signed.

3 Type the following minutes on A4 paper. Suggested left and right margins: 25 mm (1 inch). Set a tab stop or second margin a minimum of three character spaces after the longest side heading for the matter following the side headings.

NEWTOWN LEISURE CENTRE

Minutes of a committee meeting held at Newtown Leisure Centre, Hayfield Road, on Thursday, (insert date from ex1 on p.100) at 2000 hours.

Present

Charles Harper (In the Chair)
Gill Cartwright (Secretary)
Bill Lovegrove (Treasurer)
Pat Mahoney   ⎱ Committee members ← (in alphabetical order)
Margaret Madgewick   ⎰
Alan Poole
Glyn Payne

1 APOLOGIES FOR ABSENCE   Apologies were (recieved) from Graham Thompson, Anne Springett and Molly Wells.

2 MINUTES OF LAST MEETING   The secretary read the minutes of the meeting held on (insert date here from exercise 1 pg 100) These were signed by the Chairman as (bieng) a correct record.

3 MATTERS ARISING   There were no matters arising from the minutes.

4 (CORRESPONDANCE)   The secretary read a letter from Mrs Knight, whose daughter Tracy, got into difficulties whilst swimming in the pool. The letter expressed the (familys) grateful thanks for the efforts of all concerned in rescuing Tracy, who ~~is~~ has now fully recovered.

5 LEISURE CENTRE   A subctee was formed to deal with the preliminary arrangements - Gill C —, Pat M —, and Graham T — .

6 SUBSCRIPTIONS   It was agreed that membership subscriptions shd be raised from £8.50 to £10.00 per annum. All facilities are available to members, free of charge.

7 AOB (In full)   There was no other business.

8 DATE OF NEXT MTG   (Insert first Thurs of next mth.)

CHAIRMAN .... DATE ....

KEYBOARDING SKILLS

Before proceeding to the exercises below, you should type the following skill building exercises:

improve your spelling Nos 17 and 18, page 155.   **alphabetic sentence** No 91, page 156.
skill measurement No 28, page 160.   **record your progress** No 23, page 166.

PRODUCTION DEVELOPMENT

Allocating space

In examinations and in business, you may be given instructions that will require you to leave a certain amount of blank space in a typewritten document for the insertion, at a later date, of further information. For example, you may be asked to leave room for the name and address of the addressee in a circular letter, to leave a specified top margin of, say, 51 mm (2 inches), or to leave a certain amount of space in the middle of a document for the later insertion of a diagram, photograph, etc.

In an examination, you will be told how much space to leave, either as a measurement, eg leave 25 mm (one inch), or as a number of linespaces, eg leave seven single lines clear.

It is important to remember that if an instruction states 'leave seven single lines *clear*', you must turn up *one extra space*, ie turn up eight single spaces and type on the eighth line, so leaving seven clear. If the instructions ask for a space of '*at least* 51 mm (2 inches)', it is wise to leave a little extra space rather than risk not leaving sufficient space. If the words 'at least' are not used, then the amount of space left must be exact.

1   Type the following on A4 paper in single spacing.

(leave a top margin of at least 38mm (1½ inches))

THE EUROPEAN COMMUNITY

The European Community arose from a desire to establish a peaceful & prosperous Europe. The different nations of the Community hv agreed to merge their economic interests to form a 'common market' where trade may be conducted freely, people can work wherever they want, & money can be invested where it is most needed. // Four of the countries that belong to the EEC are —

1   GERMANY — Population 62 million
      Exports (inside the EEC) £55,990 million
      Exports (outside the EEC) £58,339 million

2   ITALY — Population 57 million
    (Leave 3 single lines clear)

3   FRANCE — Population 54 million
    (Leave 3 single lines clear.)

4   UNITED KINGDOM — Population 56 million
      Exports (inside the EEC) £26,885 million
      Exports (outside the EEC) £34,772 million

2 Type the following notice of meeting and chairman's agenda on A4 paper. Suggested margins: left and right 25 mm (1 inch). Tab stop for 'Notes' column: 12 pitch 52, 10 pitch 43.

LEYS ENTERPRISES

Please type the address here, on one line. You wl find it on page 39.

A meeting of sales representatives for the south-west region will be held in the conference room of the main building in Druce Road, on Tuesday, 4 September 1990 at 2.30 pm.

A G E N D A	N O T E S
1 Apologies for absence. (Geoffrey Raynor will be in Germany on business.)	1
2 Minutes of the last meeting of sales representatives held on Tuesday, 3 July, 1990.	2
3 Matters arising.	3
4 Recieve reports from Glyn Watts, Brenda Abbotts, Bob Anderson. (Bob Anderson has recently joined the company.)	4
5 Cellular telephones. (They are to be instaled in all cars by the end of next month.)	5
6 Any other business. (Mr Raynors visit to Germany and Ms Grant's impending visit next month.)	6
7 *Date of next mtg. (Some time towards the end of Oct.)*	7

2

(Leave a top margin of at least 25mm (1 inch). Double spacing.)

Florence Nightingale ← (Use any typing method to highlight this line.)

'The Lady of the Lamp'

Florence Nightingale was born in Florence,
Italy, in 1820 of English parents, but she
was brought up in England. She was always
interested in looking after the sick, but it
was not until she was 30 years of age that
Florence at last persuaded her parents to
allow her to go to Germany and Paris to
study nursing.

51mm (2")

Rule a box here.
51 mm × 51 mm
(2" × 2")
for the later insertion
of a photograph.

51mm (2")

(as a nurse)

A few years after Florence qualified, The Crimean War broke out. A large l_c

stet/ number of ~~English~~ British soldiers were wounded, but the conditions in the hos-
pitals in Turkey were appalling. Florence Nightingale was sent out
there to try to improve conditions. She worked hard & long
in often dangerous, & always very difficult circumstances.
The soldiers adored her & called her 'The Lady of the
Lamp' because she used to walk around the wards at
night tending her patients & carrying a little lamp to
light her way.//Shortly before she died in 1910*, she
was awarded the Order of Merit. F——— N———
wl always be numbered among the famous & great
women of the world.

* Florence Nightingale was 90 yrs of age when she died.

Key in document 2 (filename NURSE) for 12-pitch printout. Highlight Florence Nightingale's name each time it appears. Use the word wraparound facility. When you have completed this task, save under filename NURSE and print one copy. Retrieve the document and follow the instructions for text editing on page 171.

KEYBOARDING SKILLS

Before proceeding to the exercises below, you should type the following skill building exercises:

proofreading No 9, page 152.   **techniques and reviews** No 9, page 157.
skill measurement No 29, page 160.   **record your progress** No 24, page 166.

PRODUCTION DEVELOPMENT

Notice of a meeting

The notice should contain details of the date, time and place of the meeting and is usually incorporated with the agenda.

Agenda

An agenda contains a list of items to be discussed at a meeting. These items are usually listed in a certain order and numbered for easy reference, as follows:
1 Apologies
2 Minutes of last meeting
3 Matters arising out of the minutes
4 Correspondence
5 Reports
6 Any special points for discussion
7 Any other business
8 Date of next meeting

Agendas may be displayed in a variety of different ways. It is wise to follow the display indicated in the exercise being copied, or to use the house style when typing agendas in the office. The CHAIRMAN'S AGENDA may contain more information than the agenda for the other members of the committee, the right side of the page being left blank so that notes can be made by the chairman of any decisions reached, etc. The word NOTES is usually typed above the blank space to the right of the listed items, and the item numbers may be retyped for ease of reference.

1   Type the following notice of meeting and agenda on A4 paper. Suggested margins: Left 38 mm (1½ inches), right 25 mm (1 inch).

NEWTOWN LEISURE CENTRE

A committee meeting of the Newtown Leisure Centre is to be held in Room B, First Floor, Newtown Leisure Centre, Hayfield Road, on Thursday *(insert the first Thursday of this month)* at 2000 hours.

A G E N D A

(1) Apologies for absence

(2) Minutes of the last meeting held on *(insert the first Thursday of last month)*

(3) Matters arising from the minutes

(4) Correspondence

(5) Leisure Centre Open Day

(6) Subscriptions

(7) Date of next meeting

(8) Any other business

GILL CARTWRIGHT
Secretary

Continuation sheets

In a long document that extends to more than one sheet of paper, it will be necessary to note the following points:

1 To ensure that you do not continue to type too low down on the paper put a light pencil mark at least 25 mm (1 inch) from the bottom edge of the paper, before inserting it into the machine, and do not type below this mark. Or, rule a heavy line on a backing sheet across the complete width, at least 25 mm (1 inch) from the bottom edge of the sheet, so that it will show through your typing paper, and do not type past this line.

2 **Pagination (the numbering of pages)** The first page is not generally numbered; second and subsequent pages are usually numbered in arabic figures, approximately 13 mm ($\frac{1}{2}$ inch) from the top edge of the paper. The number may be blocked at the left or right margin, or centred on the typing line. In some documents, the pages may be numbered at the bottom.

3 **Catchwords** Sometimes the typist may be required to type the first word or two that appear on a continuation sheet at the foot of the preceding page. These words are known as catchwords. They are typed below the last line and are aligned at the right margin. CONTINUED or PTO may be used instead of the catchwords, but not the number of the next page.

4 **Reverse of paper** If a continuation sheet is typed on the reverse of the paper and the margins are not equal, the margin settings should also be reversed.

Ellipsis (*the omission of words*)

Words are sometimes deliberately omitted at the beginning, end or in the middle of a sentence. Such omission is indicated by the use of three spaced full stops with a space either side, as follows . . . When quotation marks come before the ellipsis, there is a space between the mark and the first full stop. There is also a space before the final quotation mark, eg " . . . "

3 Type the following exercise on A4 paper in double spacing.

Change the word 'authority/ies' to 'council/s' throughout.

THE COMMUNITY CHARGE

The Community Charge replaced domestic rates on 1 April 1990. The main difference is that domestic rates were a tax on property, paid by only about half the adult population and taking no account of the number of adults living in a house, whereas the Community Charge is based on <u>people</u> rather than property.

It is a charge paid by almost all adults, and shares the cost of paying for local authority services more fairly than the rating system did. This new system of paying for the services provided by the local authorities benefits some people, especially single pensioners and one-parent families.

continued/

2

The Community Charge varies from area to area. Some authorities spend ~~much~~ more and therefore charge more. (Everyones) bill will show the local Community Charge figure for (there) authority's spending and . . . so everyone can see what they are getting for their money , + can judge whether the authority is spending the money wisely + well. This is particularly so as we now all get our own separate bill whether we are a husband or wife, a parent or grand-parent — or a son or daughter over the age of 18. [Rebates are available for those on low incomes. In all, approx 9 million people in England rec rebates. This is calculated by yr local authority — but all authorities make their calculations in the same way. following the procedure wh is set down by law.

Certain people are exempt from paying the C— C— Including

Inset numbered items 5 spaces.

(1) resident hospital patients;

(2) the severely mentally handicapped;

(3) people over 18 still at school;

(4) members of religious communities; and

(5) those with no homes, sleeping 'rough'.

(Leave 6 single lines clear here)

We all benefit from the many services that the local authorities provide. These include schools, libraries, social local services, the police, the fire brigade, housing, roads, parks + leisure centres. The C— C— is felt to be a fairer system of helping to pay for these services, with nearly all the adult population contributing, instead of only abt half.

Key in document 3 (filename CHARGE) for 10-pitch printout. Use the word wraparound function and the automatic indent function when typing the numbered items. Embolden the words Community Charge each time they appear. When you have completed this task, save under filename CHARGE and print one copy. Retrieve the document and follow the instructions for text editing on page 171.